21st EDITION

INNES'S EXOTIC AQUARIUM FISHES

A Work of General Reference

Aquarium Starter Kit by Hagen.

The safest and least expensive way to start an aquarium is to buy a *starter kit* from your local pet supplier. This kit will contain everything you need to get started.

CONTENTS

From left to right: The late Dr. Leonard P. Schultz, Curator of Fishes at Smithsonian, G.J.M. Timmerman at that time (1960) the leading fish photographer, Dr. Herbert Axelrod, and the late William T. Innes who lived to the age of 95, passing away in 1969.

FOREWORD TO THE 21ST EDITION

William T. Innes first published the *Exotic Aquarium Fishes* in 1935, after the original author Herman T. Wolf sold him the rights to his book *Goldfish Breeds and other Aquarium Fishes,* which Innes and Sons printed. Because of bitter feelings between Innes and Wolf, Innes omitted all mention of Wolf in subsequent editions of the book and the book eventually became known as *The Innes Book.* This term, *The Innes Book,* was trademarked by Metaframe Corporation which itself went bankrupt and the trademark and copyright were transferred to Rolf Hagen Company. Hagen sold it to TFH, the present publisher. Innes had, unfortunately, sold the rights to his book to TFH earlier, when he was in his 90s. Metaframe and TFH were competitors, both claiming ownership of the Innes book. TFH updated the original edition, while Metaframe elected to rewrite the book almost completely, crediting Klaus Woltman as the editor. They called this edition the 20th Edition of the Innes *Exotic Aquarium Fishes.* That edition was published in 1979. The sales of that book were so poor that it was never reprinted. The *Dr.* sometimes used in connection with Innes's name was an honorary degree (L.H.D.). Innes had no formal education either in ichthyology or in writing. Innes was a printer by profession and his father's company, Innes and Sons, printed most of the aquarium literature prior to World War II. Innes and Sons eventually went out of business.

TFH took the 20th Edition and updated it, adding new color photos, changing scientific and common names to be more in keeping with modern usage, and publishing it in an up-to-date format.

It is really not correct to credit Innes with this book because neither a single Innes photo, nor any significant text written by Innes, is included herein. However, from a commercial point of view, the designation *The Innes Book* is valuable and for commercial reasons we are using the Innes name. We apologize to our readers for this misleading designation but it will, in no way, affect the quality of the book.

Designed as a work of reference, *Exotic Aquarium Fishes* listed the families of fishes in their correct scientific order of precedence, from the lowest in the scale of development to the highest. In order to reflect the latest status of the hobby, the earlier editions of the book were revised almost yearly by Dr. George Myers himself. From time to time, fishes that had become unpopular or unavailable were replaced with current species of greater interest. New information was added as a result of increased knowledge of aquarium keeping. Up until the fifties, the book had become regarded as the *bible* of the aquarium hobby. Then, in 1952, Dr. Axelrod's first book was published by McGraw-Hill. Shortly thereafter, the landmark *Handbook of Tropical Aquarium Fishes* by Dr. Herbert R. Axelrod and Dr. Leonard P. Schultz was also published by McGraw-Hill. Faced with this competition, Innes could no longer produce his annual updating. A 1955, 1957, 1964 and 1966 edition followed. Then the book was discontinued.

In the earlier editions, most photographs had been personally taken by Innes, including some color photographs of aquarium fishes that were a milestone in the art of naturalist photography. These were not truly color photographs but black and white photos that were painted in color.

In 1956, Innes retired, and the nineteenth edition was edited by Dr. George S. Myers, of Stanford University, and Helen Simkatis, Technical Editor of the now defunct *Aquarium Magazine* respectively. Dr. Myers, one of the world's outstanding ichthyologists, had supported Innes as a scientific advisor for many years.

William T. Innes died in 1969 at the age of 95. His book will stand not only as a memorial to a great aquarist, but also as a source of information and delight for many aquarists to come.

The 20th edition of *Exotic Aquarium Fishes* was the first major revision since the book was originally published in 1935. Although the principles of aquarium keeping have changed very little, the technical means of maintaining aquariums have experienced major changes. This is reflected in the expanded section on aquarium filtering devices. The most obvious and notable revision, however, is the replacement of all of Innes's original color plates and black and white photographs with modern color photographs of the highest quality. The photographs in the 20th edition and most of the photographs in this edition were taken by Andre Roth and Charles B. Cooper, who during their tenure as staff photographers at Metaframe Corporation used fishes kept in the Metaframe laboratory to produce all the pictures included in the 20th edition.

In revising the text, the editors of the 20th edition felt that some of the *Miscellaneous Information* of former editions, which could be found near the end of the book, should more properly be included in the section on aquarium management. As an example, the controlling of pH and hardness of water certainly is a function of management and is dealt with under that heading. Similarly, facts about oxygen and chlorine have been incorporated in appropriate opening chapters. Other chapters of former editions have been deleted either because they had become hopelessly obsolete (like the chapter on constructing metal-frame aquariums) or because our knowledge about the subject matter has increased to such an extent that to treat the subject adequately would go beyond the scope of this book—a case in point was the chapter on marine aquariums.

As will be noted, we have changed the layout of the book to a two-column page format, which follows the modern trend toward a more easily readable text. In addition, this layout permits a more economical use of paper which, in a time of trying to conserve our natural resources, seems no small matter. We have tried to present the revised, as well as the newly added, sections of this book in the same easily readable style Innes so successfully used throughout his book.

The original Metaframe edition had many errors and poor quality photos. We replaced the photos and made many corrections, but we left in the genus *Barbus* for the small Asian and African Barbs even though *Barbus* is restricted to the large European Barbel. For this edition, TFH set new type and made new printing plates.

Knowing that several generations of hobbyists have enjoyed *Exotic Aquarium Fishes*, we sincerely hope that the new 21st edition will help many more aquarists enjoy our pleasant hobby. In deference to William T. Innes, who inspired so many aquarists with his book and his personal advice, we hope we have succeeded.

The Editorial Staff of TFH, Neptune, N.J.   1994

The latest technology in aquarium filters is to combine efficiency with compact size. Many children keep aquariums in their rooms. They are a great substitute for TV, and the moisture put into the air is healthful for the child.

AQUARIUM PRINCIPLES

The principles of correct aquarium management are based on a few easily learned natural laws. It is our hope to explain these laws so simply that all who follow them will succeed. Except for feeding the fishes, the ideal aquarium is a self-sustaining unit. It will stay in good condition with little care. This is made possible by considering five fundamental factors:
water quality
water surface
temperature
light
waste control
Let us discuss each of these five factors in order.

WATER QUALITY

Most water furnished by the public systems of cities and towns is well suited to our needs. Perhaps the most serious faults from our standpoint are extreme hardness, fluorine and chlorine, but these are easily corrected. If the natural water of a community is so hard that it is difficult to make soap suds, this condition is usually corrected either at the pumping station or by private water-softening equipment. Water so treated is fit for aquarium use. Water softeners may be sold by petshops, too.

Fluorine and chlorine may be contained in most public water systems. They can be removed by exposing the water to air. Except where fishes are in running water, these gases can be slowly evaporated off. That is the main reason for aging or seasoning tap water for at least twenty-four hours before using it in an aquarium. The process may be greatly shortened by adding a fluorine and chlorine neutralizer which is readily available in most pet shops.

Aquarium fishes and plants have considerable tolerance to the type of water in which they are kept. Ordinarily the water's quality is the first thing considered when looking for the cause of failure. With some of the more fussy species, it may be of major importance not only for their breeding but also for keeping them alive.

If failure persists after running down such common causes as overcrowding, temperature, light, or feeding, the difficulty may be the kind of water used for the affected fishes and plants. Occasionally we hear of aquarists who are generally successful, but who fail with specific fishes or plants. Their failure could well be caused by water unsuited to a particular species. As an example, if light and soil conditions are good and most plants prosper but *Vallisneria* habitually turns yellow, the fault is probably the quality of the water. The aquarist then has to decide either to correct the water quality or to give up the troublesome plant or fish species. There are those unusual cases where the water may be totally unsuited for fishes or plants, even though, it is drinkable. In such extreme cases a different source of water is needed. The local pet shop should be of use here. Ask them for advice.

There is no evidence that the normal amount of fluorine added to drinking water is injurious to fishes or plants since the standard dilution used is only one part per million. If fluorine hardens the teeth of humans, it might even be beneficial to fishes.

Such complexities of aquarium chemistry as pH and water hardness are dealt with in more detail in the chapter on "Management."

WATER SURFACE

At the surface of every inhabited aquarium two seeming miracles are constantly occurring and both are vital to the life of fishes. One is the dissolving of air into the water to replace that extracted by the gills of the fishes. Fishes sustain life by using the oxygen content from the water. The action of oxygen on their body tissues results in the creation of carbon dioxide, a harmful gas, which is then exhaled by the fishes. This gas, not the lack of oxygen, causes suffocation when it becomes too concentrated. Happily the carbon dioxide is carried off at the water's surface. The larger the surface the more rapidly the double action of dissolving oxygen and the releasing of carbon dioxide takes place. There are some fishes, like the anabantoids, which do require atmospheric oxygen directly from the atmosphere. The importance of water-air contact can be strikingly demonstrated: float a sheet of plastic or paper so that it completely covers the water surface. Soon the fishes show signs of distress and in several hours they suffocate. The wa-

ter surface is truly the "window of the aquarium."

The dissolving of oxygen and the releasing of carbon dioxide is further promoted by mechanical aeration and, to a lesser extent, by plants under good light. Both of these will be considered in detail later.

AQUARIUM PROPORTIONS

From what has been said, it is obvious that those aquariums designed with a liberal air surface in relation to water surface are best for our purposes. Tall narrow tanks for window sills or for special spots in decorative schemes should be populated only on the basis of their water surface. Water depth should be disregarded altogether.

Aquarium Starter Kit by Hagen.

Buy the largest tank you can afford; complete starter kits are the least expensive way to get started.

Though it appears that a deeper tank can hold more fishes, the initial supply of dissolved oxygen in the water would soon be absorbed by the overcrowded fish. It is only when actively growing plants are kept, or when the aquarium is aerated artificially, that a few additional fishes can be maintained in the deeper tank.

It should also be clear that ordinary fish globes should be filled only a little more than half way in order to bring as much water into contact with air as possible, though fish globes are not recommended.

TEMPERATURE

The word *tropicals* places too much emphasis on the idea of high temperature for all exotic fishes. A number of these exotic fishes are not from the tropics and quite a few of them from the tropics do not come from particularly warm water. It is true that most of our exotic aquarium fishes cannot stand chill. On the other hand, many of them do not prosper in high temperatures because they may need more oxygen than such water can carry.

The kind-hearted aquarist who thinks he is doing his fishes a favor by keeping their tank at 80°F or more is actually making them uncomfortable. Nor should one believe that there is an exact degree of heat which is best suited to each species. Most fishes can tolerate at least 10° changes and overnight can stand a change of 5° without injury. For example, if a fish has a safe toleration range from 70° to 80°F— and most of them have—it would be safe for such a fish to experience a drop from 75° to 70°F spread over a period of several hours.

When planning an aquarium, the temperature range of each species should be considered. The more tender fishes require warmer, evenly heated tanks; the hardier fishes can be kept in cooler tanks. For most species described in this book an approximate temperature range is given.

A great deal of needless worry and expense is incurred in trying to keep aquariums or aquarium rooms within 2° of a fixed point. Almost nowhere does nature supply such an environment. It has often been observed that fishes are stimulated by a reasonable change in temperature.

Aquarists should not be seriously concerned about the variation between the heat at the top and the bottom of the aquarium. The temperature difference in native waters is often considerable, and the fishes negotiate it without trouble. In a modern aquarium, which is usually equipped with a filter or an aerator—often with both—such stratification of temperature does not occur. The circulation in the aquarium insures an even distribution of heat.

Tolerant as fish may be they should never be forced to acclimate themselves to new temperature ranges. Experiments of this sort always result in disaster.

In practice, it comes down to this: the average exotic aquarium fish is perfectly happy at a temperature of 72° to 76°F. For short periods the temperature can drop to 68° or rise to 85°F without trouble. Even these extremes may be safely passed in aquariums that are in extra fine condition and where the fishes are not crowded. If, through uncontrollable causes, the temperature drops to the extreme danger zone of the low sixties or even the fifties, one should slowly raise it to about 80°F and keep it there for twenty-four hours or more.

LIGHT

Natural daylight is by no means a necessity for the health of aquarium fishes. Artificial light, in fact, has its advantages. It allows one to place the tank in the darkest corner of the room and it can stimulate plant growth without encouraging too much algae, since the intensity and duration of the light can be controlled easily. However, if one is going to rely on natural light, several things should be kept in mind about the location of the aquarium.

With the exception of a few species (top swimming fishes), aquarium fishes do not require light for health and can live satisfactorily in a quite subdued light. On the other hand, plants require light. They should be in a location where one can easily read a newspaper by natural light alone without the aid of artificial light. For plants of mixed varieties there should be medium light. A position by a window where there is good diffused light and, about two hours of direct sun is ideal, but not indispensable. A strong north light without sun is satisfactory. A position by a south window is likely to give too much sun and a certain amount of shading becomes necessary. The great difficulty about excessive light is the growth of too much algae. This results either in green water or a green mossy coating on glass and plants. Too much summer sun is apt to overheat small aquariums. The location of

an aquarium presents the interesting problem of securing just enough light to stimulate plant activity, but not so much as to develop other unwanted growth. Given the choice between a location with too much light and one with too little light, it is always better to select the former since one can always shade off the excess illumination.

WASTE CONTROL

Many aquariums, even those without a filter or aerator, often stay fresh and clear for very long periods of time. Such aquariums usually contain only a few fishes, but have a lush growth of various aquatic plants. They receive a proper amount of light (natural or ar-tificial, or a combination of both) and have well-fitting covers to reduce evaporation. Their owners have mastered the art of feeding their fishes the right type and amount of food at the right time. But even though the fishes breathe and produce carbon dioxide, feed and excrete solid and liquid waste materials directly into the water, the aquarium does not become a cesspool, and the fishes do not perish in their own excrement. This is a most amazing fact and the reason that makes aquarium keeping possible in the first place. How, then, are the waste products removed from the aquarium, especially if the water is not filtered? We already know that carbon dioxide, which fishes breathe out, leaves the water through the surface. But it is also used up by plants during the process of photosynthesis. The removal of the other waste products, however, which accumulate through the fishes feces and urine is a little more complicated. It is accomplished by certain bacteria which are found in any aquarium. As soon as fishes or other aquatic animals are present and produce organic waste, these bacteria start to multiply in tremendous numbers, since organic waste is food to them. The most dangerous by-product of animal waste is ammonia, which even in small quantities can be dangerous to fishes. Luckily, it is quickly attacked by these ammonia-loving bacteria, which by their action change ammonia into much less harmful nitrite. Then, as nitrite accumulates, another group of bacteria takes over to change nitrite into nitrate, which is completely harmless to fish. Nitrate does accumulate in the aquarium, but, to our knowledge, no fish has ever died from it. Actually some of the nitrate is discharged from the system into the air by a certain reversed process, again involving bacteria, in which nitrate is changed into nitrogen. In addition, growing plants incorporate some nitrate into their tissue, and if the excess plant growth is periodically removed (as it should be), a certain balance in the nitrogen cycle of an aquarium is achieved.

As we have seen, the ability of an aquarium to almost maintain itself is not dependent upon filters or aerators. Nevertheless, filters and aerators are of great help in maintaining an aquarium. Aerators will speed up the discharge of carbon dioxide and the dissolving of oxygen, and filters will rid the water of suspended solid materials, giving the water the sparkling clear quality which is so much enjoyed by the viewer. In addition, since the bacteria which are so essential to the well-being of the aquarium must settle on some solid surface to be able to do their work properly, the tremendously large surface area of the filter materials provides the perfect place for them. Therefore, biological filtration, as the conversion of waste products is called, can function even better.

With this knowledge, we can set up an aquarium, stock it with the right kind and number of fishes and plants and be reasonably certain that it will function properly. Occasionally we fail, something goes wrong: a tank may become foul, fishes die for unexplainable reasons. But fortunately, failures have become very infrequent. This is undoubtedly due both to our increased knowledge of the internal workings of an aquarium, and the ability of manufacturers to produce better products that complement the natural functioning of an aquarium.

The state of the art in aquarium filtration is Wet/Dry Filter systems.

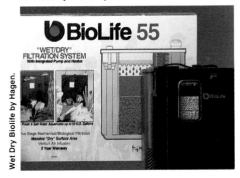

14

MANAGEMENT

A freshly filled aquarium is usually not safe for fishes. Various additives to tap water, in most cases chlorine, are toxic to fishes and have to be removed before the aquarium is stocked. Simply letting the filled tank age for a few days will usually make the water suitable. Chlorine will completely evaporate within that time. Even well water, which contains no chlorine, improves with age. Aeration and filtration will speed up this process considerably.

AERATION

In this convenient technique, a small electric pump forces the air through a tube connected to a diffuser or an airstone at the bottom of the tank, sending up a spray of small bubbles. It is a common impression that some of this air is *forced* into the water, but such is not the case. All the air is picked up by absorption, some from the bubbles, but most at the water surface. The real value of aeration lies in the fact that the rising column of bubbles sets up a circulation in the aquarium by bringing bottom water to the surface, where it is exposed to the air above it. Thus, fresh oxygen is distributed through the whole aquarium. Aeration is particularly valuable at night for those aquariums that partly depend on day-time oxygen from plants. At night plants give off no oxygen and produce carbon dioxide, a gas that should be eliminated. Aeration is almost indispensable in hot

weather, when the oxygen capacity of water is low due to the higher temperature of the water. In addition, where overcrowding of fishes is unavoidable, a stream of air through the water has the effect of practically doubling the fish capacity of the aquarium. At times a cloudy gray (not green) tank can be cleared in a few days by constant aeration.

Usually a thin stream of bubbles is sufficient for ordinary purposes. Small bubbles, using a constant flow of air, are more efficient than large ones.

OXYGEN AND WATER

The importance of oxygen to all life, and especially to the welfare of fishes, has already been explained in general. A more detailed understanding, however, is useful to the aquarist. Air is composed of approximately four parts nitrogen to one part oxygen. However, when water absorbs air it does not take the two gases in that proportion. It takes two parts of nitrogen to one of oxygen, a ratio of oxygen which is twice as rich as that which we breathe. Furthermore, the amount of oxygen that pure water can absorb depends on the temperature of the water as shown by the following table:

At 50°F, 7.8 parts per 1000 by vol.
At 60°F, 6.9 parts per 1000 by vol.
At 70°F, 6.3 parts per 1000 by vol.
At 80°F, 5.7 parts per 1000 by vol.
At 90°F, 5.0 parts per 1000 by vol.

As the table shows, oxygen content in water rapidly decreases as the temperature increases.

Under ordinary aquarium conditions, the amount of dissolved oxygen present is about half that shown in the table. This is due to the unavoidable presence of certain gases that displace the oxygen. These are generated mostly by the decomposition of organic matter (fish waste, dead leaves, etc.) and the carbon dioxide from the breathing of the fishes.

While the theoretical capacity of water to hold free oxygen at a temperature of 75° is about 6.0 parts per 1000, as a matter of fact, fishes are fairly comfortable with an oxygen content of 3.3. This is what they get in an ordinary, good aquarium at 75°F. Therefore, keeping an aquarium at about this temperature is recommended. With clean water, growing plants in good light (or the use of artificial aeration), and not too many fishes, the dissolved oxygen content can remain between 3.3 and 5.0 parts per 1000 by volume, which is good.

Contrary to popular belief, fishes are injured or killed more by an excess of carbon dioxide than by any lack of oxygen. Ample water surface areas and aeration are necessary, not only to provide the fishes with oxygen, but also to liberate poisonous carbon dioxide.

FILTERS
A number of good aquarium filters are sold commercially. Some fit into the inside corner of a rectangular aquarium, some on the outside. The outside models are usually larger and more easily cleaned and serviced. All inside filters are operated by small electrical air pumps. They are efficient enough for small tanks, but their presence inside the tank greatly detracts from the beauty of plants and fishes. Outside filters, on the other hand, can be hung on the back or side of the aquarium. Some of these are operated by air pumps, others by electrical motors. In many models, water from the aquarium is siphoned into the filter tank, circulated through the filter medium, and returned clean to the aquarium either by means of an airlift or by a motor-driven pump mechanism. Other models pump rather than siphon the aquarium water into the filter tank. After the water has passed through the filter material, it returns to the aquarium via a spillway. The latter type is somewhat easier to operate. It has fewer parts, does not rely on siphon tubes, and consequently does not depend upon a high water level in the aquarium for efficient operation. The best filter medium for inside and outside filters is a layer of filter wool coupled with a layer of activated carbon or bone charcoal. The filter wool removes dirt particles from the water and the carbon absorbs some dissolved waste products and other pollutants.

Changing the filter material periodically is a matter of good housekeeping. Normally, the filter material should be changed every two to three weeks, or whenever it looks dirty. Filters should be cleaned by scrubbing in clean water. No soap or detergents should be used. In severe cases use a bleach and rinse well.

A third type of filter is the undergravel, sub-sand, or biological filter. Most models have a perforated tray covering the entire bottom of the tank. Gravel, not sand, is placed on top of the filter and an airlift is attached to one corner. Water is filtered through the entire bottom layer of gravel and then airlifted back into the tank proper. Naturally, an air pump is needed to

absorb certain concentrations that are bound to build up where animal life is maintained in a confined space. For that reason alone, an aquarium with

Your local pet shop has starter cultures to help with sludge removal and water clarity.

Every aquarist who worries about overcrowding should have an emergency battery pump in case he needs more aeration or the electrical supply is cut off.

Pet shops carry vibrator pumps of varying capacity; a pump must be matched with the filter and air outlets.

operate this filter. As the water passes through the gravel, certain types of bacteria begin to multiply and colonize the gravel bed. These "good" bacteria convert harmful waste products into less harmful substances and thereby help maintain a biological balance in the aquarium.

An aquarium, whether it be equipped with some type of filter or no filter at all, has its natural filters in the form of plants and bacteria. Plants

healthy plants is better than one without them. Bacteria, by converting fish waste into substances plants can more readily utilize, have an important share in maintaining good water conditions. These reactions between fish, bacteria, and plants gave rise to the very good, though not quite accurate, expression "balanced aquarium."

There are chemical substances that accumulate in an established aquarium which even the best filter cannot remove. Some of these build up because water lost through evaporation is replaced by water from the tap. Since most waters contain various amounts of dissolved minerals which stay behind as water evaporates, these minerals become more and more concentrated each time water of the same chemical makeup is used to top the tank off. Adding distilled water to compensate for the evaporated water would alleviate the problem, but this is both expensive and unnecessary. A partial change of water, about ten to twenty-five percent, every four to six weeks will help to prevent a dangerous mineral buildup.

There are other little-known substances that may accumulate through fish waste or other fish secretions. These may cause fishes to grow at a slower rate than normal. Experience has taught us that partial water changes—other conditions being equal—will maintain a good growth rate and improve the well-being of fishes. This advice is in direct contrast to a theory, popular some years ago, that the older the water, the better it is for fishes.

Aquarium power filters make the job of keeping the tank clear an easy one.

Power heads attach to the undergravel filter to filter more efficiently.

The gravel can be cleaned of fish droppings and uneaten foods with a gravel cleaner.

Aquarium Gravel Cleaner by Hagen.

Heavy metals in water, like zinc and iron, are toxic and cumulative. These metals are brought into the aquarium by feeding flake fish foods that contain them in excessive amounts. Write to the manufacturer of the fish food you are using if you experience unexplainable deaths, or if you are unable to spawn fish that should spawn. Books focusing on fish health or fish physiology list the heavy metals that are toxic and the levels tolerated by fishes.

GREEN WATER

The facts about green water appear to be so simple that its control should be an easy matter. Quite the contrary is true. Unaccountably, green cloudiness arises in the tanks of the ablest aquarists and confounds even those who instruct others on how to keep water

clear! We know that the color is produced by microscopic algal cells that must have food and light in order to develop. By taking away either of these stimulants, or both, we would have no green water. But that is not easy since the plants and fishes present require light themselves and enrich the water by their breathing and by their waste products.

On the other hand, it is perfectly true that there are numberless aquariums that are healthy and clear year after year. It would seem that we should be able to reproduce the same condition at will. To a great extent we can. In such aquariums we nearly always find plenty of strong, growing plants. The reason may be that the plants successfully compete with the green cells (suspended algae) for both food and light.

In these perpetually clear tanks two other things will be observed. The fishes are not crowded and there is only sufficient light to keep the plants in good condition. That is to say, when the supply of life elements is just enough to keep the plants going and there is practically no excess left, then the green organisms are kept under control.

Many of these green water cells go through periods of activity. If allowed to subside naturally, the water may remain clear for a long time. Then, with only a partial change of aquarium water, they may again become stimulated and start out on a fresh rampage.

The two principal rules to follow to maintain clear water are: (1) have no more fish than the tank can easily support *without aeration*, and (2) use only enough light to keep plants healthy. If necessary, green water can also be reduced in several other ways: by interposing a suitable thickness of paper on the light side of the aquarium; by applying tinted crystal varnish to the outside glass; by using a mantle of floating plants such as Duckweed, *Salvinia*, or Water Fern. Such a canopy upon the surface of the water will not significantly reduce the dissolving of oxygen and the releasing of carbon dioxide from the water if slight aeration is used.

Remember that green water is not an unmitigated evil. In moderation it is healthy and depleted fishes sometimes improve in it.

Remove some fishes if crowding is suspected. Feed less. Every scrap of food becomes fertilizer. Siphon the bottom frequently.

When green water reaches the *soupy* stage and is very opaque it is dangerous, especially in hot weather. It is liable to decompose suddenly and kill fishes. A change to a slightly yellowish tinge is the danger signal. This calls for an immediate change of water—minutes count!

CLOUDY WATER

Green water is cloudy, but cloudy water is not necessarily green. There is a difference. The causes of gray cloudiness are usually decaying food (overfeeding) or too many fishes. The cloudiness is actually a population explosion of bacteria due to the sudden availability of food in the form of decaying organic matter. Newly-set-

up aquariums are particularly prone to gray cloudiness because the plants have not yet begun to function fully. In such aquariums clouding can also come from sand that has not been well cleaned. For these and other reasons, it is best to have an aquarium planted and in a favorable light a week before the fishes are introduced. Even then, the aquarium should not be taxed immediately to its full limit of fishes. Start with a few fishes and add more from time to time.

CLEARING WATER

The best way to clear up cloudy water is to correct one or more of its underlying causes. However, there are ways in which clearing can be accelerated. Gray cloudiness can be reduced in a few days by constant aeration. If fishes are temporarily removed from a green-water aquarium, the water can be cleared by introducing live *Daphnia*. These small crustaceans feed on suspended algal cells, thereby cleaning the water. After the water has cleared, the fishes can be returned to the tank to feast on the *Daphnia*. Normal filtering apparati will remove neither suspended algae nor cloudy-water bacteria, since both are too small to be retained by filter wool and charcoal. There are, however, a few specialized filters on the market which use diatomaceous earth as the filter medium. They are designed to filter out minute particles and are an excellent tool for clearing cloudy water. As a permanent filter they are less useful, since an excess of larger debris causes them to clog very quickly.

Activated Carbon by Hagen.

Above: A fluorescent aquarium hood protects the tank from airborne contaminants. **Below:** *Activated carbon in a filter removes dangerous gases, heavy metals and discoloration from aquarium water.*

There are also a few chemical products available which are useful in clearing cloudy tanks. Read the label and follow the instructions. However, if the underlying causes are not corrected, the tank will become cloudy again no matter what method is used. Copper sulfate in proper dosage is used by professionals, but it is very toxic, as are most heavy metals.

WATER CONTAMINANTS

Water absorbs not only beneficial oxygen but also injurious gases and fumes. Fumes from varnishes, varnish removers, paints, turpentine, shellac, insecticides, or anything containing wood alcohol are all injurious to aquarium water and often they are fatal. An excess of tobacco smoke can be hazardous too. With the advent of the all-glass aquarium, metal contamination is much less likely to occur. However, troublesome condensation can collect on defectively plated or aluminum top reflectors and run into the tank. Be sure to place a glass cover between the water surface and the fixture or use an enclosed reflector. A glass cover keeps room dust from falling into the water, cuts down evaporation, and prevents the fishes from leaping out.

ALGAE ON GLASS

A green film of algae on glass is one of the aquarist's greatest griefs. It is bound to occur at one time or another. It can be removed easily with an aquarium scraper. Many fishes, especially Mollies, Swordtails, Kissing Gouramies, and some Catfishes are extremely fond of algae, which is undoubtedly beneficial as food. Two species of fish in particular are sold in pet shops for the purpose of keeping glass and plants free of algae: the South American suckermouth catfish (*Plecostomus*) and the Indian algae eater (*Gyrinocheilus*). These fishes do much toward keeping the glass and plants clear. *Plecostomus*, however, are apt to grow unpleasantly large for the average aquarium and two of them will often fight with each other. Though not very hardy, the little *Otocinclus* is the best plant cleaner, for it works both sides of the leaves. Your local aquarium shop has plenty of exotic scavengers, from time to time, so visit it regularly. It should be remembered that algae are not an unmixed evil.

Rusty brown algae are obnoxious and hard to eliminate. They usually grow in tanks which are dimly lit. Equally hard to eliminate are the smelly blue-green algae that sometimes infest tanks kept at tropical temperatures. If left alone, they create a mantle over everything and suffocate the plants. They are soft and easily wiped off.

Long, hard, hairy types of algae sometimes take over a tank. These algae cannot be rubbed from plants. The sole remedy is to remove the fishes, destroy the plants, disinfect the aquarium with a wash of weak ammonia, bleach or strong salt, and start again with clean plants—and hope for the best.

SCUM ON WATER

The cause of scum on water, a disagreeable condition, is often puzzling. It may come from decomposing vegetation, oily food, atmospheric settling, or from domestic frying or greasy cooking. Persistent removal by drawing a paper over the surface may overcome it. Covering the tank with glass helps. Mechanical aeration of the water dispels it.

SCAVENGERS

Many aquarists, especially beginners, ask too much of so-called *scaven-*

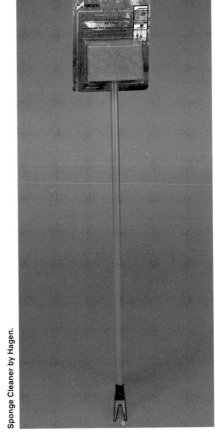

Sponge Cleaner by Hagen.

Sponge Cleaner and Planter is a useful gadget.

gers. It is unreasonable to expect any creature to take all undesirable matter out of an aquarium and utterly destroy it or to keep the glass cleaner than the aquarist would. The original aquarium scavengers were Freshwater Snails. Other important assistants are Weatherfishes, Armored Catfishes, Tadpoles, Freshwater Mussels, and Freshwater Shrimp. All, except the Mussels, hunt out and eat particles of food that have been missed or rejected by the other occupants of the aquarium. This is a very important service

Basic Aquarium Products by Hagen.

Don't buy junk. Only buy nationally advertised products guaranteed by the manufacturer to be free of defects.

for it prevents the evil chain of conditions and events that are caused by the decomposition of such food. It has been argued that scavengers only convert this food into humus. But that is precisely the service they render: the humus they produce (their droppings) is far less harmful than the decomposing food.

Unfortunately, scavengers are often added after the aquarium is fully stocked with other fishes. This practice overcrowds the tank. Scavengers should be counted as part of the entire fish population. Some snails keep down the film of green algae from glass and plants, but none of them get *all* of it. They cannot, unassisted, make a polished plate-glass parlor of the aquarium.

Many fishes kill small snails. Big "Mystery Snails" fare better. Snails eat fish spawn, but never attack live fishes, not even very small ones. This makes them valuable in cleaning up uneaten food in the aquarium nursery. When big Mystery Snails die, they usually cause pollution since their death is rarely noticed.

SNAILS

The popular European Red Ramshorn Snail (*Planorbis corneus*) continues to hold interest. Bright red ones, free from chippings or blemishes, are always in demand and their breeding is a matter of some commercial value. In order to get them clear red, they must be grown rapidly, and to be grown quickly they must have plenty of room, warmth, and food, together with slightly alkaline water. The preferred foods are spinach, lettuce, and boiled oatmeal containing powdered shrimp. They should be fed as much as they can possibly eat. This has a tendency to foul the water which, in turn, produces erosion of the shells. Therefore, the bottom of the tank should be siphoned off frequently and fresh water added. *Daphnia* tends to clear the water and to prosper at the job. The flat, amber egg-masses appear freely in the early spring. If properly raised, snails will be ready for the market in October, although the demand is greater in midwinter. The eggs hatch in anywhere from ten to forty days, according to temperature. Nearly all fishes destroy newly hatched Red Ramshorn Snails. Freshwater Limpets are very small snails completely covered by translucent shells, like low parasols, rather oval in outline, usually about ⅛ inch across. They are really miniature scavengers and quite harmless. They appear unaccountably, often coming in with aquarium plants.

Pond Snails (*Physa*) are considered the best by many aquarists. Their clear, jelly-like spawn brings forth young that are too hard for most small fishes to eat. Some consider this snail a pest since it multiplies so freely.

Colombian Striped Ramshorn (*Marisa cornuarietis*), reaching a diameter of 1½ inches, is the best of several South American introductions. It is very handsome but eats the softer plants.

The Australian Red Snail is a most prolific breeder outdoors and a handsome creature with a yellowish red body.

The handsome and once popular Paper-shelled Snail dislikes warm water. It breeds rapidly but lives only a year. Like the native snails, such as *Physa* and *Lymnaea,* it survives winter outdoors if not actually encased in ice.

The Apple Snails are the big, round, four-horned *Pomacea* from South America and Florida. All except one are ravenous plant eaters. They are sometimes known as "infusoria snails." The exception is *Pomacea cuprina*; for some mysterious reason it is known in the trade as the Mystery Snail. It does not eat living plants and is a fair scavenger. If not getting enough pick-ups, it should have some boiled spinach.

It may be distinguished from the destructive *Pomacea* by the depressed channel around the turns of its rather high spiral. The destructive *Pomacea paludosa* has a low spiral and no channel. All these snails spawn great masses of eggs above the water, generally at night. The young fall into the water as they hatch. Hatching (in about two weeks) requires a warm, moist atmosphere.

The Japanese Live-bearing Snail, like Goldfish, prefers cool water and is therefore popular mainly among Goldfish fanciers. Being large and meaty, these snails are also relished in Japan as food. The young, about the size of a pea, are born alive and fully formed. The right horn of the male is slightly shorter and serves as a sex indication. Once impregnated, a female appears to be fertile for life. Identification of species is by the high spiral and slightly raised keels on the big turn. The so-called American Potomac Snail, sometimes sold as the Japanese species, is generally similar but has no keels. It is sluggish, spending most of its time buried in the sand.

One other species of snail that is popular is the Malaysian Burrowing Snail (*Melanoides tuberculata*), a very effective scavenger. This snail spends much of its time foraging through the gravel bed where it cleans up much of the decomposing matter. It is a prolific breeder.

Full Range Aquarium Products by Hagen.

Your local pet shop should have nationally advertised products for EVERY one of your aquarium needs.

Mussels remove suspended green algae from the water to some extent, but they require checking to see if they are alive. We are inclined not to recommend mussels, especially since heat does not agree with them. The risk is hardly worth the doubtful benefits.

Several species of fishes called *Corydoras* are generally considered the best aquarium scavengers. They belong to the Armored Catfishes and

are illustrated and described later under their own headings. They are popular as well as effective in cleaning up leftovers. Their rooting activities tend to stir up sediment which the filter can then remove from the water.

CHANGING THE WATER

The most popular question put by the beginner is, "How often must I change the water?" As stated earlier, a partial change of water (replacing of ten to twenty-five percent of aquarium water every four to six weeks with seasoned tap water) is a good practice. With good management and sensible feeding practices no other water changes are required. There are two main qualities in water to be considered: acid-alkaline and hard-soft. These characteristics are not related to each other (except that hard-alkaline and soft-acid conditions often go together) and require different tests for detection.

WHAT IS pH?

Under usual conditions water is either acid or alkaline, seldom exactly neutral. The term *pH* has reference to those opposite factors and their degree of intensity. A scale has been set up by chemists in which 7.0 represents neutral. Higher figures are alkaline, lower figures are acid. The scale is set up logarithmically, rather than arithmetically: there is a ten-fold value between full numbers. For example, a reading of 6.0 is ten times more acidic than a reading of 7.0.

Readings are arrived at by taking a small specimen of the water to be

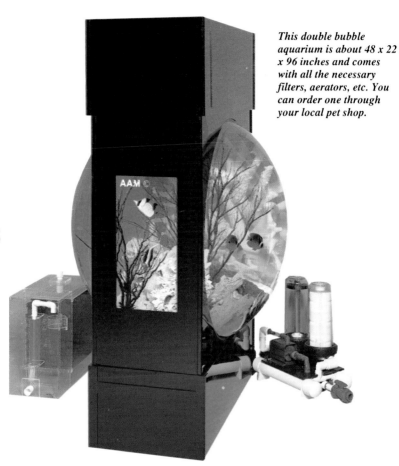

This double bubble aquarium is about 48 x 22 x 96 inches and comes with all the necessary filters, aerators, etc. You can order one through your local pet shop.

It is necessary to control the pH of your aquarium water. This is easily done with buffering solutions for the short term.

tested and placing in it a few drops of a sensitive dye called indicator solution. The color to which the specimen turns is compared with a standard comparison scale consisting of several numbered shades. Readings are determined by finding the shade most nearly matching the water into which the dye was placed. Testing sets are sold by aquarium dealers and by scientific instrument firms. Those sets in which the matching shades are on printed cards should be kept out of long exposure to light, especially daylight. Very accurate, but very expensive, electronic pH meters are available, too. But it is questionable whether that degree of accuracy is really important enough to warrant the high price.

Chemicals for pH adjustments are sold in petshops. However, such adjustments in established aquariums are temporary and they usually return to the original pH in a matter of days. Most well-managed tanks settle in at a pH of 6 to about 7.5, which is fine for almost all fishes.

HARDNESS

The degree of hardness of tap water is usually determined by the ease or difficulty with which soap suds form in it. Hardness is mainly caused by compounds of calcium and magnesium. Unlike pH, there is no neutral point between hard and soft water. It is simply a question of *how much* of the hardening minerals are present. From 0 to 50 parts per million is considered soft; from 50 to 100, moderately hard; from 100 to 200, hard

and above 200, very hard. (One grain per gallon equals 17 parts per million.) Contact with limestone formations is the main cause of hardness. Deep wells have higher hardness content than open streams in the same locality.

Similar fishes are found prospering in either moderately hard or moderately soft water. However, hardness has certain effects on both fishes and plants. It has been found that some of the hard-to-spawn fishes are stimulated to breed when changed from hard to soft water. This seems to carry out what happens in nature. A long dry season concentrates the mineral content of the water, thus making it hard. Spawning often comes with the rainy season and consequent softening of the water.

The addition of distilled or clean rainwater will correct too much hardness. There are also filter materials which reduce hardness as long as they are not overworked. Nature's waters, are used in whole or part by some breeders for fishes that require specific water conditions.

There are hardness testing sets that can be purchased in aquarium stores. Boiling removes some hardness, however boiled water should be thoroughly aerated before use.

Due to concentration by evaporation, hardness increases in an aquarium over a period of months if no water is drawn off. As pointed out earlier, it is occasionally advisable to siphon away about ten to twenty-five percent of the water and replace it with fully aged water.

Hardness is increased by the presence of a large number of shells from dead snails as well as by sand or gravel containing much lime. Although they have no place in the freshwater aquarium, pieces of coral and empty sea shells are sometimes used as decorative items. These pieces contribute greatly to hardness of the water.

HEATERS

Most heaters on the market today are thermostatically controlled. They consist of a partially or fully submerged tube in which there is an electric coil. The coil is usually placed at the lower end of the tube in order to contact the cooler strata of water and thus produce circulation in the tank. The upper end of the tube houses the thermostat with a knob to set the heater for any desired temperature. Heaters are made in different wattages, most commonly from twenty-five watts to two hundred fifty watts. The best rule for selecting the proper heater is to allow five watts for every gallon of water. Thus, for a ten-gallon tank, a fifty-watt heater should be used. Most fishes will do well at a temperature between 70° and 82°F. Since few heaters are made with a built-in thermometer, a separate thermometer is needed to check the temperature. There are many models available and most of them are accurate enough for our purposes. A heated tank should also be filtered or aerated to insure an even distribution of temperature.

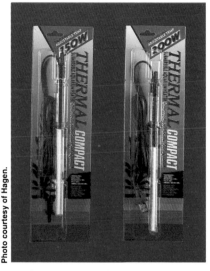

Photo courtesy of Hagen.

Modern heaters are thermostatically controlled.

SUDDEN CHANGES OF TEMPERATURE

While most fishes can tolerate a slow change of temperature over a range of 10° to 15°F, changing fishes from a tank at one temperature to another having a different temperature of several degrees, either up or down, is one of the things that absolutely *must not be done*. Bad results may not be apparent at once, but they are seldom escaped. The fishes usually get the shakes or shimmies, *Ichthyophthirius* (ich), fungus, or general decline. Changes should be made within 2° of the same original temperature.

REFLECTORS AND HOODS

The ordinary artificial illumination of a living room, even though it penetrates into the aquarium, is worthless

Light is necessary for the aquarium. New types of fluorescent lamps simulate the sun's spectrum are available through your local pet shop.

for plants. Electric light, to be of value to plants, must be *very close, preferably overhead.* Various devices are manufactured for holding bulbs in position over aquariums. The reflectors sold for aquariums are generally rather narrow, covering only part of the tank. Hoods are complete covers with a light fixture built in. Halogen lights and other high intensity sources can be remote from the aquarium. Halogen might well be the best light, and it requires neither a reflector nor a hood. In the usual reflector, either incandescent or fluorescent bulbs are used, but occasionally a full hood incorporates both types. It should be kept in mind that incandescent light produces a warm light, generates heat, and the bulbs burn out quickly. Fluorescent light, on the other hand, produces practically no heat, consumes less electricity, and the bulbs have a long life. However, it is more expensive to install. When selecting fluorescent light, the warm white fluorescent tubes gives the best illumination.

Special bulbs, which have been developed for growing plants, can also be used for the aquarium. These tend to exaggerate the colors of fishes, making them appear more brilliant.

How much light and how long it should be kept on during the day depends upon the availability of daylight. However, a tank receiving very little daylight (one not close to a window) should be lit for ten to 12 hours daily. When using fluorescent light there is no choice about the wattage of the tube. The length of the tank determines the length of the bulb and therefore its wattage. With incandescent bulbs, care should be taken not to overheat the tank. Two twenty-five watt bulbs are the maximum for a ten-gallon tank. A larger tank may require forty-watt bulbs. No tank needs stronger bulbs, provided they are placed in a reflector directly above the tank.

Along with the petty cruelties to fishes that might be mentioned is the thoughtless practice of suddenly placing them in powerful light when they have gotten used to darkness. If the aquarium is in a darkened room, the room lights should be switched on a few minutes before the aquarium light is turned on. The fish give every evidence of experiencing the same distress we would feel under like circumstances. A little care in this matter is a kindness that is not misspent.

COVERS

Tanks should be covered both to keep the fish in and the dust out. A cover also reduces evaporation. Care should be taken so that spray does not wet the electrical fixtures of a hood or reflector.

NUMBER OF FISHES PER AQUARIUM

If you have a well-proportioned tank with liberal water surface, you can make a rough calculation of the number of fish it will support from the following example for a ten-gallon tank: small fishes (1 to $1^1/_2$ inches long), such as Guppies, Zebras, Cardinals—about twenty fishes per tank; medium fishes (2 to 3 inches long), such as Swordtails, Mollies, Platies—ten to twelve fishes per tank; large fishes (4 to 5 inches long), such as grown Clown Barbs, Discus, Angelfish—two to four fishes per tank.

SELECTING AND BUYING FISHES

Look for fishes with fins that stay erect most of the time. They should swim in a relaxed manner, not jerkily or with nervous dashes. The belly outline is also a good indication of a fish's condition. Good specimens have a rounded belly outline; poor specimens have sunken-in stomachs. This is especially important when buying some of the live-bearing fishes, such as Mollies, Platies, Swordtails and Guppies.

Don't buy out of a tank where fishes shimmy, that is, they go through violent shaking and swimming motions while standing still.

Make sure fins are intact. The fins should not be split or frayed and the body should show no marks or injuries.

Avoid fishes with small white spots or blotches on their body or fins.

Fishes should be alert and actively avoid the net when being caught.

INTRODUCING FISHES

Before the trip to the store, the tank should be fully prepared with the water properly aged and the temperature set. The container—plastic cup, paper cup or plastic bag—with the fishes should then be "floated" in the tank to gradually equalize the temperature of the two waters. Slowly mix the waters and let the fish swim out. This procedure is usually sufficient since most fishes are able to withstand gradual changes. In cases where waters are known to be very different in temperature, hardness, or pH, the change should be made more slowly.

CATCHING FISHES

Approach the task of catching fishes with confidence but not conceit; with determination not to lose patience nor ruin the plants. Any fish can be outwitted and outwaited by man. Each species has its peculiarities, but initially captured, all individuals of that species can be caught by the same method. Many species yield to very slow movement. This is the first thing to try. When a fish seems nearly caught by the slow-motion method, it is almost sure to dash away if the net accidentally taps the glass. This is often difficult to avoid, but should be kept in mind. A net in each hand often helps—a large one for a catcher and a small one for a persuader.

Very small, newly hatched fishes had best not be handled at all. But, if necessary, a good way is to raise them near the surface with a fine net and then dip out fishes and a little water in a spoon.

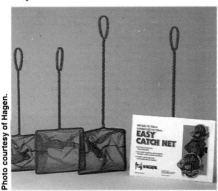

Properly shaped nets.

NETS

Except for use in globes, all nets should have straight edges. Suitable nylon netting is preferable to knotted threads. Nets should be hung up when not in use. It is a good practice to rinse all nets in clear water before drying. Every aquarist loses fishes by having them leap from a net while being trans-

ferred. We can only suggest to take extreme care at this moment. A net should be deep enough so that the free hand can form a little bag to close off the fishes. A net should not be so deep as to entangle the fishes and tear their fins when they struggle. Small nets, up to about three-by-four-inch frames, should be as deep as they are wide. Larger nets can be proportionately shallower. With large aquariums a large net is almost indispensable. Professionals, who must catch their fishes without wasting much time, often have a square net nearly the full width and depth of the tank. With this the fishes are raised to the surface and then removed by a smaller net.

BULLIES

Sometimes an individual fish, possibly of a peaceful species, learns that other fishes will flee if chased. This becomes a sport with that fish, to the misery of its fellows and the discomfort of its owner. It should either be disposed of, partitioned off (perhaps in a corner like a dunce), or placed in another aquarium with larger fishes. There, among strangers, it may reform. Like the rooster taken out of its own barnyard, it will not fight so well.

TEMPERATURE AND MEASUREMENT SCALES

In practically all aquarium literature, except that written in English, Centigrade measurements (often abbreviated as C) are used to designate temperature. Centigrade measurements translate into these Fahrenheit

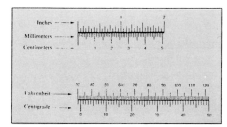

is the same as a cubic decimeter.

The great advantage of the metric system is that it is based on the decimal system. The denominations are in multiples of ten so that multiplication or division, within the range of those multiples, is accomplished by merely moving the decimal point forward or backward.

equivalents: It will be noticed that Centigrade zero is the freezing point, 32° in Fahrenheit. On the higher part of the scale, not shown, the Centigrade boiling point at 100° equals Fahrenheit 212°.

In most foreign aquarium literature we find measurements expressed in the metric system, which is gradually coming into general use. For those who have not been reared to think in those terms, we give a few of the most important equivalents. There are three principal measurements of this kind which foreign aquarists use.

Two of the measurements met with most often in foreign publications are the *centimeter* and the *cubic centimeter*, abbreviated respectively as *cm.* and *cc.* For all practical purposes there are five centimeters to two inches, as shown on the accompanying parallel scale. The ten subdivisions to be seen in the centimeters are *millimeters*. These are universally used by scientists to designate the lengths of the smaller fishes, such as we keep in our aquariums and of small objects, such as fish eggs.

The third measurement we often read is the *liter*. It expresses capacity and is just a trifle over a quart. It comprises 1000 cubic centimeters and

That extra tank doesn't have to be hidden. Hanging on your wall can be a living picture. It can house the extra fish; it can be an isolation tank; it is a great maternity tank, too.

Wall Aquarium by GM Aquatics.

FEEDING

How fishes are fed is just as important as *what* they are fed. A poor food properly handled may give better results than an excellent one used without judgment.

HOW OFTEN TO FEED

Temperature and oxygen directly influence the amount of food a fish can properly consume. The life processes (metabolism) of all cold-blooded animals are very much affected by temperature. The warmer they are, within their own established limits, the faster they breathe, digest, eliminate, and grow. Such animals as frogs, turtles, and alligators offer extreme examples of this law. With a few degrees deficiency in temperature they will refuse food for months on end. Lizards, lightening fast in the sun, are torpid in the cool of the morning and can be picked up. A warm water aquarium fish has an indifferent appetite at 67°F, a good one at 72°, and a ravenous one at 77°. Its appetite does not increase above 80° because of the diminished oxygen content of the water at the higher temperature. Appetite and digestion are twins and both require oxygen as well as warmth. It is well to keep in mind that exotic fishes, mostly from tropical countries, normally lead a life that is speeded up and needs a fair supply of fuel delivered frequently. In practical terms this means adult fishes should be fed at least twice daily instead of once. Such a practice not only doubles the pleasure of aquarists, who usually like to feed their charges, but also makes fishes bigger, better, and happier.

Regardless of all other rules, theories, practices, or printed instructions, the aquarist should stick tenaciously to this one: *Feed only enough prepared food at one time so that practically ALL of it is consumed within three minutes.* The rigid application of this rule will prevent many mysterious ills, as well as much clouding of water.

If it is impossible to feed more than once daily, the morning is the best time, especially if the aquarium contains healthy growing plants. The oxygen the plants develop during the day aids the digestion of the fishes. At night, the plants give off carbon dioxide which inhibits digestion. In addition, any leftover food particle is likely to be consumed during the day while the fishes can find it. At night, it would only decay. I have never seen a fish die of starvation. I have seen millions die from overfeeding. As a matter of fact, overfeeding is the principle cause of fish death in the aquarium.

CARE DURING ABSENCE

If one must be away for a week or two, it is safer to let the fishes go hungry rather than entrust their feeding to someone without experience. It is quite extraordinary what number of things can go wrong when aquariums are in unfamiliar hands. In leaving the fishes unfed, it may relieve the mind to remember that when fishes are shipped and are on the road several days they arrive without signs of starvation. Should the aquarist be away two weeks or more and finds it is necessary to call in a substitute, let that person first do an actual feeding with instructions and under supervision. Substitute caretakers should tend towards *underfeeding* and be most particular to replace glass covers.

A very good plan is to leave with the novice caretaker a set of one-meal packets of food designating the aquarium in which each is to be used.

When fishes must be kept without food for several days, it is better to maintain them at a temperature of 70° rather than at a higher temperature range.

FISH FOODS

It is generally conceded that living foods produce the best results and it is, therefore, the ideal of every amateur or professional maker of prepared foods to produce a compound that will be approximately as satisfactory as a living food, such as *Daphnia* and brine shrimp. This is a fine ambition; a prepared food that is perfect would answer every aquarist's prayer. Each manufacturer of food believes his own to be the best, but as yet no impartial, competent comparison has ever been made. Aquarists, bewildered by a chorus of claims, often use several brands, hoping to combine the merits of all. Not a bad idea, if one has no time to make systematic tests. The fishes surely give evidence of enjoying a change, so why not let them have it? Heavy metal content of flake foods may be a serious problem. Stay way from foods with contents of iron, zinc, copper or cyanide.

PREPARED FOODS

Prepared foods come in many forms: granular, flake, pelleted, paste, and freeze-dried (irregular lumps). When selecting a prepared food one should keep in mind whether it sinks or floats. Granular, pelleted, and paste foods often sink rapidly and get lodged in gravel where they can quickly cloud water. Great care should be taken when using them. Flake foods float much longer and, if not eaten immediately, cloud water less. It is also easier to judge the amount eaten by the fish when using flake foods. Flake foods are usually more expensive, ounce for ounce or gram for gram, than pelletized or granular foods.

Lumps of freeze-dried foods, especially brine shrimp, are ideal for larger fishes.

A splendid moist food, though a bit of trouble to make, and suited to all but very small fishes, is made as follows:

One pound of beef or calf liver, finely chopped and put through a blender twice. Strain through fine wire sieve. Add one level tablespoon of salt. Mix with spinach in the form of baby food. Add fourteen level tablespoons of a cereal-base baby food and six of wheat germ. Stir well, pack in small screw-top jars. Pasteurize thirty minutes. Cool and store in refrigerator. This is known "Dr. Gordon's formula," named after Dr. Myron Gordon, who used it while he was a geneticist at the New York Aquarium. The

Frozen Brine Shrimp and other foods by San Francisco Bay Brands.

Your local pet shop should carry a full line of frozen aquarium fish foods. Vary your fishes' diet.

formula was developed by his assistant, Dr. Herbert R. Axelrod. He and Axelrod used mostly Platies and Swordtails in their cancer research and produced many of the now common color varieties of these fishes. Because of Axelrod's involvement with aquarium fishes, all of the color varieties developed in Gordon's lab on the roof of the American Museum of Natural History in New York City ended up in fish farms in Florida where

Flake foods and pellet foods are staples. Vary your fishes' diet between flakes, pellets, frozen and live foods.

Photo courtesy of Hagen.

they were mass produced for the aquarium hobby. A great debt of gratitude is owed to these two scientists.

FROZEN FOODS

Pet shops offer more than twenty varieties of frozen fish foods among which are brine shrimp, *Daphnia,* bloodworms, and *Tubifex* worms. Like frozen food for human consumption, these foods should be kept frozen all the time. Any thawed-out portion not used at once should be thrown out. To feed frozen foods, it is best to break off a piece of appropriate size, thaw it out in a jar of water, stir, let food particles settle, pour discolored water off, and then feed.

LIVE FOODS

Except in a few cases, live foods are not indispensable, but they are always desirable. They are important for baby fishes and they round out a needed ingredient which few, if any, prepared fish foods possess.

Daphnia

Daphnia are the best known of the living foods. They are of almost universal distribution. However, one can not go to any body of water anywhere and get what the fish might describe as a delicious dish of *Daphnia*. It is not as easy as that.

While it is true that this little aquatic flea-like crustacean occurs in fresh water almost everywhere, it only appears in concentrated numbers in a comparatively few places—rather unpleasant places as a rule. At the margins of pools in city dumping grounds we sometimes find the true hobbyist enveloped in a cloud of mosquitoes, patiently swirling a net through evil-looking water, hoping to land a few million of the bugs. What none but the initiated can understand is that the fish fan likes to do it.

Cyclops

Cyclops are found in *Daphnia* ponds. They are a slight, small animal with one central eye which moves rapidly in a straight line through a series of jumps. Sometimes there is a double tab on the end of the body; this

Live Adult Brine Shrimp

is the female's egg pouch and soon drops off. It is nearly impossible to gather enough *Cyclops* to make a substantial food, but for fishes that catch them on their own they make a good food.

Flies

Houseflies freshly swatted, are very fine food for larger species. Once fishes become used to them, they are always on the lookout for their owner to give them a few as a special treat.

Live Brine Shrimp

The live food most often stocked by pet shops is adult Brine shrimp. Slightly larger than *Daphnia,* they are nevertheless relished by as small a fish as the Neon Tetra. Brine shrimp are col-

Brine Shrimp Hatching Device

lected daily in the shallow salt ponds of the San Francisco Bay Area and several other brine or alkaline ponds and shipped via air freight to most dealers in the United States. They are also available in England, Australia and other countries where they are collected from solar evaporating ponds where salt is harvested. Being sea creatures, they need to be kept in salt water of a rather high density, specific gravity 1.025 (four to six ounces of salt per gallon of water). For feeding, therefore, they must absolutely be strained through a net instead of poured into the tank. Adult brine shrimp are able to live in fresh water for two or more hours. Store in refrigerator or with aeration.

Brine Shrimp Eggs

Dried eggs of the brine shrimp (*Artemia salina*) are now sold by most dealers and are a godsend to all breeders of aquarium fishes. About the size of ground pepper, they are sprinkled on salted water (six ounces of non-iodized salt to the gallon). After a day or two at temperatures between 70° and 80°, they bring forth thousands of tiny visible brine shrimp nauplii, living tidbits of food for baby fishes and those up to and over one inch long. No serious breeder can be successful without newly hatched baby brine shrimp. They are the first food for almost all egg-laying and live-bearing fishes.

Live Tubifex Worms

Even full-grown fishes such as Swordtails gorge themselves on them. Various devices are now on the market for hatching them.

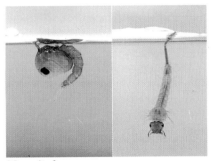

Mosquito larva
Left: pupa, Right: larva

***Tubifex* Worms**

Sometimes in *Daphnia* pools one finds a rusty edge around the shore that looks hopefully like *Daphnia* but turns out to be a mass of wriggling, threadlike worms called *Tubifex*. When they are alarmed they become quiet and draw back for a short time into their cases. It is quite impractical to either collect or propagate *Tubifex* worms, nor is there usually a need since they are obtainable the year round from professionals.

The best way to store these worms for use is to place them in a pail under a small stream of water from the tap. The worms remain in a mass at the bottom of the container. Occasionally one should break up the mass using a strong stream in order to wash away the dead worms. The colder the water, the longer they last. They can also be stored in the refrigerator in a shallow pan without water.

Sometimes these worms infest the

soil of aquariums. A few of them do no harm; in fact, they provide fishes with an occasional homegrown and quite wholesome snack. Heavy infestations, however, consume oxygen.

Some of the gravel-chewing Cichlids (*Geophagus*), many of the Armored Catfishes and most Loaches rout them from the gravel bed.

Mosquito Larvae

Here we consider a living food that is often present in *Daphnia* pools and in many other pools as well. In season it is found in almost any pool that is free of fishes, especially in water containing decaying vegetation, such as old leaves. In many instances mosquitoes place their eggs in rain puddles. This is the reason we have more mosquitoes in rainy seasons. The eggs hatch in a few days and become wrigglers. They are usually dark and straight; they have a big head at one end and a Y-shaped ending at the other. In length they average perhaps 1/4 inch when fully developed. When not eating they congregate in masses to breathe at the surface of the water, but are ready to wriggle to the bottom when alarmed. For this reason it is necessary to approach them rather carefully and make one quick sweep with the net. They can be carried in water in a crowded state and need no ice. Mosquito larvae are good for fishes large enough to swallow them readily. Fishes about an inch in length have been known to choke on them and larger ones to over-eat on them. Vessels containing stored mosquito larvae should be covered with gauze to prevent es-

Glass Worm

cape of the flying pests. Their egg rafts look like 1/8 inch bits of floating soot. It is well to learn to recognize and collect them, for on water they hatch into numerous very small larvae that make splendid food for any fishes the size of newly born live-bearers. When larvae are collected from suspiciously foul pools, it is just as well to give them a rinsing in fresh water before feeding or storing.

Glass Worms

In many lakes and ponds throughout the land one may break the ice in midwinter and net out a liberal supply of live food called Glass Worms. They are the larvae of a fly, are about half an inch in length and are nearly transparent. From a top view they look some-

Blood Worms

thing like a miniature pike. Although popularly called worms, they are not worm-like in appearance. They last remarkably well in crowded conditions and will keep for weeks in cool water. Their value as a live food is fair. They have been known to eat fish spawn and newly hatched fry.

Bloodworms

Often in *Daphnia* ponds and other bodies of water one sees deep red, jointed worms, about half an inch long, wriggling awkwardly through the water. They are bloodworms, the larvae of *Chironomus* midges. Wild fishes eat them ravenously, and they are an extremely nourishing food for all ex-

cept the smaller varieties of aquarium fishes.

White Worms

White worms, little relatives of the earthworm, are about an inch long. They are cultivated; cultures may be had commercially. Advertisements in *Tropical Fish Hobbyist* magazine can lead you to sources of supply if your local dealer cannot supply them. Under proper conditions they may multiply very rapidly. Keep in covered, damp soil that is spongy and contains plenty of leaf mold or similar matter. Every two days stir in as much dry baby cereal or oatmeal as they will consume in that time. Or they may be fed a

The River Tank is the latest thing in aquarium beauty. It is an aquarium, a terrarium and you can grow aquatic and bog plants in it, too. Almost ALL living aquarium plants grow out of the water, too. Photo courtesy of Finn-Strong Design.

variety of foods placed in holes in the soil and covered over. Mashed potatoes, cheese, bread wet with milk, or shelled boiled lima beans are some of the offerings they like and prosper on. Overfeeding sours the soil. Mite-like creatures usually accompany them but do no particular harm, nor are they related. The principal enemies of white worms, or *Enchytraeids*, are ants, mice, and heat. They like a temperature of about 60°F. It is difficult to keep them over the summer. Most amateurs buy a new culture each fall. Petshops can usually order starter cultures for hobbyists, or they can be purchased directly from mail order houses which specialize in aquarium supplies. There are many methods of getting the worms out for feeding purposes. A pair of tweezers dipped into a mass of the worms seems to be about as good as any. As worms in general are hosts to various parasites, it is good practice to cleanse and purge them in clear water for an hour or more before using. They won't drown.

Earthworms

Known also as the garden worm, rain worm, and fishing worm, the earthworm is nature's gift to fishes, and man cannot improve on it. Even vegetarian fishes take it with relish. Game fishes probably suspect the hook but cannot resist the worm. Not much need be said about collecting this choice food. That is a matter of local experience. The one thing to avoid is taking the evil-smelling dung worm, usually inhabiting manure piles and exuding a disgusting yellow secre-

tion. Even wild fishes will not touch them.

Small worms are more tender and generally preferable. Most aquarium fishes require them chopped up, although some the size of large Cichlids can take them whole. A pair of old scissors does the job very well. These worms are fine for putting fishes into breeding condition. Gather a big supply of them in the fall for winter use. Keep in damp earth, but not wet. Feed lightly on mashed potatoes, corn meal, or rolled oats. They may be cleansed by keeping for a week in moist sphagnum moss, or for a day in water. They won't drown. For safety one can scald them. Most live-bait stores sell earthworms.

Gammarus

Gammarus is a widely-distributed, hard, shrimp-like creature, sometimes arriving with the plants. It hovers about the bottom of the aquarium, plowing through sand, sometimes loosening leaves of *Vallisneria*, etc., but it is otherwise harmless. Multiplies rapidly. Too tough for small fishes, but is eaten by Cichlids.

Infusoria

To the fish breeder the word "infusoria " means almost any aquatic animal organism that is of a suitable size to feed young fishes before they are large enough to negotiate small *Daphnia* or brine shrimp nauplii. Many of these little animals, such as the important group of rotifers, are not infusoria at all, but we aquarists are used to making scientific blunders without embarrassment, so without apology we are going to use the word in its popular sense. "Animalcules" would be correct and inclusive. There are a number of ways to cultivate infusoria. One is to set up a mild decomposition in water and wait for infusoria spores from the air to settle on the water and multiply on the products of decay. A handful of crumpled lettuce placed in a quart of water produces results in about four days. So does chopped hay. One of the best mediums we know is dried *Anacharis* sprinkled on the water, but many organic substances may also be used. A tank containing those lettuce-devouring snails, *Ampullaria paludosa* (infusoria snails) soon brings forth infusoria that prosper on the snails' half-digested droppings. Cultures depending on decay should be started in rotation every few days if a continuous supply is needed. Aeration freshens such cultures and prolongs their life.

A second method is to prepare a boiled and cooled culture medium and then inoculate it with selected organisms, usually *Paramecium*. These organisms are commonly found in old aquarium water, in barnyard drainage, or they can be purchased at biological laboratories. Only a little is needed. Boiled cultures do not foul and last well. Rice, chopped hay, canned pea or black bean soup, and dried lettuce leaves are among many suitable stocks for boiling. Use about three tablespoons of mixed ingredients to a quart of water. This may be kept covered as stock and further di-

luted with water when poured into culture vessels (preferably shallow trays) for inoculating.

A new method has dried skim milk as a culture medium, about two pinches to a pint of boiled and cooled water. The milk and the seed micro-organisms should be put in at the same time. A rich growth takes about four days. A pinch of milk powder added every three or four days keeps the culture going. We have also used liquid skim milk, a teaspoon to a quart of water. "Infusoria tablets," too, have their advocates. They are standard items in aquarium stores and provide the cleanest and easiest method for cultivation of infusoria. Do not place these tablets with the fishes. Make culture water and dip as needed. A liquid formulation is also available.

The "Slipper Animalcule," or *Paramecium*, is the commonest organism produced in the artificial culture of infusoria. It thrives on the products of organic decomposition and can live in either foul or good water.

Well-established aquariums with old settlings contain infusoria, but only enough to give the fish a start. A separate rich supply is needed. It is impossible to specify exact feedings; three tablespoons daily of good culture to a five-gallon aquarium with fifty fry would be conservative. The nursery needs a constant supply, to be determined by magnifying a drop of its surface water. Youngsters are kept on this diet until they have about doubled in size. Infusoria are too small for live-bearer or Cichlid fry. These, as well as the fry of many other species, are able to use newly hatched brine shrimp as a first food.

How to judge the ripeness of a culture is one of the most difficult (and important) things to impart to the inexperienced. The organisms usually seek the top surface towards the light. Touch the tip of the finger there and place a drop on a piece of glass. Hold glass over something dark, and with the light coming across the drop, examine with a magnifying glass, preferably a folding "thread-counter." If it is swarming with life, the culture is ready. Or the water may be examined in one of those thin pill vials. This slightly magnifies the contents so that a sharp pair of eyes can detect life moving about like particles of fine dust. Or, use a microscope magnifying not over fifty times.

Mikroworms

These tiny worms (*Panagrellus silusiae*), barely visible to the naked eye, were originally found in beer felts in the presence of yeast fermentation. They serve the same purpose as newly hatched brine shrimp in feeding baby fishes that have outgrown the need for infusoria. They nicely supply the next step upward in size and are far less expensive. A constant supply is easily kept. Many dealers sell them. The growing culture is usually four parts of baby cereal (or boiled oatmeal) to one part of yeast, either in granulated or paste form. This is diluted with water to the consistency of thin paste and kept about $1/4$ to $1/2$ inch deep in a covered glass container. Temperature, 70° to 80°F. The worms are live-bearing and multiply fast, once well started. They creep up the sides of the glass, or will cover blocks of water-logged wood which are thick enough to stand just above the level of the liquid. From there they are easily rinsed off into the aquarium water. As they sink rapidly, it is advisable to drop them into a small net suspended just under the surface of the water. Nylon with openings of suitable size does nicely. Through this the worms escape gradually and are eaten as they fall. These worms are also well suited as a *first* food for larger fry, such as Cichlids, the Livebearers and Goldfish. Even a fresh culture has a mild odor of yeast sourness, but if it becomes offensive, save a portion with which to seed a new batch and discard the remainder. Life remains in the culture, even though the appearance is bad.

OTHER LIVE FOODS

While there are many good live foods other than those we have described, such as *Asellus*, freshwater shrimp, fairy shrimp, mayfly larvae and others, they only amount to interesting conversation for aquarists when other subjects give out—if they ever do. They cannot ordinarily be gathered in quantity. Brown mealworms, such as those sold in pet stores for feeding birds, are good food for strong-jawed fishes like Cichlids. Since it is not practical to cut them, they should be used whole, and only fed to larger fishes. If placed in plenty of bran in a large covered tin box and allowed to go through their natural beetle stage, they will multiply greatly in a few months. Brown mealworms serve as a good food especially in winter when other live foods are less available.

During the winter one can also gather bottom scrapings from ponds which, when carried home and brought up to house temperature, yield an amazing amount of life of many kinds. The surface of decaying wood is particularly likely to produce a harvest of Blood Worms. After the worms are revived in this way, the same care must be exercised as in summer for the exclusion of fish enemies; if present, the enemies are easily discovered when the water life awakens. Bloodworms keep best in cotton rags in a cup in a refrigerator, using only a little water to keep the rags wet.

Of course, for those who do not have the time or desire to procure or propagate their own live foods, brine shrimp and *Tubifex* worms, which are two excellent live foods, are available the year round from pet shops.

RAW AND BOILED MEATS

However excellent any dried food may be, fishes should have an occasional change, especially in the long winter months when live food is less obtainable. With very little trouble fish can be served chopped raw fish, shrimp, crab, or clam—all fine foods that can also be boiled. Mincing them in the hand with scissors is easily done. Blot up clam or oyster juices before feeding. Minced raw chicken liver or beef liver is a good change. One of the standbys is fresh, frozen, or canned shrimp. Practically all aquarium fishes like it and it agrees with

them. For use, cut the shrimp into thin slices with scissors, cutting across the grain.

A boiled, lightly scored shrimp suspended on a string hanging from a light stick across the aquarium gives the fishes sport and exercise. Leave the suspended shrimp in the tank as long as the fishes enthuse over it and consume the fallen bits.

Stress Coat is not a food but is a health supplement. It conditions the water, removes the chlorine and aids the fishes' slime coating. It can be used to clean the live foods before you offer them to your fishes.

Stress Coat by Aquarium Pharmaceuticals.

ENEMIES

Fortunately there are few serious enemies of fishes in the aquarium. The three outstanding ones all smuggle themselves in with your supply of live foods. Since one of these enemies is far more destructive than all others combined, we will give it first consideration.

WATER TIGER

A sleek, spindle-shaped creature, the Water Tiger is the larval form of a large Water Beetle (*Dytiscus*), which itself is also a powerful enemy of fishes. There are several species, but in effect, as far as the aquarist is concerned, they are all one. The pincers, or mandibles, are hollow, and through these Water Tigers rapidly suck the blood of their victims. Growth is rapid and they soon attain a size where they attack tadpoles, fishes, or any living thing into which they can bury their strong bloodsuckers. Vigilance is the only protection against them. Large, hard-mouthed fishes will eat them. Destroying them gives double pleasure to parent Cichlids while tending their flocks of young.

The Water Tiger breathes air through its rear end and, therefore, must occasionally come to the surface.

DRAGONFLY LARVAE

Although not nearly so deadly as Water Tigers, Dragonfly larvae have a more widely heralded reputation as killers. Their disadvantage is that they have to lie in wait for their victims and seize them from below with a much smaller and less effective pair of pincers than the Water Tigers. These pincers are located on the end of a "mask," which is a contrivance having hinged joints. These normally lie contracted just below the head but are ready to be extended in an instant when within striking distance of a victim. Although there are more Dragonfly larvae than Water Tigers, they are less likely to be collected with *Daphnia,* for they usually lie half concealed in the mud, whereas the Water Tigers are swimming about.

Damselflies are about half the size of the Dragonfly, and when at rest the wings lie parallel to the body. Their larvae are proportionately smaller and more slender, but they are also killers. They may be identified by three long bristle-like gills at the rear end of the body.

The flies themselves have their uses to man. Dragonflies (Devil's Darning Needles) devour mosquitoes while flying. Damselflies eat mosquitoes and other small flies.

HYDRA

Hydra are low forms of life and are enemies of any small water creature that can be caught by their peculiar method of stinging their victims. So far as the aquarist is concerned, Hydra catch baby fishes up to a size of $3/16$ of an inch. They also devour *Daphnia* and brine shrimp nauplii. Their shapes

are extremely variable. They can contract themselves almost to the point of
invisibility so that it is impossible to
detect them in a can of *Daphnia.* Even
worse, any broken bit of a Hydra soon
regenerates into a new complete individual.

Colonies of Hydra usually appear
like pendant, slowly swaying gray or
green hairs, about ½ inch long or less.
From the main thread are from three to
seven tentacles, spread starlike. They
are usually found attached to the glass
and plants. It is rather surprising to
find that they can move about, using
alternately their tentacles and their
suction foot in a clumsy kind of locomotion.

The body and the tentacles contain
many sharp barbs filled with a numb-
ing poison. As a prospect brushes
against a tentacle, the apparently inert
Hydra springs into action. It injects a
"shot" into its victim, draws the victim
into a mouth from which the tentacles
radiate, digests it and presently dis-
charges the undigested portions from
the same opening. When business is
brisk, a Hydra may have a *Daphnia* or
a young fish held by each tentacle, to
be swallowed at leisure.

Immediately following a "strike,"
the creature undergoes a marked
change in form, becoming much more
compact. Multiplication usually takes
place by budding, and, under the influence of plenty of food, is rapid.

The larger live-bearers, like Mollies, are a little too big for Hydra to
negotiate. Their favorites are the babies of the egg-laying species. In either case they compete seriously with

young fishes for live foods, especially for baby brine shrimp and *Daphnia.*

The easiest and safest way to get
rid of this rather interesting pest is by
introducing into the aquarium several
Three-spot, Blue or Pearl Gouramies.
Give them no other food and they will
soon devour the Hydra. A complete
change to fresh water from the tap
usually puts an end to them in a day.
Remove all fishes during treatment.
Some of the available fish medica-
tions containing copper are probably
effective as well.

OTHER ENEMIES

Two questionable intruders that
sometimes enter with *Daphnia* are
Water Boatmen (Corixidae) and Back-
Swimmers (Notonectidae). They may
be introduced while very small or
they may slip in unnoticed in larger
sizes. Though they are commonly
believed to be enemies of young fishes,
our experiments indicate a "not guilty"
verdict. Dr. G. C. Embody, a noted
fish culturist, says that Back-Swim-
mers are dangerous, but that Water
Boatmen are harmless. Both swim
with a rowing motion of their two
long oar-like legs.

Beetles

Most Water Beetles live on other
insects or animals. They seldom get
into the aquarium, but should be immediately removed when discovered.

Fish Lice (*Argulus*)

These are free-swimming, translucent, tenacious, wafer-like parasites

that become fatally epidemic mostly in Goldfish pools from July to October. Argulus are about $3/16$ of an inch across and may attack exotic fishes. To get rid of them, catch fish in a net, lift out of tank for a minute or two. Fish lice will usually leave their host when out of water. A new chemical marketed under the names of "Dylox" and "Masoten" has recently been introduced as being effective against *Argulus.*

Anchor Worm

While in the small free-swimming stage the Anchor Worm, a parasite, embeds itself in the flesh of Goldfish and some exotics. It develops a big anchor foot in order to attach its $5/8$ inch long, thread-like body to the host. The body is so tough that it does not break when given a hard yank. A drop of formaldehyde on the infested area usually kills it. "Dylox," as recommended against fish lice, is also said to be effective against Anchor Worm.

Planaria or Flatworms

These pale little creatures, growing up to $1/2$ inch long and gliding like snails, sometimes distress aquarists by appearing on the glass sides of tanks. They are carnivorous and live on various fish foods, including live *Tubifex* worms, as well as dead fish and snails. They may fairly be rated as scavengers. Placed in clean water they starve and in an immaculate aquarium they do not last long. They do no harm and will not overpopulate an aquarium, provided good housekeeping is practiced.

There are aquarium water neutralizers at your petshop that slowly dissolve in the water, maintaining pH and assisting your fishes to ward off **Planaria** *and anchor worms.*

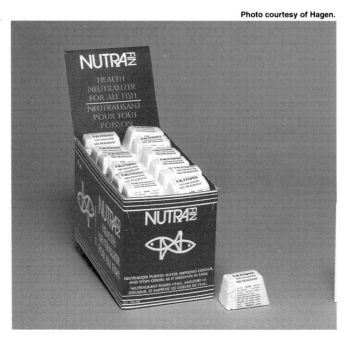

Leeches

Reports of leeches found in aquariums are not rare. Aquarists do not always recognize them. While there are other animals that travel like the measuring worm, it is a good guess that anything in the water travelling that way is a leech, especially if it has the ability to contract and extend its length. In North America there are about fifteen genera, divided into thirty species. Only a few attack fishes. Most of them are parasitic on snails or consume small worms, etc. Some prey on each other. It is rare to see one attached to an aquarium fish, but it is a possibility. Therefore it is good policy to get rid of any such suspicious characters. They are extremely tough. No known chemical affects them that may not also kill the plants. They hate salt; also nicotine. If things become too unpleasant for them, they climb out of the water.

After a meal and at night, they seek a dark spot, such as under a stone. If an inverted saucer is placed loosely on the bottom of an aquarium, and leeches are present, they will likely be found in the morning, clinging to the dark side. Destroy them and continue until no more appear. Most leeches carry their young on the underside of their bodies, but the species most often encountered in aquariums lays eggs. Under-gravel filters are the best breeding grounds for these leeches. Their egg cases, usually containing two developing larvae, are about ³/₁₆ of an inch long, oval

in shape, and light brown. They are often attached to the filter plate and inside the tubes of an under-gravel filter.

Most often they are introduced as eggs (on plants) or as young leeches (among *Tubifex* worms). They do not attack fishes.

Your pet shop will have specialty chemicals like Rid-Ich to control ich in your tank. Use of untreated tap water is also dangerous and can be treated with conditioners. Photo courtesy of Kordon.

DISEASES

Fortunately, far fewer diseases and parasites attack fishes in the aquarium than they do in nature. This is probably because the aquarium does not furnish favorable conditions for the life cycles which many of them undergo.

ICHTHYOPHTHIRIUS

The only very common disease which gives us much concern is popularly called "ich," being short for *Ichthyophthirius*, the name of the parasitic protozoan causing the trouble. The malady is aptly called by some the "pepper and salt disease," because in its advanced stage there are small white specks on the fins and body of the victim which resemble seasoning. At first only a few specks are seen. Unless treatment is given these specks multiply rapidly until the body and fins are almost completely covered. A coating of fungus appears and death soon follows the fungus. The cause of attacks of *Ichthyophthirius* is usually chill or exposure to the parasite. An affected new fish can create havoc in an entire tank. Chill works against the fish in two ways: (1) its own resistance is reduced and (2) the vitality of the parasite is increased at lower temperatures.

The organism that causes the trouble is one of the low forms of animal life, a simple cell covered with swimming hairs. It burrows just below the outer skin of the fish, the irritation causes a tiny pimple. In this pimple the parasite prospers on the fluids and tissues of its host, causing an itching which is evidenced in the early stages by the efforts of the fish to scratch itself against objects in the aquarium.

In a few days the parasite reaches its maximum size of one millimeter, leaves the fish, drops to the bottom of the aquarium, forms a cyst, and breaks up into from 500 to 1200 young. Not all these young succeed in reaching a host, but enough do so that the progress of the disease sweeps on like wildfire.

The important thing, of course, in checking the parasite is to break into its life cycle at the weakest point. This is in the early free-swimming stage. Several methods have been developed. Most methods call for heat of about 85°F., either with or without medication. Some aquarists hold the extreme view that simple heat is the best and the only effective remedy. Most aquarists, however, believe in the value of other aids.

Methylene Blue, two drops of 5% aqueous solution to the gallon, has no such reaction, but it is deadly to plants. Therefore treatment with this dye should be in a bare container. It is one of the best remedies. The use of quinine at a proper strength has neither of those disadvantages and can be used without high temperature. A half grain of quinine sulphate to each gallon of aquarium water is approximately correct. Place the required amount of powder in a cup, add a few drops of water, and with the point of a spoon mix it into a thin paste. Add warm water to fill the cup. A short stirring will then fully dissolve the powder. Empty into the aquarium and stir gently.

The quinine treatment, which originated in Germany and is generally accepted there as being the best method, has its critics as to its reaction on both plants and fishes. Perhaps it has been used in too strong concentrations. A strength of one grain to the gallon is highly effective, but may injure some plants.

Acid water of 5.8 readings is said to make life hard for the parasites. Sea salt, one heaping teaspoonful to the gallon of water, is also recommended in conjunction with high temperature. Fishes of the Gourami family (Anabantidae) can be treated in a unique way. These fishes possess an auxiliary breathing apparatus, the labyrinth, which permits them to "breathe" atmospheric air at the surface, thus they can survive in water of very low oxygen content while the parasite cannot. If kept in a small aquarium without aeration and filtration at a temperature of 85°, the fishes will be completely cured in a few days without further medication.

The germs of this organism are not carried through the air as are the spores of fungus or of greenwater algae. In an absolutely sterilized aquarium, fishes will die of chill without developing Ichthyophthiriasis, but in ordinary practice it is difficult to produce or to maintain water in that condition. Biologists state that the microscopic

young die in sixty hours if they fail to find a host. If this is true there must be some unknown way in which the life of the organism can be indefinitely suspended, for an epidemic has often been produced by chilling an aquarium that had been subject to no recent contamination and which for a long preceding period had not been attacked. In any case, all aquarium implements should be well sterilized and water splashings into other tanks should be avoided when handling an afflicted fish.

Aquarists are often puzzled as to why in a tank of mixed species only certain kinds may be affected by "ich." There are several reasons: the parasites prefer certain hosts; some fishes withstand chill better than others, and certain fishes in an aquarium will be in better health than their companions. Several species of *Ichthyophthirius* exist. This probably accounts for variable results in treatment.

It should be remembered that it is by no means a sure indication of "ich" if fishes scratch or rub themselves against objects. It could very well be flukes or some other parasitic disease. Treatment for Ichthyophthiriasis should not be given unless the little white spots are observed. When these are seen, no time should be lost.

Occasionally, fishes will scratch or rub themselves against plants, stones, or gravel as if they were infected with "ich," but no white spots develop. This is usually not a cause for alarm. If the scratching persists, it is probably caused by numerous microorganisms which have devel-

For marine and brackish water species like Monos and Scats, use **Organi-Cure** *as ich remedies for freshwater fishes won't work.*

Life Bearer *is supposed to eliminate gill flukes, fish lice, anchor worms and leeches. Your pet shop should have this drug.*

oped from infrequent water changes and uneaten decaying food in the aquarium. Siphon the bottom, draw off about half the water, and replace with clear, conditioned water. Pet shops have several excellent remedies for curing Ichthyophthiriasis.

DROPSY

One of the strangest of fish diseases is dropsy. It is also one of the most unpleasant in appearance. The fish becomes puffed and the scales stand out at an angle to the body. Sometimes the eyes have a tendency to bulge. The puzzling thing about the malady is the unaccountable way in which it singles out individual fishes. Although some aquarists believe that the trouble arises from faults in diet, the fact remains that it strikes without

apparent regard to what the fish has been fed and it is just as likely as not to single out a fish in a pool where the conditions seem to be perfect. Some species seem to be more subject to dropsy than others. *Colisa lalia, Danio malabaricus*, and *Brachydanio rerio* are among the more susceptible.

The disease is fatal in from one to three weeks.

There is no reliable cure for this disease. Since it is usually not very contagious in the aquarium, the removal of the infected fish will prevent an epidemic in most cases.

FLUKES

A malady not often attacking aquarium fishes is flukes. It is caused by parasitic animals called *Gyrodactylus* and *Dactylogyrus,* which lodge in the skin and gills. The fish dashes wildly about and then when exhausted comes to a sudden stop. There are other maladies which cause fishes to act in this way, but since we know little or nothing about them, the treatments described here may as well be applied. These flukes can be highly contagious. Treatment is twenty drops of formaldeyhyde to a gallon of water. Leave the fish in this bath until it shows signs of exhaustion, usually in from five to ten minutes. If necessary, repeat in a day or two. Petshops have highly effective chemical remedies to treat this parasitic infection.

FUNGUS

There is a white slimy coating on fishes that usually follows the first stages of *Ichthyophthirius* but that sometimes appears independently. In either case, it is caused by a fungus called *Saprolegnia*. Four level teaspoons of salt per gallon of water is the best treatment. Fishes are made susceptible to fungus by bruises, attacks

Quick Cure works on lymphocystis or hole disease.

of other fishes, sudden temperature change, chill, overfeeding, and poor general conditions.

MOUTH FUNGUS

A wicked disease with serious consequences is mouth fungus. A light-colored fluff appears at the lips, gets into the mouth, and soon starts eating the jaws away. Unless action is taken very quickly, it is likely to kill all the fishes that have been exposed to it. It is highly contagious. Gouramis, Barbs, and Live-bearers are particularly subject to mouth fungus. For a long time no remedy was known; today many antibiotics cure the disease. Among the best are chloromycetin, aureomycin, and terramycin. Dosage should be fifty milligrams to each gallon of water. Follow dissolving procedure described under "ich" for dissolving quinine. Cure is usually effected in a few days. At specified strength this will not harm plants or fishes. Expensive but effective. Petshops sell these remedies. You might need a prescription if you buy it from a druggist.

FIN ROT

Fins sometimes become frayed without having been bitten by other fishes. Treatment is the same as for fungus. If the entire fins start to rot away (not just the membrane between the fin rays), the treatment described for mouth fungus should be used.

VELVET

Another disease among domesticated fishes is velvet. It mostly affects labyrinth fishes and members of the Carp family, such as White Clouds, *Brachydanios*, Barbs, and the live-bearing Tooth Carps. It first shows as a yellowish brown patchy film usually beginning on the body near the dorsal fin. If untreated, this spreads quickly and develops into a series of small raised circular crusts. Fry usually succumb before the disease is detected. The trouble is caused by a protozoan parasite (probably *Oodinium limneticum*) which has a free-swimming stage before becoming parasitic. The best remedy for this ailment is one containing copper sulphate and salt. Since copper sulphate is highly toxic in unskilled hands, it is advisable to purchase a ready-made solution in an aquarium shop. Many brands are available, most for use in marine aquariums, but all are suited for freshwater fishes as well. Use as directed for marine fishes, but add four *level* teaspoonfuls of salt per gallon of water to be treated.

SHAKES OR SHIMMIES

A description of shakes or shimmies is not easily made, but most aquarists have seen it. Once seen, it is always remembered. The fish usually stays stationary, wobbling its body from side to side in a slow, clumsy motion. It is like swimming without getting anywhere. There are several causes. The principal cause is chill. Many aquarists declare their fishes to have been afflicted in this way without having been chilled, but they are probably mistaken. A short drop in temperature may do it and the effect lasts long.

Fishes with *Ichthyophthirius* are apt to shimmy. This shaking is merely a manifestation of trouble and is not a definite disease in itself, any more than chills are with people. Aside from treating the disease causing Shimmies, the usual successful treatment is a persistently applied temperature of about 78-80°F.

Indigestion is, no doubt, another cause. There is reason to believe that an overly dirty aquarium gives rise to quantities of microscopic organisms which cause the fish to act in this way. Cases have often been instantly cured merely by a complete change of water. The new water should be seasoned.

WASTING

Like shimmies, wasting is not a disease, but a symptom. However, it may be caused by internal parasites. In any case, there is little or no hope for a hollow-bellied fish with a big head and shrunken body. Usual causes are

Clout is one of the most widely used general drugs available for tropical fish hobbyists.

Photo courtesy of Aquarium Products.

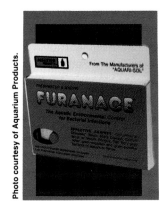

Photo courtesy of Aquarium Products.

Furanace is a wide spectrum drug that controls many aquarium fish diseases. Ask your pet shop about it.

lack of fresh or living food, infrequent and too small feedings, over-crowding, and continuous cool water. The trouble may be old age. Whatever the cause, an emaciated fish seldom survives, although it may last for some time.

SWIM-BLADDER TROUBLE

The great majority of fishes are equipped with a very wonderful mechanism that enables them to remain balanced, almost without effort, in any reasonable depth of water. It is a flexible bladder, filled, not with air, but with gas generated by the fish. For this balancing system to be effective, the amount of internal pressure must be precisely right. With too little gas the fish sinks; with too much it floats. Sometimes floating is temporarily caused by intestinal gases. Usually, floating or sinking is caused by some derangement of the swim bladder and is incurable.

WOUNDS

Nothing seems to be better for wounds than touching them with 2% Mercurochrome. Repetition may be necessary.

CROOKED BODIES

It is probable that deformed spines in fishes sometimes result from constitutional or tubercular weakness similar to rickets in man and are just about as incurable. Malnutrition and vitamin deficiency are contributing causes. The body often assumes a crescent shape. It may accompany swim-bladder trouble or another internal disturbance. In many years of experience we have never seen or heard of a recovery from any of these deformities and death is usually not far off.

OTHER TROUBLES

There is a list of rare troubles that are difficult for the amateur to diagnose. These include cysts, lumps on fishes, blindness, partial paralysis, worms eating through from the inside, and sudden death with no outward sign of disease. No doubt there are internal parasites which defy treatment. Many of them must have free-swimming stages in which they can be killed.

SUDDEN DEATHS

Occasionally, a fish in apparently perfect health is found dead in an aquarium that seems to be in ideal condition and in which other fishes are in good health. This could be the result of a stroke. Man is not the only creature subject to that malady, nor to the sudden results of over-eating. Unless this little tragedy is repeated too often, it seems best to file it under "unsolved mysteries."

SALT

Salt is nature's remedy for many ills. It is effective in most troubles of freshwater fishes, causes no bad reactions, and is safe to try on obscure cases or when in doubt. Its one fault is that when strong enough to check disease, it is too concentrated for plants. Place fishes in a bare tank or enamel receptacle in seasoned water containing two level teaspoons of salt to the gallon. Gradually over twenty-four hours build it up to four teaspoons. If no improvement appears by the third day, go to six teaspoons if the fish shows no signs of distress. Species vary. Guppies and Mollies can stand eight. Aeration helps. At end of treatment, before returning fish to aquar-

The old and most recommended of all remedies is plain aquarium salt. It is the best first aid remedy until you have identified the problem and can treat it effectively with a specific drug.

ium, slowly add fresh water until the salt content is low. Sea water is still better than salt crystals. One part to five of fresh is a good strength, about equal to three level teaspoonsful of crystals to the gallon.

CHECK-UPS

Aquarium conditions frequently seem to be ideal, the aquarist has been careful about feeding and temperature, yet the fishes are low in vitality or otherwise ailing. All conditions have their causes, however obscure they may be. Sometimes these causes are beyond the range of our knowledge, but there are several important points on which a re-check can be made. Is there a possibility of dead fish or snails? Does the water have an unpleasant

Formalin is a long time favorite remedy for fish parasites and bacterial infections.

smell? If so, it should be partially changed and aerated, either by pump or hand pouring. A sprinkling pot serves temporarily. If the cover is down tight, raise it a little.

Is there enough light for the plants? Do they have a good green color? Are they growing? Are there plenty of them? Plants which are not prospering are a detriment.

Is there any chipping away of nickel or chromium plating at any point in direct or indirect contact with the water? This is poisonous.

Unsuspected overcrowding is the commonest trouble. When in doubt, use fewer fish.

Has the water been thickly green and then turned yellow? In that case, the microscopic suspended plant life is dying, and the water should be changed.

Have the fishes been chilled within a month or are they being kept at 68° or a little lower?

On the other hand, there are heat

An ounce of prevention is worth a pound of cure. Genesis is used to protect the fish before it gets sick.

fanatics who never let the aquarium water drop below 80°. If and when the fishes weaken in this tropical temperature, try something about 74°-76°.

What about insecticide sprays, paint fumes, or excessive tobacco smoke?

Has the water become too acid or too alkaline? Has it become too hard by adding water from the original source to make up for evaporation without ever actually changing water? If this is suspected, remove half the water and use soft water, such as distilled, clean rain or melted snow that has not been in contact with metal or new wood to refill the tank. In industrial and urban areas where air pollution is a problem, rainwater may also be unsafe to use, unless it is collected after the air has been "cleaned" by a long steady rain.

One of the commonest of mysterious troubles is caused by the use of new copper boilers and piping in residences. Let standing water run out of pipes before using water for the aquarium, or try water from some source not so contaminated.

To control snails is to control many diseases, too. Too many snails means too many plants being eaten and too many diseases being brought into the tank.

PLANTS AND PLANTING

We now come to the point of considering plants not only as renewers of life, but also as purifiers and beautifiers. As it is with garden flowers, a few old friends are the ones we find to be best. In over one hundred years of organized aquarium study, about a dozen kinds of plants (with their variations) have come into general use. Several other good plants are growing in popularity, but are not yet universally available. Finally, many authentic looking, artificial plants are available and petshops usually have racks full of them.

THE PLANTS

Vallisneria spiralis
(Eel Grass, Tape Grass)

Its tall, graceful, grass-like form, with narrow, silken, light-green leaves, rises vertically in undulating lines. The plant in moderately good light multiplies rapidly and forms a dense but not impenetrable thicket or screen. It is one of the very best oxygenators and its roots tend to purify the soil.

Propagation is principally by runners. The plants are male and female and, peculiarly enough, the plants from runners are all the same sex as the parents. Nearly all of them are female. Their little floating, white cup-shaped flowers are on the ends of long thin spirals, rising from the crown of the plant. The word *spiralis* refers to the shape of these flower stems. The flowers of the rare male plants are close to the crown. Pollen rises from them and fertilizes the floating female flowers. The seeds from these fertilized flowers may produce both male and female plants, but very few of the seeds ever germinate. In planting *Vallisneria,* care should be taken to keep the crown just at the surface of the sand.

Photo courtesy of Tetra/Second Nature.

Live plants are best, but when fish eat the plants or your tank doesn't get enough light, plastic plants are there to help. Your pet shop should have a large selection.

A giant species with leaves about ⁵⁄₈ of an inch wide and several feet long with bristly edges is propagated in Florida. It is splendid for aquariums that are at least eighteen inches high.

Corkscrew Vallisneria
(Vallisneria spiralis)

An attractive mutation from the tall *Vallisneria spiralis*, but instead of growing from fifteen to twenty inches and sprawling on the water surface of small tanks, its charming twisted leaves average only seven to twelve inches. Very popular. Prefers hard water and fairly strong light. Getting *Vallisneria* to flower in an aquarium is difficult because they require more light than is usually safe for the aquarist to provide.

Sagittaria
(Arrowhead)

This famous old aquarium plant is another one having a grass-like form. It comes in many more species than *Vallisneria,* most of them being bog plants rather than pure aquatics. Their barb- or arrow-shaped aerial leaves, common along watery borders almost everywhere, are responsible for the naming of the plant after the mythological Sagittarius, the Archer.

About half a dozen species, some of

them of doubtful identity, are being successfully used as aquarium plants. The three most important are *Sagittaria gigantea* (believed to be a cultivated form of *Sagittaria sinensis*), *Sagittaria natans*, and *Sagittaria subulata*.

The strong green leaves of *Sagittaria gigantea* are ½ inch or more wide, and from seven to eighteen inches in length. They are rather firm and withstand a fair amount of buffeting by nets once they are well rooted. As their roots are eventually quite vigorous, they should be planted in sand about two inches deep. The plant is a comparatively slow grower in the aquarium, but aquarium-grown specimens are best. These are easily distinguished by a large mass of yellowish

Sagittaria species
(Probably S. subulata)

roots, whereas those grown in ponds have fewer, shorter, and white roots. It takes about a year to get pond-grown plants acclimated to the aquarium.

Sagittaria natans. This is the original *Sagittaria* of the aquarium and was at one time very popular, especially in the early days of the fancy Goldfish. In the Goldfish tank it was largely replaced by *Sagittaria gigantea* which was better for that purpose. Since the advent of "tropicals" it has again come into its own, for it has advantages that make it welcome in the small aquarium. The main point is that it does not grow very long and, therefore, does not easily get into a tangle. The six to twelve-inch leaves are tough and the plant is a very good oxygenator.

Sagittaria subulata. This is a species that has become very popular in recent years. It is different from the two foregoing kinds in two respects: the leaves are narrower and thicker, they are straighter and of a darker green. Under favorable conditions this plant propagates rapidly. The leaves are from five to ten inches long and are rather wiry.

While not quite as beautiful or as long as *Vallisneria*, we believe, all

things considered, it is the most valuable plant for use in the average household aquarium. Among its other merits, it is long-lived.

A vigorous two-inch *Sagittaria* "*microfolia*" has its appropriate uses.

All these truly aquatic species of *Sagittaria* throw up summer stalks which develop long, lance-like leaves above the water. Flower stems bear trusses of pretty cup-shaped white flowers with a yellow ball in the center. *Sagittaria* and *Vallisneria* are rivals. They seldom prosper together.

Hygrophila polysperma
Young Cuttings

Hygrophila polysperma

This popular and comparatively new addition to aquarium plants is one

Temple Plant (**Nomaphila stricta**), *a close relative of* **H. polysperma, but not as easily grown.**

"*Micro*" *Sagittaria*

of the most important. It adapts remarkably well to a wide variety of conditions, especially to weak light either natural or artificial. Propagates easily from rooted cuttings. It is the only aquatic member of an otherwise terrestrial genus. Introduced from India to aquarists through the late Joe Johannigman, Jr., Loveland, Ohio.

Cabomba
(Washington Plant, Fanwort, Watershield)

While we by no means claim this to be the best of aquarium plants, it is most largely sold and has its good points. It fell out of fashion in the Goldfish aquarium because it is brittle and those husky fishes picked it to

Cabomba (Cabomba caroliniana)

pieces. Very few exotics munch on plants and that objection to *Cabomba* is thus removed. Certainly when in good condition, it is one of the brightest and most beautiful of aquarium plants. It is used chiefly for its attractiveness and for the fact that it is always in supply.

The fan-shaped, light-green leaves on a running stem form good refuge for young fishes, but they are not sufficiently dense to make a satisfactory spawning plant. *Cabomba* is apt to become long and stringy unless kept in a strong light.

Myriophyllum
(Water Milfoil)

A plant of delicate beauty, its fine leaves make a perfect maze for catching the adhesive eggs of egg-dropping

Milfoil or Foxtail
(**Myriophyllum** *species)*

fishes or a wonderful refuge for newly hatched fish babies. Broke or cut-off bits of its feathery leaves precisely suit the needs of those fishes which entwine a bit of such material into their nests (Dwarf Gouramis, for example). It is beautiful in the aquarium but

Pool-grown Anacharis, *left & Aquarium grown Anacharis* (Elodea (Egeria) densa), *right.*

requires strong light to avoid becoming thin and leggy. Long a popular favorite, it is generally in good supply. Rinsing well under a tap of water removes most of the possible fish enemies from wild stock.

Sold bunched, it should be separated unless used as a spawn-receiver.

Anacharis
(Elodea, Ditch Moss)

Early dealers claimed that *Anacharis* was the best of oxygenators. This was generally accepted and has become something of a tradition, although the claim is open to question. It is probably based on the undoubted fact that it is the most rapid-growing of all aquarium plants—an inch a day for a long strand is not unusual. However, growth and oxygenating power bear little, if any, relationship to each other. Rapid stem growth occurs in poor light, producing plants lacking vigor.

Anacharis is only at its best in outdoor ponds that are partially protected from the full light of the sun. In the aquarium it gradually becomes stringy

Ceratophyllum demersum

Ambulia (Limnophila sessiliflora)

and pale. Some aquarists claim that a good supply of it clears green water.

Ceratophyllum

Ceratophyllum, or Hornwort, has a decided beauty that would make it one of our standard aquarium plants, but for two fatal faults. It is brittle and it has no roots. It is like a thinned-out *Myriophyllum*. Placed in a concrete pool in summer, where it will receive about three hours of sunshine per day, it grows in magnificent scrolls floating just below the surface. It is excellent in breeding and rearing tanks which generally contain no gravel.

Ambulia

This plant roughly resembles *Cabomba*, but is a little smaller, is a lighter shade of green, and does better in the aquarium. The life-like drawings of sections of the two plants show the difference in leaf formation and

Ambulia   Cabomba

arrangement. The alternating pairs of fan-like leaves of *Cabomba* form only a semi-circle, the cylindrical effect of the plant being produced by the next and opposite pair. *Ambulia* completes its leafy circle from one point. Imported from India in 1932, *Ambulia* has grown steadily in favor and as it easily multiplies from cuttings, it seems sure to join the surprisingly small circle of best sellers. Sold bunched. Separate the strands when planting. Correct name, *Limnophila*.

Water Sprite
(Ceratopteris thalicroides)

Possibly dependent on the species, the leaves are sometimes much broader than shown here, although we have seen both broad and narrow leaves on the same plant. The genus occurs in the tropics around the world and is most variable.

If left to itself and untrimmed, it spreads to the surface where the baby plants, formed on the old leaves, assume the floating form. In a warm moist atmosphere, they pile up into veritable islands.

Another peculiarity is the stiff, narrow, aerial leaves that adult submerged specimens sometimes produce. With age the parent plant becomes soft and should be replaced. Snails attack soft plants.

Water Sprite (Ceratopteris thalicroides)

Amazon Swordplant **(Echinodorus** *species)*

Amazon Swordplant
(Echinodorus species)

The Amazon Swordplant seems to be nature's special gift to aquarists as a centerpiece for a fifteen to twenty-nine gallon tank or it will suitably colonize a more massive container with a family of giants. Runners from the crown (a king's crown indeed) are free and far reaching. Press runners into sand at points where new plants develop. Do not cut them off until well started.

Several other aquatics with large leaves have long stems making them rather rangy, but the Swordplant has short stems that give a compact sturdy effect. When the plant appeared here in 1937 it was a truly valuable acquisition for the artistic aquarist. It is now well established.

It likes a good but not powerful light. A moderate amount of daylight suits it very well.

Melon Swordplant

Here we have a recent introduction of great merit having a marked individual character and unusual toughness of texture. It reproduces in the same manner as the other members of the family.

Comparatively slow of propagation, it took some time to build a commercial supply. That desired end has now been reached and while not widely offered, it is not difficult to secure from leading specialists.

Some aquarists rank it as the handsomest of the Swordplants.

Pigmy Chain Swordplant

This plant, one of the latest introductions among the numerous

Melon Swordplant

Pigmy Chain Swordplant

Above: Aponogeton undulatum

Below: *Madagascar Plant*
(Aponogeton madagascariensis)

the surface of the soil.

Perhaps its greatest value is in small tanks (one to five gallons), as there are few rooted plants that do not get too tall for them. If used as a centerpiece in a small aquarium the runners should be pinched off, forcing it into a bushy fountain shaped miniature Swordplant.

It gets along well in subdued daylight or under good electric illumination from a standard reflector over the aquarium.

Aponogeton undulatum
(incorrectly *A. crispus*)

The somewhat translucent leaves of this striking plant look like green swords with rippled edges. Heights, six to eighteen inches, depending on strong or weak light. In the taller plants the leaves do not broaden in proportion, thus making them more strap-like. Mostly grown from seed, but

Echinodorus family, has several points of value. It is a first-class addition to the low-growing plants of which we have few. It only reaches from three to four inches in height according to conditions. Reproduction from runners is rapid. In a big aquarium it virtually carpets the floor in a few months. Runners should be pressed just below

bulbs are often available in petshops. They have a resting period in December. The plant has a shepherd's crook flower stem above the waterline bearing small white flowers. Flowering in the aquarium is rare.

Madagascar Lace-leaf Plant
(Aponogeton madagascariensis)

Although the Lace-leaf Plant is one of the earliest used by aquarists, and many rivals have appeared that are really better aquarium plants, this aristocrat somehow continues to be the classiest of them all. Its moderately high price, its slowness of propagation, and its unique beauty easily account for the distinction it maintains.

The plant is tricky, either succeeding or failing for reasons that are not clear. It does well in the alkaline waters of California, but poorly in the acid conditions of New England—yet at the Botanical Gardens of the University of Pennsylvania, it flourished in half-casks of oak, which certainly ought to be acid. It does prefer soft water.

A moderate light is best. New plants occasionally appear at the root. Recently imported bulbs produce good plants.

It has resting periods when the leaves die but the bulbs are viable.

Spatterdock

One of the forms of this plant from the southeastern United States makes a striking centerpiece in the aquarium. The large, long leaves are of a delicate, translucent, light green. Propagation is from a heavy, trunk-like rootbase

called a rhizome. Unfortunately, when broken off, decay may set in and finally destroy the rhizome. The break heals better if planted in soil. Seedlings from northern Spatterdocks produce smaller plants with much more rounded leaves. While the parent stocks of most of those seedlings have aerial leaves which are seen by the millions along the edges of rivers, they seldom, if ever, become sufficiently robust in the aquarium to reach that stage of development. Usually they are pretty little submerged plants not over six inches in height. The Cape Fear Spatterdock is collected in the wild in the Carolinas and shipped worldwide to petshops.

Dwarf Lily

A dwarf lily from Southeast Asia has been introduced under the name of *Nymphaea stellata*. It is a hardy, fast-growing plant, but rarely blooms under aquarium conditions.

Cryptocoryne

Cryptocoryne, long-lived Asiatic plants, were once rarities, but their valuable special uses, together with intensified commercial production, have brought them into popular demand and fairly good supply. Besides an attractive individuality different from all other true aquatics, they have the great merit of thriving in situations where the light is rather weak. This obliging characteristic should not be pushed too far. They come from well-shaded jungle streams, but need a reasonably strong diffused light. Where an aquarium contains a variety of

Cape Fear Spatterdock
(**Nuphar sagittifolium***)*

Dwarf Lily
(**Nymphaea stellata***)*

plants, it may not be possible to give all of them light ideally suited to their natures. With *Cryptocorynes* in the picture, it is well to place them out of the full glare of strong light.While there is fascination (especially among beginners) about decorating aquariums with a wide variety of plants, there is also a simple, pleasing, and, perhaps, more successful scheme in which only one or, at most, two kinds are used in one tank. *Cryptocorynes* adapt themselves well to this treatment. They are all long-lived.

Hair Grass

Growing along the edges of many ponds and streams in the eastern and southern parts of North America are short, hair-like grasses suited to aquarium culture. The majority of them

propagate from runners, but the one shown here divides on the leaves and sends down rootlets. Plants of this character offer not only interesting variety in contrast with other aquarium vegetation, but also make perfect thickets for harboring baby fishes finding themselves in a dangerous world.

Ludwigia

Ludwigia is not a true aquatic, but a bog plant which does fairly well under water. It never completely forgets its habit of having some leaves above the waterline. There are about twenty-five species in North America usually growing at the shallow edges of ponds and streams. *Ludwigia* is somewhat similar to Watercress, but, unlike that plant, it does not require cool water. A very beautiful red strain of this species

One of the many **Cryptocoryne** *species* **(probably C. wendti).**

Cryptocoryne affinis.

Eleocharis vivipara.

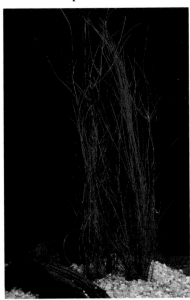

is cultivated in Florida where conditions exactly suit it, but elsewhere it soon loses most of this peculiar character. For best results *Ludwigia* should be rooted in earth and placed in strong light, otherwise the leaves drop prematurely. It is easily propagated from end cuttings. Nurserymen stick these in small pots containing earth and a top layer of sand. This is not done under water, but on trays of saturated sand or ashes. As soon as growth starts, the pot may be placed in the aquarium—this is a most satisfactory method.

Fontinalis or Willowmoss

A dark green plant, native to small, cool, clear swift streams. Usually attached to a stone or a bit of waterlogged wood, it does moderately well in the aquarium, especially if settlings are regularly knocked off or the whole plant rinsed. In nature, the small leaves on a firm stem conceal an infinite variety of tiny crustacea, etc., mostly fishfoods. Useful as a spawn receiver, especially for fishes breeding near the bottom. Some dealers carry it.

Najas

Aquarists receiving shipments of plants from the southern United States sometimes find masses of the above used as packing material. Of a pleasant translucent green color, like a small *Potamogeton*. Grows into masses useful to fish breeders. It may take hold in a pool with soil bottom. Grows wild from Florida to Labrador.

Ludwigia *species*
A bog or semi-aquatic plant, long used by aquarists.

Cardamine lyrata
A beautiful light-green plant from northern Europe and America.

*Moneywort (*Lysimachia nummularia*) A common creeping terrestrial, sold in quantity to aquarists. Does fairly well under water.*

Baby Tears
Often used by florists in moist terraria. Submerged, its tiny, light-green leaves make a novel and pleasing effect.

Willow Moss (**Fontinalis gracilis***)*

Najas *species*

Nitella

This is a native American plant distributed largely throughout temperate North America. It is interesting in several ways. Classified for years as one of the algae, there is now considerable doubt on this point. It has a great deal of sap for so slender a plant, and through its beautiful, translucent, pale green walls the flow of protoplasm is easily seen with the aid of a microscope of moderate power. Used extensively in classrooms and for scientific research. There are no roots.

Young live-bearers among a loose mass of *Nitella* nearly filling an aquarium need no other protection from hungry parents.

Some fishes, especially *Scatophagus*, greedily eat large amounts of it.

Growth in a sunny situation (in neutral to alkaline water) is rapid.

Nitella flexilis

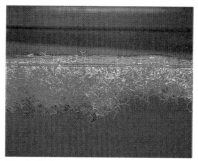

Riccia fluitans

FLOATING PLANTS

Riccia

To the breeder of aquarium fishes, *Riccia* is one of the most valuable plants. Its green, crystal-like formation produces masses which are compact enough to catch and hold the spawn of the surface egg-layers, yet open enough for new baby live-bearing species to use as a perfect refuge. When it is desirable to produce top shade in an aquarium, we can depend upon *Riccia* to do it in any desired degree. For some aquarists it grows tremendously, but the surplus never should be thrown away as there are always those in need of it. When a mass grows over an inch thick so that the sun cannot force light through it, a thinning is necessary so it will not turn yellow and soft and pollute the water.

Under the influence of sun these little plants are enormous oxygenators. Large bubbles of that precious gas become imprisoned among the massed leaves and stay there until absorbed by the water. This takes several hours and favorably affects the fishes long after sunset.

The great enemies of *Riccia* are algae, which get among the leaves and choke it. A plentiful supply of small snails usually keeps it clean. When used for spawning purposes, no snails should be present.

While *Riccia* is native to the fresh waters of the middle and southern Atlantic states, it appears to grow better in a well-lighted aquarium than it does outdoors. All-day sun seems to shrivel it. *Riccia* naturally floats just below the surface of the water and beautiful effects can be obtained by anchoring small bunches at a depth where they will not be disturbed and where good light penetrates. Under these conditions *Riccia* develops into gorgeous green masses, even up to six inches across.

There are few fishes that eat *Riccia,* but *Scatophagus argus* is extremely fond of it. This seems strange, as nothing even distantly resembles this plant in this fish's native salt and brackish waters.

Duckweed (**Lemna minor***)*

Water Lettuce (**Pistia stratiotes***)*

Salvinia species

Duckweed

A despised pest in *Daphnia* ponds, but not without its use in the aquarium. Some fishes like to eat it and it is a good producer of shade where a tank gets too much top light. No fear need be entertained about introducing it in aquariums where it can be kept under control, but in large containers and lily pools it is apt to gain too much headway and getting rid of it proves difficult. A native plant of almost universal distribution. For so small a floating leaf it develops quite long roots if they are not nibbled by fishes. Dried Duckweed is a good producer of infusoria.

Water Lettuce

A beautiful floating plant about four inches in diameter, having fluted, velvety, light green leaves and long roots. Requires warm, moist atmosphere and diffused light. Propagation is by runners. Does exceptionally well in shallow water (three to five inches) with roots dragging in earthy soil.

PLANTING

Sand or Pebbles?

Coarse sand is best, or a mixture of sand and small pebbles, such as Jersey gravel. Washed building sand is satisfactory. Fine sand packs too hard for the roots to penetrate easily and allows no beneficial circulation of water. Pebbles, stones, shells, or marbles alone are bad because they have open spaces which catch and hold fish food where no scavengers can reach, thus causing the water to turn foul. Large and small stones, well selected, may be very ornamental and natural in an aquarium, but they should be set in sand for the reason given.

Depth of Sand

This is a more important subject than is generally recognized. The planting medium should be only deep enough to be certain of holding down the rooted plants. *Vallisneria* and the smaller *Sagittarias* need only about 1 ½ inches, while giant *Sagittaria* requires two inches or more. It is a good plan to root the larger plants in deeper sand in the back of the aquarium and then let the level slope lower towards the front. This serves the double purpose of giving the smaller plants a place in the light and of working the aquarium sediment forward where it is more easily removed. Some aquarists place a glass bar or other stop about an inch wide between the front edge of the sand and the front glass of the aquarium, making a one-inch trench the entire length an excellent dirt trap. The stop may also be made of well selected small stones placed in the form of a semicircle.

Use Soil?

No. Theoretically it might be a good idea to provide soil substance in the form of a substratum for plants, but in practice it does not work well. It is apt to become foul and any stirring clouds up the aquarium. Besides, we expect the plants to get their sustenance by absorbing the waste products of the fishes. Professional growers use garden soil below the sand. Some soil benefits potted aquarium plants.

How to Plant

Enough has been said as to the characteristics of available plants for the aquarium, so that here we are concerned with the mechanics of the job. The first thing is to make sure that the plants are kept moist while the work is being carefully done. A half-drying may set them back for weeks. If they are laid in water or covered with a wet newspaper, there will be no danger.

The water in the aquarium should be about five or six inches deep while most of the work is being done. If the sand is fairly clean, the water can be kept clear by placing a piece of paper over it while filling. Pour on the paper. When rockwork is to be used, it should be placed before the plants are set. The only real difficulty is in arranging the grasses that have spreading roots, but it is not very troublesome when the water is shallow. Spread the roots of *Sagittaria* and *Vallisneria* as widely as possible and cover them well with sand; be careful not to bury the leaves. If there are tall, stiff leaves, partly in the air, be sure to sprinkle them often during the balance of the work. Sometimes a large plant is so buoyant that it is necessary to place a small stone or two on the sand over the roots, or to wrap the base of the plant with a plant weight. Each rooted plant like *Sagittaria* or *Vallisneria* should have sufficient space so that there will be room for new runners to expand.

The smaller plants and those with long strands, like *Anacharis*, should be placed last. Old yellowish leaves should be removed before planting.

Planting Sticks

If plants must be added after the aquarium is filled, or if any of them ride up, a planting stick is most useful. Many algae scrapers are designed for use as planting sticks. The end of the handle is notched which makes them very handy tools. Most petshops sell these handy tools.

Bunched Plants

Plants in wired bundles look very attractive and one is tempted to plant them in the way they are received. They never grow that way naturally and should not be planted in that way. Stemmed plants, like *Anacharis*, *Cabomba*, and *Myriophyllum*, ought to be slightly separated so that water and light may pass between the stems at the base.

Fertilizing Plants

This is a "noble experiment," but a dangerous one. It belongs in the same category as placing a layer of soil under the sand, only it is a few degrees more dangerous. It has been proven many times that fish fertilize plants. If there are enough fish present, the combined effects of their breathing and their droppings give the plants all the chemical stimulation they need. The author has seen many well-planted aquariums degenerate without the presence of fish life, and to revive beautifully upon the reintroduction of fishes. However, if any readers feel that their plants are in need of added stimulation, any of the plant foods available in petshops can be tried. These fertilizers were developed especially for aquarium plants.

Selecting Plants

As in other branches of horticulture, it is best to select young or half-grown plants rather than fully developed specimens that have arrived at the zenith of perfection. The young adapt themselves better and last longer. Avoid plants covered with algae or "moss." It chokes the plants and spreads through the aquarium.

Cleaning Plants

It is, of course, desirable to have new plants free of germs and "bugs." Any known treatment fully accomplishing this would sicken or kill the plants. New plants should first be rinsed and then placed for a day in a shallow, white tray for observation. Perhaps some unwanted snails or leeches will appear, although inspection of the tanks is necessary to detect snail eggs which look like small gelatinous clumps filled with numerous poppy seed sized eggs. Plants like *Vallisneria, Sagittaria*, Swordplants, and *Cryptocoryne* are often infested with egg cases of certain leeches. These are light brown, oval shaped, about inch long and are often attached at the base of the leaves near the roots. Both snail eggs and the egg cases should be removed by gently scraping the leaves with a dull knife.

CLASSIFICATION OF FISHES

The pleasure of aquarium study can be doubled by organizing it. The following explanation has been prepared in the hope that it will clear up, in the beginning, a number of simple facts that aquarists ought to know. These are facts which may not previously have been reduced in plain enough terms for popular use; here they are brought together within the compass of a few pages. These pages may be skipped without regret (but not without loss) by those who are science-shy.

Anyone who is familiar with the ordinary run of aquarium fishes, if asked whether the Cardinal Tetra is a Characoid or a Cichlid, will not hesitate to say it is a Characoid. But if you ask him why, he is likely to tell you that it is similar to other Characoids, that it has an adipose fin—and stop right there. Very probably he has never considered what other differences there are between a Cichlid and a Characoid; *he has learned to recognize the two families by sight* without attempting to analyse the whys and wherefores. In this particular instance, he is just like the professional ichthyologist, who can place most fishes in their proper families by sight, without recourse to books.

There is more to the subject than this, however, and since we have decided to present the different families of aquarium fishes in their correct ich-thyological order-of-precedence, a brief explanation of why this has been done should prove helpful.

IDENTIFICATION BY ANATOMY

Under each family heading throughout the book there are a few sentences calling attention to some of the external features that will help the aquarist recognize a member of that group. To understand *why* the families are placed in the order in which they stand, something else is required. This is supplied by the bird's-eye-view of fish classification given in this chapter. Before this classification or the notes under the families can become intelligible, we must learn a few simple names for certain parts of a fish's anatomy, especially the fins. Every aquarist ought to be familiar with these few terms, for they are used continually in describing the form and color of all fishes. The great majority of fishes have seven fins. Of these seven, four are *paired*, that is, there is one on each side of the body opposite its mate. The first or forward paired fins are the *pectoral* or *breast fins*, one on each side of the body just behind the head. These correspond to the forelegs of land animals or the arms of a human being. The second paired fins are the *ventral* or *pelvic fins*, placed close beside each other on the under-

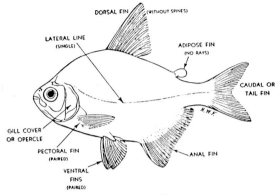

OUTLINE DRAWING OF A CHARACIN
It will be seen that there are no fin spines, and that
the ventral fins are *behind* the pectoral line.

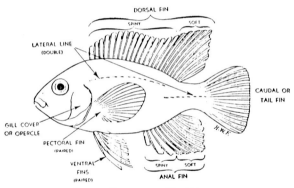

OUTLINE DRAWING OF A CICHLID
Note presence of 2 sets of fin spines, and the forward
position of the ventral fins, *under* the pectoral fins.

side of the fish, either before, directly below, or behind the pectoral pair. Aquarists frequently misname these the breast fins. The ventral fins correspond to the hind legs of land animals and the legs of man. The remaining three fins are unpaired or single. They are placed exactly on the midline of the fish as viewed from the top or front. The most important of the unpaired fins is the caudal or tail fin. With most fishes it is the caudal fin that provides the chief propelling power in swimming. It may be forked as in most swift-swimming fishes, cut off straight, rounded at the end, or pointed. On the back of the fish is the dorsal or back fin and on the underside behind the vent is the anal fin.

These fins are formed of a delicate *fin membrane* supported by fairly stiff but jointed *fin rays* that usually branch somewhat as they approach the outer edge of the fin. In certain fishes the front rays of some of the fins are bony, unjointed, and sharp. These bony rays are called *fin spines* and in groups like the Cichlids these spines may make up more than half of the rays of the dorsal and anal fins. In such cases it is usual to refer to the two parts of the dorsal fin as the *spiny dorsal* and the *soft dorsal*. Fishes that have several spines in the dorsal and anal fins form a group called the *spiny-rayed fishes*. In the Gobies, the Silversides, and some other families, the spiny dorsal has become completely separated from the soft dorsal so that there are two entirely separate dorsal fins, the first spiny, the second soft.

Other fishes, notably most Characoids and Catfishes as well as Salmon and Trout, have another small fin on the back. It is behind the dorsal and near the tail fin. This, the *adipose fin*, is unlike the other fins in that it is not usually supported by rays, but consists of fatty or adipose tissue. In the Armored Catfishes the adipose fin is supported by one stiff spine.

The similarities and differences in these fins as well as in other, mostly internal, characteristics are utilized by ichthyologists to classify fishes. In some groups the teeth are important in classification.

HOW FISHES ARE CLASSIFIED AND PRESENTED IN THIS BOOK

All the fishes in this book, with the exception of the Stingray, *Paratrygon*, belong to the great class of bony fishes, Osteichthyes, which is split up into a great number of *orders*, the orders into *families*, the families into *genera* (singular form, *genus*), and the genera

into *species*. There are good reasons for this arrangement, and the aquarist who takes a little time in spying out the similarities in his fishes can easily find out much about fish classification for himself. The order in which the species and families are treated follows rather closely that in which the ichthyologist places fishes. Those families that resemble most closely the primitive types of fishes of bygone ages, as revealed by the study of fossils, are placed first; the rest are arranged in an ascending order determined by the advancing degree of complexity of their structure. This complexity is shown externally chiefly by the greater number of spines in the dorsal and anal fins and the more forward position of the ventral fins. For instance, a Characoid has no spiny dorsal fin and there are never any spines in the anal fin. Furthermore, the ventral fins are set well back along the belly of the fish. These are relatively "primitive" fishes and belong well towards the beginning of the series. On the other hand, the Cichlids have well-developed spiny dorsal and anal fins and their ventrals are placed well forward, under the pectoral fins. The Cichlids are highly developed "spiny-rayed" fishes. The Killifishes (egg-laying tooth-carps) and *Poeciliidae* (live-bearing tooth-carps) are about midway between the Characoids and the Cichlids in their make-up. They have not developed any spines in their fins, but their mouth structure and other points show that they are measurably nearer the end of the series than are the Characoids.

We now proceed with a few notes on the orders, in which the families in this book are placed.

The Herring-like fishes (order Clupeiformes) are "primitive" bony fishes, lacking fin spines, and having the ventral fins well back. Only a few species are included in this book: the Butterflyfish, *Pantodon*; the Arowana, *Osteoglossum bicirrhosum*; the Feather-fins, *Notopterus*; and the Elephant-nosed fish, *Gnathonemus*.

The true freshwater fishes (order Cypriniformes) include probably three-fourths of all freshwater fishes throughout the world. The Characoids, the South American Gymnotid Eels, the Cyprinids, the Loaches, and the Catfishes all belong to this order. As a group they resemble the Herring-like fishes. They differ from them and from all other fishes, however, since they have a complicated series of bones (the Weberian ossicles) that connect the air bladder with the inner ear. The exact function of this complex organ is not known with certainty, but it is probably of use as an accessory organ of hearing or in detecting differences in water pressure.

The egg-laying Killifishes and live-bearing *Poeciliidae*, together with some lesser families, are placed in the order Cyprinodontiformes, generally known as the Cyprinodonts. These are much like the Beloniformes in the fins, but differ in the mouth and other points.

The order Perciformes, or Perch-like fishes, includes the majority of spiny-rayed fishes. Among our aquarium fishes, the Cichlids, the Perches, the Sunfishes, the Theraponids, the Nandids, the Monodactylids, the Archer Fishes, and the "Scats" all belong here. All of them have well-developed spiny dorsal and anal fins and ventral fins placed forward under the pectorals.

The Labyrinth fishes are now usually placed with the above families in the Perciformes, but are often relegated to a suborder (Anabantoidei). They differ in having a chamber above the gills with which they breathe atmospheric air. They are Old World freshwater fishes.

Another group often separated from the Perciformes but usually included in that group as a suborder (Gobioidei) are the Gobies. This suborder includes the true Gobies and the Eleotrids or Sleeper Gobies, and a few little-known families, perculiar fishes found on the coasts of all the continents. A few inhabit fresh water. The spiny and soft dorsal fins are separate, giving the appearance of a double dorsal; the ventrals are far forward, either set very close together or united into a sucking disk.

The order Mastacembeliformes, or Spiny Eels, includes elongated, long-snouted freshwater fishes of the Old World with a great many free spines in front of the dorsal. The only fish in the book belonging to this order is *Mastacembelus*.

Finally, we have the order Tetraodontiformes which includes the Puffers and Trigger-fishes. Nearly all are saltwater fishes, but a few come up into freshwater rivers. A few are used as aquarium fishes.

USING SCIENTIFIC NAMES

If the reader has scanned the foregoing with care, he will see at once that the terms "order," "family," "genus," and "species," all mean something definite in fish classification. The term "family" is the one most frequently misused by aquarists. We see many references to the "Panchax family," the "egg-laying family" or the "live-bearing family." Such uses of the term *family* have no meaning and will not be followed by the careful aquarist. Instead of the *"Cheirodon* family," one should say the "genus *Cheirodon"* (which belongs to the Characoid families). Further, all live-bearers do not belong to one family. The first word in the name of a fish is the genus to which it belongs. The second word is the species and ordinarily is the last subdivision. However, at times a less important peculiarity is taken into account and made into a subspecies, race, or variety: *Xiphophorus maculatus, var. ruber,* for instance. "Variety" should never be used in any other sense. It is always *within* a species.

When no specific name is given a fish, but the word "species" is used, it means that we know the genus to which it belongs, but not the species. An example would be *"Corydoras species"* or *"spec.,"* as it is often written.

It should also be noted that the singular of species is species, not "specie." The plural of genus is genera.

Sometimes after a fish has just been referred to by its full scientific name, the generic name is abbreviated on following repetitions, such as *Scatophagus argus* being repeated as *S. argus.*

CHANGES IN SCIENTIFIC NAMES

Changes in scientific names present a constant problem to the scientist and aquarist. We can only say on this point that names do change in accordance with the progress of ichthyological research. The chief source of confusion has been the hurry and carelessness of some aquarists in sticking any name on a newly imported fish before it has been carefully identified. Later study usually shows such names to be erroneous. Often modern research has made changes necessary, but when the job has been done well, we may expect relative permanence before a particular group is again subjected to revision.

NAMES OF PEOPLE DESCRIBING SPECIES

In the main heading for each fish the name of the scientist who first described it is given. This is in accord with universal practice. There is one point in connection with this that is not always understood. It will be noticed that sometimes this name is in parentheses. This means that there have been developments since the original naming which require that the fish be moved into some other genus (the first name) instead of that in which it was originally placed. When this is done, the original describer is retained, but his name is placed in parentheses.

FISHES

All fishes in this book are arranged in family groups. At the start of each family its general characteristics and breeding habits, when known, are described. These are not usually repeated for the species comprising the group because most of them follow the same life pattern. Special traits, if any, of species, however, are covered on their individual pages.

THE STINGRAYS
FAMILY DASYATIDAE

Most stingrays are strictly marine fishes, but a few enter the brackish water of estuarine river systems. As far as we know, only two species exist in freshwater. Both are found in South America and are occasionally imported. They are often difficult to keep in an aquarium, but once acclimated, make very interesting objects to study.

Paratrygon species
Popular name: Freshwater Stingray
Length: to 15 inches
Northern and Central South America

Stingrays are fascinating fishes, but they need an aquarium properly set up for their mode of life. A large aquarium of at least 30 inches in length and 12 inches in width is necessary. Instead of coarse gravel, a layer of sand should be used, since rays spend much time resting on the bottom half buried in sand. But, they also need plenty of swimming space. While lying on the bottom, they breathe through special openings, called spiracles, which are equipped with valves and are located on the upper side of the head, just behind the eyes. This is a marvelous adaptation, since normal breathing through the mouth would inevitably result in sand and other foreign matter to be inhaled and irritate the gills.

Their feeding habits are equally interesting. Although newly acquired specimens are often very reluctant feeders, hardly any can resist the temptation of a meal of live ghost or grass shrimps. These shrimps are often sold as scavengers in petshops. If live shrimps are not available, frozen ones often are and should be tried instead. Rays capture their prey by literally "pouncing" on it with the whole body. Once they are feeding well on their preferred food, other, more readily available foods can be substituted. Earthworms, bloodworms, *Tubifex* worms and pieces of fish and shrimp are among the most likely foods to be accepted. Many stingrays like live goldfish. Temperature, 72° to 82°F.

THE BICHIRS
FAMILY POLYPTERIDAE

The Bichirs are a small family of primitive African fishes. All are carnivorous and, with the exception of the reedfish, *Erpetoichthys,* are better kept with fishes of their own size. Few species of *Polypterus* are imported, but *Erpetoichthys* is usually available. Few have been bred in captivity.

Paratrygon *species*

Erpetoichthys calabaricus
(Smith)
Popular name: African Reedfish, Rope Fish
Meaning of name: Erpetoichthys, reed-like fish; calabaricus, from Calabar
Length: about 20 inches
Western Africa

The dorsal fin of this odd-looking fish consists of a series of small, one-rayed finlets set about one-half inch apart and starting about midway between head and tail. The scales are quite prominent, hard, and rhomboid in shape. They are fairly quiet fishes and only occasionally swim about with eel-like motions. They do not bury themselves as true eels sometimes do and, therefore, do not dislodge plants. Food is hunted at the bottom. Pieces of fish, beef heart, shrimp, *Tubifex* worms, frozen, adult brine shrimp, and live or frozen blood worms are some of the foods they will take. Dried foods are not accepted. Smaller fish are safe with them. Though they are sluggish fish, their tank should be covered; when frightened, especially at first introduction to the tank, they are quite nervous and many a Reedfish has met its untimely death by slipping out of the tank unnoticed.

Reedfishes have gills like other fishes, but also possess lungs of sorts. These enable them to survive in fairly stagnant water by occasionally taking gulps of atmospheric air. The fish has not been bred in captivity, but secondary sex characteristics are present, the male showing a peculiar thickness in the anal fin. Temperature, 75° to 82°F.

Polypterus species
Popular name: Bichir
Meaning of name: Polypterus, with many fins

Calamoichthys calabaricus

Polypterus *spec.*

Length: 15 inches

Central Africa

A rather secretive fish which should be provided with adequate hiding places. Once acclimated to aquarium conditions, it loses much of its original shyness. Bichirs have large mouths and cannot be trusted with fishes of platy size and smaller. The fish prefers to feed near the bottom on small earthworms, blood worms, brine shrimp and other larger types of live food. Rarely accepts prepared food. Temperature, 72° to 85°F.

THE FEATHERBACKS
FAMILY NOTOPTERIDAE

This is a small, specialized family of fishes widely distributed throughout Southeast Asia and Africa. The small, featherlike dorsal fin is characteristic of the family, although in one species, *Xenomystus nigri*, the fin is absent. All have a long anal fin which is continuous with the small tail.

Wavy motions of this fin can propel them forward as well as backward.

Notopterus chitala
(Buchanan-Hamilton)

Popular name: Featherback Knife Fish, Clown Knife Fish

Meaning of name: Notopterus, with feather-like fin; chitala, a native name

Length: Up to about 30 inches in nature

Southeast Asia, India

Featherbacks spend most of their time in the lower half of the tank, although they rise to the surface periodically for a gulp of atmospheric air. They are omnivorous when young,

Notopterus chitala

Xenomystus nigri

but usually change to a diet of live fish and shrimp as they mature. Among themselves they are somewhat quarrelsome, but are peaceful towards other fishes of comparable size. Only the large specimens have to be kept alone in a tank. They are not bred in the aquarium. In the wild, eggs are deposited on smooth, hard surfaces, such as stones or logs, and are guarded by the males. There is no apparent sexual dimorphism. Temperature, 72° to 85°F.

Xenomystus nigri
Guenther
> *Popular name:* African Knife Fish
> *Meaning of name:* Xenomystus, with strange mustache; nigri, black
> *Length:* about 8 inches

West and Central Africa
Although these fishes resemble the South American Knife Fishes in form and finnage, they are not at all related to them. Their mode of locomotion is much more eel-like, and their bodies appear to be more flexible than the somewhat rigid body of the South American Knife Fishes. In the aquarium, they move about at a fairly sluggish pace.

They are generally peaceful towards other fishes, but often quarrelsome among themselves and, therefore, should be kept in large tanks. Various live and frozen foods should be offered; dried foods are only reluctantly eaten. One should provide sufficient hiding places for these Knife Fishes, not because they like to stay hidden most of the time, but because they are much more at home in such an environment. Occasionally they surface to take gulps of air.

The fishes have no known secondary sex characteristics and no information exists about their breeding habits.

Temperature, 70° to 82°F.

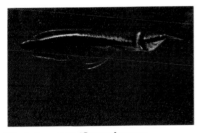

Black Arowana (Osteoglossum ferreirai), juvenile

THE BONY-TONGUES
FAMILY OSTEOGLOSSIDAE

Only five species of this ancient family of Herring-like freshwater fishes still exist: *Scleropages leichardti* in Queensland, Australia, and New Guinea; *S. formosus* in S. E. Asia, Borneo and Sumatra; *Clupisudis niloticus* in tropical Africa; and three in northern South America: *Arapaima gigas, Osteoglossum bicirrhosum,* and *O. ferreirai.* All grow to two feet or more in length; the Pirarucu of the Amazon (*Arapaima*) grow to about eight feet. All are voracious and have sharp teeth, all have notably large scales, and all seem to be mouthbrooders.

Osteoglossum bicirrhosum
(Vandelli) Spix and Agassiz
Popular name: Aruana or Arowana

Osteoglossum bicirrhosum, juvenile

Meaning of name: Osteoglossum, bony tongue; bicirrhosum, with two cirri or barbels

   Length: To over 3 feet

   Amazon River and Guyana

   Young Aruana are sometimes im-(flies, etc.), mosquito larvae, and live, adult brine shrimp are the foods most likely to be accepted in the beginning. Later, mealworms can be offered, as well as lumps of freeze-dried brine shrimp, for which some specimens

Arapaima gigas

ported and make interesting and striking aquarium pets if kept alone or with fishes too large to be swallowed by their capacious mouths. They are probably the most graceful, smooth-flowing swimmers of our aquarium fishes. The two forward-projecting barbels which are leaf-like, though narrow, the large alert eyes, and the continuous graceful motion make this fish unique. The Aruana likes live food and prefers to take it off the surface. Most of the time, young three- to four-inch specimens that have just absorbed their yolk sacks are imported. Small insects develop a particular liking. Importation is problematic. Temperature, 75° to 80°.

Arapaima gigas
Cuvier

   Meaning of name: gigas, giant like

   Length: Up to 8 feet

   Northern and Central South America

   As is obvious from the adult size of this fish, only very young individuals can be kept in the average home aquarium. They are seldom imported and command a high price. Young Arapaimas are very active, extremely graceful swimmers, spending much time in midwater. Occasionally, they take a gulp of air. They feed almost exclusively on live fishes. Arapaimas that zon, one of the largest of freshwater fishes. The chief distinguishing features of *Pantodon* lie in the teeth and certain peculiarities in the skeleton.

Pantodon buchholzi

outgrow a hobbyist's tank should be donated to the nearest public aquarium. There they will be much appreciated since they make excellent show fishes. Importation is forbidden. Temperature, 70° to 82°F.

THE AFRICAN FRESHWATER FLYING FISH
FAMILY PANTODONTIDAE

This family includes only one species, the Butterflyfish, which comes from West Africa. Its nearest relatives are the members of the Osteoglossidae, a family of large fishes, which includes the Arapaima of the Ama-

Pantodon buchholzi
Peters

Popular name: Butterflyfish

Meaning of name: Pantodon, with teeth everywhere (in the mouth); buchholzi, after the naturalist Buchholz

Length: 5 inches
West Africa

No finely drawn description of this bizarre fish is needed to help the reader single it out from close relatives, for it has none. However, when we see such an extraordinary fish, we wish to know something of its peculiarities and the uses for its fantastic fins.

In reality, this is a freshwater flying fish. The fish spends much time at the surface of the water, and is said to skim along it for at least six feet at a leap.

The fish is strictly a surface feeder and can be trained to take food from the finger, such as chunks of freeze-dried brine shrimp, strips of lean, raw beef, mealworms, inch-long live fish, or bigger earthworms.

Breeding Butterflyfish is a rare achievement. Males are slimmer and have bigger "wings" in proportion, also longer anal fins. Very large floating eggs hatch in a week at 75°F. Young look like little tadpoles. They remain at the surface and must have newly hatched mosquito larvae or else a sufficiently large supply of food, like small, sifted *Daphnia* so that much of it reaches the top of the water. Lowering the water level about two inches helps to bring the baby fish and food together. The young can presently be weaned to taking some dry food that floats. The species is naturally long-lived, but often comes to an untimely end by leaping out when a forgetful aquarist fails to quickly replace the cover on the tank (which should be fifteen gallon size or larger). They snatch and swallow small surface fishes that come too close.

THE MORMYRIDS OR ELEPHANT-FISHES
FAMILY MORMYRIDAE

These curious-looking freshwater fishes are found only in tropical Africa. Some kinds have the jaws short and blunt, some have the lower lip extended, while others have a long, down-curved snout. All have weak electric organs, probably used as an alert system against potential aggressors. Finally, they have the largest brain for their size of any known fishes. Several species have been imported, since regular air service was established from Africa; prior to that most came from the Congo via Belgium, having been collected and shipped by the legendary Pierre Brichard. Perhaps the best known mormyrid is the following:

Gnathonemus petersi
Guenther
Meaning of name: Gnathonemus: jaw-thread; petersi for Dr. Wilhelm Peters, Berlin zoologist
   Length: Up to 9 inches
   Niger River to Congo River in Africa

Although this odd-appearing fish has a rather stiff body and often remains still, it is nervous and is capable of rapid movement. Should be kept in

Gnathonemus petersi

a large, well-planted tank. While aggressive toward its own kind, it seems not to kill. The extension of the lower jaw is flexible and has taste buds which are probably used in locating worms in the soil. They take brine shrimp, white worms, or other live foods, eating in a manner similar to other fishes. Breeding habits unknown. Temperature about 75°.

THE CHARACOIDS
FAMILIES CHARACIDAE, ANOS-TOMIDAE, GASTEROPELECIDAE AND HEMIODONTIDAE

Once treated as one very large family, the Characoid fishes are now considered by taxonomists to comprise over fifteen separate families. They are all from tropical America and Africa. They belong to the great order Cypriniformes, together with the Carps and Catfishes. Many Characoids look much like some species of Carps (Cyprinidae), but the aquarist seldom has trouble distinguishing members of the two families. No Carp ever has any teeth in the jaws, or any adipose fin. Most Characoids possess both teeth and an adipose fin. Some lack one or the other, but few or no species lack both, and if aquarists will remember this "one-or-the-other" combination, they will seldom be puzzled. The presence of teeth in a small live fish is easily determined by running a pin or needle lightly along the upper jaw of a fish held gently but firmly in a wet cloth or net. (Some Characoids have teeth only in the upper jaw.) Internally they differ from the Carps in the bones of the throat. All Characoids have scales, excepting two very rare species from Argentina.

While there is considerable variation in members of the family as to size, shape and habits, ranging from the brilliant little Cardinal Tetra to the blood-thirsty Piranha, there is usually a suggestion of uniformity that is not hard to discover.

Most of them are fairly hardy, considering that they come from tropical regions. Generally speaking, they are not fighters, although any fish with good teeth is liable to use them. This sometimes results in a little sly nipping of fins. It takes place so seldom, and without any outward appearance of fighting, that it is hard to detect. On the whole they are peaceful and seldom kill.

Of course, this is not true of Piranhas.

"Tetras"

In those earlier days of the exotic fish hobby, a number of Characoids were included in the genus *Tetragonopterus*, a generic name still used for a small genus, but under which many of our aquarium fishes used to be placed. It became the trade practice to apply "Tet" or "Tetra" as a blanket name to all Characoids, especially the small ones, such as "Tet from Rio," "Lemon Tetra," "Black Tetra," has become well entrenched in popular usage, but has no present scientific standing.

Care and Breeding

In the matter of food, most Characoids are easily pleased with an average fish diet. They appreciate variety especially when it tends towards live foods, but seem to enjoy various freeze dried and frozen foods as well. The brand of fish food called *Tetra* has nothing to do with the fish called *Tetra* and is merely a trade name. Few tetras demand special water conditions for their well-being, as long as the water does not become too hard. In general the Characoids do very well in water at from 70 to 75°F although for breeding, it should, in some instances, be raised to 80°F. Very few of the species are easily bred. They offer an interesting challenge to the aquarist in that respect. A number of them yield to skillful handling, yet several of the most desirable species, such as Cardinal Tetras (*Paracheirodon axelrodi*), Rummy-nosed Tetras (*H. rhodostomus*), Bleeding Heart Tetras (*H.rubrostigma*), and many of the African species still oblige us to import wild specimens in order to keep up our stocks.

With the few exceptions to be noted, Characoids drop adhesive or semi-adhesive eggs, to which they pay no attention, except, perhaps, for the doubtful compliment of eating them. Failing this, they are likely to make up for the oversight by devouring the young. Very few of them fight in defense of their fry, as do the Cichlids and Bubble Nest-builders.

Only fishes in the best physical condition should be used for breeding. In many cases it is almost impossible to distinguish between the sexes unless the fishes are in excellent shape.

In general the requirements for breeding the various species of Characoids are similar. The aquarium should have a reasonable amount of open space, but with thickets of plants having finely divided leaves, such as *Myriophyllum, Nitella, Fontinalis* or artificial spawning grass. To ensure cleanliness, and for better observation of eggs and fry, no gravel should be used. Water in the breeding tank should be clean, well aged, and possibly a little softer than the water in the aquarium where the prospective breeders are normally kept.

It has been found that some of the species spawn more readily in "soft" water. Indeed it may be hoped that this is the key to unlocking the difficulty of breeding this large and important family of fishes.

Many fishes are more apt to spawn if previously separated a few days from their mates. "Absence makes the heart grow fonder." It is usually best to place the female in the breeding tank a day or two in advance of the male.

If all goes well, spawning will take place in the morning after the male has been placed in the breeding tank. If the fishes do not spawn within a few days, try a partial change of water. If that does not stimulate spawning, remove them and try again in a week or two. In the interim, feed rather often with the best foods available.

If the fishes have spawned, remove them immediately.

The greatest problem in fish culture is the first food. Most fishes, when hatched, are more egg than fish. Some of them seem like a splinter attached sidewise to a ball. Gradually the fish enlarges and develops fins, while the ball contracts until it is a mere lump on the abdomen. It is the yolk sac. So long as it is visible, it is nature's reservoir of nourishment. Usually the babies are not much in evidence during this period. Being helpless to avoid enemies, they hover or hop about the bottom. Sac soon absorbed, the fish becomes more streamlined and takes to the open water. It is on its own.

The aquarist's problem is right here, and for the next week or two, is to have enough of the right sizes and kinds of food ready. Standard directions say "feed infusoria." Sounds simple enough, and it *is*, if we are lucky. Infusoria covers a multitude of sizes and kinds of organisms. The predominating one in most prepared cultures is *Paramecium*, which happens to be a fair food. In addition, many other tiny organisms are usually present in such cultures, providing a varied menu.

Having passed the feeding point where infusorians are outgrown, something larger must be found. Newly hatched brine shrimp is the food of choice. For hatching instructions, see the chapter on fish foods. With newly hatched brine shrimp, the youngsters can be raised until big enough to handle the normal food for the species.

Repeatedly it has been found that more youngsters can be brought through early infancy in an oversized, long-established tank. This is no doubt due to its containing more microscopic food of suitable sizes and quality. About the only way to bring through a large proportion of very small fry in a *small* tank is to feed them often on natural pond infusoria. As these organisms appear in usable quantity at unpredictable times, we have here an element of luck. It may be asked why scientific aquarists do not make con-tinuous pure cultures of the best of the live micro-foods. This would indeed solve a problem and at least quadruple the output of fishes. It has been tried, but not successfully. However, it is the observation of experienced breeders that pond infusoria gives much better results than the cultured kinds.

Despite the difficulties considered here, the fact remains that most species of aquarium fishes *are* successfully reared.

How much infusoria to feed is an important question that cannot be answered in any exact way. *The bellies of the babies should bulge.* One soon learns to judge this. On the other hand, there ought not be *too much* live food present. It depletes oxygen and annoys the fishes. The amount of liquid to feed depends on the richness of the culture and the number of fry. It might be a spoonful or a cupful. A low-power microscope is important here. Examine the culture. It should be rich in life. Use with judgment. A test drop of water taken from the surface of the light side of the aquarium should show plenty of organisms.

Unfortunately it must be recognized that many, many ambitious aquarists are neither able to secure even a few *Daphnia*, nor any good infusoria. By care they can succeed in a lesser degree. As has been mentioned elsewhere, there are fairly good substitutes for *Daphnia*, such as finely minced white worms or grated raw shrimp. Some fishes have been reared on prepared dry foods, starting with flour size. Mashed yolk of hard-boiled egg, shaken in a bottle of water, spar-

Hyphessobrycon callistus

ingly fed, is an acceptable early food. It is almost impossible not to overfeed with prepared foods, so when using them it is well to have a number of small snails present to consume the surplus, but only after the eggs have hatched.

Inequality in the size of youngsters always puzzles the beginner. None can tell why it is any more than in human beings. Some fishes are no doubt born more vigorous than others. They get "the jump" by bolting the biggest and best food. Presently they become large enough to eat the smallest of their brethren. As these make the best of food, the disproportion increases. It is nature's way. A plentiful early supply of the small live foods tends to equalize growth.

Ordinarily the young should not be placed with their parents or other fishes, unless there is enough difference in size, or they *might* be eaten!

Hyphessobrycon callistus
Boulenger
   Popular name: Serpae Tetra
   Meaning of name: Hyphessobrycon: little Brycon; callistus, pretty sail, in reference to the dorsal fin. Formerly known as *H. serpae*
   Length: 1½ inches
   Parana-Paraguay System
   The Serpae Tetra, overall soft red set off by the black of the dorsal fin and shoulder spot, is one of the most beautiful of small aquarium fishes. The black marking on the dorsal fin suggests *Pristella riddlei,* but fins are a

Hyphessobrycon flammeus

little shorter and more intensely red. For those who like their fishes quiet, and restful to contemplate, this species is perfect. They seem to prefer a level about a third of the way up from the bottom, but are always on the alert to dash upward to catch falling food. Adipose fins are transparent.

They were first imported to Germany in 1931 and into the United States two years later. As they were hard to spawn, they disappeared for some years. We were without them until large fresh inportations to the United States in 1948. They are now bred with good success and are usually available. They breed like *Hyphessobrycon flammeus*, but it seems that only a small portion of females spawn. A charming species, neither timid nor aggressive, and an ornament to any collection of fishes of its own size. They respond well to feedings of "color foods" which intensify the red and are now on the market. Temperature, 70° to 80°F.

Hyphessobrycon flammeus
Myers

Popular name: Tetra from Rio, Red Tet, Flame Tetra, and Flame Fish

Meaning of name: Hyphessobrycon, little Brycon; flammeus, flamelike

Length: 1½ inches

Vicinity of Rio de Janeiro

The beauty of a fish by no means depends on bulk. In fact, many aquarists consider the inch-and-a-half length of the Flame Tetra the ideal size at which a fish can be viewed and appreciated. In addition, the Flame Tetra's brilliant color pattern is so simple that nothing is sacrificed to its small size. It is harmless, reasonably hardy, easily cared for, and can be bred—but not so easily as to become uninteresting.

Like many other exotic fishes, *H. flammeus* needs favorable conditions in order to develop its best colors. Plenty of room in a well-planted aquarium, an occasional extra meal of *Daphnia* or other live food, and a temperature of about 75° will soon bring on "show condition."

The sexes may be told in several ways. The males have the characin hooks on the end of the anal fin which stick to a fine-mesh net when the fish is netted. The anal fin of the male has a more pronounced black edge, and the female appears fuller in the body outline. Color is not a dependable index.

This species should be bred where at least a part of the aquarium has a thicket of finely divided leaves, such as *Myriophyllum*. After lively driving by the male, the fishes take a close parallel position among the plants. Accompanied by a little trembling, about ten eggs are dropped and fertilized. This is repeated until 100 or more small, nearly transparent eggs are produced. The eggs are slightly adhesive and they will stick fairly well to the plants if not disturbed. Those that fall may also hatch. The young, kept at a temperature of 75°, appear in three days and are almost as transparent as the eggs. They will feed on infusoria and flour made of ordinary fishfood. Considering the almost mi-

Hyphessobrycon herbertaxelrodi

croscopic size of the young when hatched, it is surprising to find that they will be two-thirds grown in less than six months when well fed.

When two males are used with a female, a higher percentage of eggs have been found to hatch. For small fishes they are rather long-lived, attaining a ripe old age of from three to four years.

Dr. Myers found them not far from Rio de Janeiro in gorgeous color in brown, swampy waters at temperatures in the low seventies.

Hyphessobrycon herbertaxelrodi
Gery
    Popular name: Black Neon
    Meaning of name: Hyphessobrycon, little fish with teeth; herbertaxelrodi, after Dr. Herbert R. Axelrod
    Length: 1¼ inches

Hyphessobrycon pulchripinnis

Brazil

A small Characoid requiring much the same care as the Neon Tetra, *P. innesi.* Fairly soft and slightly acid water, a diet rich in newly-hatched brine shrimp or *Daphnia*, some thickets of fine-leafed plants such as *Ambu-*

lia, Myriophyllum or *Cabomba*, a dark background and peaceful tank mates bring about a feeling of well-being and therefore the most pleasing colors.

Sexes are easily distinguished as long as the fishes are mature and healthy. Females are somewhat larger and deeper bodied than males. They are more easily bred than the Neon, and eggs are less prone to fungus. Fry can take newly-hatched brine shrimp immediately after becoming free-swimming. Brine shrimp eggs from the Great Salt Lake in Utah are large, and the fry of small fishes may not be able to swallow them. The brine shrimp should also be offered as soon as they hatch.

Temperature, 75 to 80 degrees.

Hyphessobrycon rosaceus

Hyphessobrycon pulchripinnis
Ahl
> *Popular name:* Lemon Tetra
> *Meaning of name:* Hyphessobrycon, little Brycon; pulchripinnis, pretty-fin
> *Length:* About 1¾ inches
> Rio Trombetas, Amazon basin

The popular name of this species is well given. While the fish has a faint yellowish overtone, the color character is accentuated and brought out mostly by the intense yellow edging in the anal fin and, to a lesser extent, in the dorsal. Both those fins are usually well spread, giving the species a lively, saucy bearing. As seen here, bodies are somewhat translucent, the only spot of warm color being the bright red in the upper half of the eye.

Eggs are quite small and the spawn-ing fishes are very successful in gobbling them almost as fast as dropped, which is not surprising in this family of fishes. For this reason it is desirable to provide them with dense plant thickets and with water that is not too deep—say about six to seven inches. They have been known to spawn on the exposed roots of plants.

An average temperature of about 73° to 75° suits them very well, but for breeding it should be raised to 78° to 80°F.

Hyphessobrycon rosaceus
Durbin
> *Popular name:* Rosy Tetra
> *Meaning of name:* Hyphessobrycon, little Brycon; rosaceus, rosy, sometimes known as H. ornatus
> *Length:* 1¾ inches
> Guyana and Brazil

A fish flying a black flag, but by no means a pirate. In fact it is one of the gentlest and best of aquarium species.

The handsome, over-arching dorsal fin with its great, black blotch, made more vivid by contrasting whites, is nearly always carried with military erectness as the fish darts about the aquarium in its busy way.

The fish is somewhat translucent, the color, consequently, varies according to whether it is viewed by transmitted or reflected light. At one time, it is pale yellow; at others, it is gently suffused with red. The red shown along the spinal column seems to be an internal color. Like other species of this type, it appears best under strong overhead artificial light.

The male at maturity develops the longer dorsal fin, while the female shows a brighter red tip atop the white edging. Breeds the same as *H. flammeus*. Difficult to spawn. Temperature range, 72° to 82°. Ahl identifies a similar fish as *H. ornatus*.

Hyphessobrycon rubrostigma
Hoedeman

Popular name: Bleeding Heart Tetra, Tetra Perez

Meaning of name: Hyphessobrycon, little Brycon; rubrostigma, with red mark

Length: 2½ inches

Colombia

When fully grown, this is one of the most handsome Tetras. They develop best in medium to large tanks in water of low hardness and slightly acid pH. Their tank mates should not be too active or aggressive, since Bleeding Heart Tetras seem to dislike having to compete for food. In more serene surroundings, they feed well on many kinds of food. Males develop long, flowing dorsal fins, sometimes reaching beyond the tail. They are not commercially bred, and our stock consists only of wild specimens. They have rarely been spawned in captivity.

Hyphessobrycon scholzei
Ahl

Popular name: Black-line Tetra

Meaning of name: Hyphessobrycon, little Brycon; scholzei, in honor of aquarist, Scholze

Length: 2½ inches

Lower Amazon

Through no fault of its own, nor of Ahl, who correctly named it in 1937, this species was later introduced to aquarists as *Aleta nigrans*. This name was probably concocted by some dealer who made "confusion twice confounded" by stating that it came from Africa, instead of South America, thus confusing it with *Nannaethiops unitaeniatus*, a similarly marked Tetra from that continent.

Usually the white first rays of the anal fin are more pronounced in the female, but this is not a dependable means of telling the sexes.

Black-line Tetras are prolific and easily bred. They are active, vigorous, and hardy in all ways. Individuals are apt to develop bad chasing habits in a community tank, but if kept in small groups of four or more, this does not become a problem. Temperature, 65° to 80°.

Paracheirodon axelrodi
Schultz

Popular name: Cardinal Tetra

Meaning of name: Cheirodon, with fins and teeth; axelrodi, in honor of Dr. Herbert R. Axelrod, the world's leading aquarist

Hyphessobrycon rubrostigma

Hyphessobrycon scholzei

Length: 1½ inches
Upper Rio Negro, Brazil
According to a decision made by the International Commission of Zoological Nomenclature, this fish was incorrectly and improperly named *Hyphessobrycon cardinalis* by Prof. George Myers and his student, Dr. Stanley Weitzman. The original name given by Dr. Leonard P. Schultz still stands as correct, besides having priority by publication prior to the Myers' description. The species appeared on the aquarium scene in the winter of

from brown, very soft, very acid water, pH 4.8 to 5.2. It is probably due to the lack of such water that most of the early shipments did not live. Temperature, 75° to 82°F. Interestingly, Dr. Axelrod also discovered this same species some years later in Colombia, but the Colombian fishes are almost impossible to keep alive for any extended period of time, while the Brazilian Cardinals live out their natural lifespan in the home aquarium without any difficulty if their water and feeding needs are supplied.

Paracheirodon axelrodi

1955-56 after it was discovered and imported by Dr. Axelrod. It has since become the most popular of imported aquarium fishes. The red of the *Paracheirodon axelrodi* is radiant and runs the entire length of the fish; the bluish green line is brilliant. The fish comes

Paracheirodon innesi
(Myers)
    Popular name: Neon Tetra
    Meaning of name: Paracheirodon, resembling Cheirodon, innesi: for William T. Innes
    Length: 1¼ inches

Brazilian-Peruvian border; far western Brazilian Amazon; extreme eastern Peruvian Amazon

As this fish is generally regarded as one of the aristocrats of small aquarium personalities, surpassed only by the Cardinal Tetra, *Paracheirodon axelrodi*, some comments regarding its introduction and its peculiarities should be of interest.

Early in 1936 a young French ments. They arrived in due course and made an instant hit; the universal acclaim with which they were greeted established history in our hobby. Other larger importations followed, the second being of 10,000. As these were sold to a New York importer at an unheard-of high price for a wholesale quantity, this probably constituted the largest single deal in the history of the trade up to that time. Since then deals

Paracheirodon innesi

banker, J. S. Neel, in the course of correspondence with the author, wrote that he had received from Brazil, through M. Rabaut, a French collector, "the most beautiful of aquarium fishes," and offered to prove his case by sending two pairs. The offer was accepted, but casually with mental reservations born of former disappoint-

for *Symphysodon*, the discusfishes, have taken the lead! Dealers quickly dried up the apparently inexhaustible supply and everybody was happy, except perhaps the breeders who hoped to cash in on the young of this new, sensational fish.

Nothing would please us quite so much as to be able to give our readers

98   FISHES

a simple, sure-fire method of breeding this little beauty, but no such formula is known. Enormous numbers have been imported since their introduction, and many aquarists have tried to breed them. Relatively few have succeeded, and still fewer have been able to repeat their success. The old "law of compensation" seems to be at work here. Thus, for its surpassing beauty, hardiness, and perfect disposition the Neon Tetra pays with two weaknesses. First, it is subject to a mysterious "Neon disease," causing body wasting and loss of color. Second, of concern to us here, is the dissolving of the eggs that is caused by the penetration of bacteria. Overcoming that tendency among these frequent spawners is the most important and difficult step toward success.

Select young, and, if available, tank-raised breeders. Water should be slightly acid, soft, and reasonably sterile. Distilled water with two level teaspoons of salt to the gallon is one way of producing such conditions.

Sexes look alike, but the ripe females are easily distinguished by their increased girth. Prepare breeders by separating them and feeding them live foods, such as brine shrimp or white worms. The breeding tank should first be treated with salt brine or other germ deterrent that can easily be washed away with distilled water. The tank should be bare (no gravel), and a small bunch of fine-leaved plants or artificial spawning grass should be placed at the bottom. Use light aeration. Place the pair together in the breeding tank in the evening, and arrange for very soft light the next day. Spawning is difficult to detect; the use of a flashlight will help. Eggs are non-adhesive and may be lifted by a dip tube. Whether left where they fall or transferred, they must be kept in virtual darkness until they hatch in two days and are free-swimming. Gradually increase light.

Their first food should be the yellow of hard-boiled eggs strained through fine cloth and placed in a half-filled, stoppered bottle of distilled water. Boil bottle and contents ten minutes; cool and place in refrigerator. It will keep for two weeks. To feed, shake the bottle and use single drops very sparingly. Artificially raised infusoria should also be used. In two weeks they should be put on newly hatched, brine shrimp (from the San Francisco area), which are small enough for the fry and which can also make an excellent food throughout the life of the adult fish. Once they are on brine shrimp they are as good as raised.

During the past few years, fish breeders in the Orient have developed a method of breeding these little fishes. They are now supplying hundreds of thousands of Neons every year for the European and United States markets.

Suitable temperature for Neons is between 72° and 76°.

Paracheirodon simulans
Gery
Popular names: Green Neon, Long-lined Neon
Meaning of name: Paracheirodon, resembling Cheirodon; simulans, imitative

Length: 1 inch

Brazil

It differs from the regular, well-known Neon Tetra for it has a blue-green line extending the whole length of the body—from the gills to the tail—with a much fainter red band below it that only covers the area from the anal fin back to the caudal peduncle. It grows to about the same size as the Neon and can be kept under the same conditions.

Nematobrycon palmeri

Feeding them presents no problem at all, as they eat all types of live, frozen, and dried food as long as the particles are small enough. The breeding habits of these fishes are unknown at present, but we suspect they are not much different from those of other small tetras. However, proof of this is lacking and it may well turn out that they are one of the toughest fishes to get to spawn. Temperature, 75° to 82°F.

Nematobrycon palmeri

Eigenmann

Popular name: Emperor Tetra

Meaning of name: Nematobrycon, having a spike; palmeri, after a personal name

Length: 1¾ inches

Colombia

Introduced in the early 1960s by Dr. Axelrod, the Emperor Tetra became a favorite as soon as it was

Paracheirodon simulans

available. A black line running from
the eye to the caudal peduncle fades
and picks up again to reach the center
point of the three-pronged tail. The
tapered dorsal, the prongs of the tail
and the anal and ventral fins are all
outlined in black, giving the species an
ethereal beauty. Blue and red shadings
follow the black body line. The females carry the same distinguishing
features but are less vividly colored
and the prong in the middle of the tail
is much shorter. A rather hardy fish
with no critical water requirements. A
few days of live-food feedings seem to
promote spawning activity, but for a
successful group spawning, the males
should be of equal size. One large
male will have a tendency to herd the
females away from the others. Mops
or bunch plants such as *Nitella* or
Myriophyllum may be used as a spawning medium. The male attracts the
female by trembling movements. The
actual spawning takes place when the
male pursues the female into a mop or
plant, and as the fishes emerge the
eggs are expelled.

Within three days after becoming
free-swimming, the fry are ready to
take newly hatched brine shrimp.
Growth is rapid.

Hemigrammus armstrongi
Schultz and Axelrod
Popular name: Gold Tetra
Meaning of name: Hemigrammus,
half-line; armstongi, personal name
Length: 1¼ inches
Guyana
This is another aquarium favorite
discovered and described by Dr. Herbert R. Axelrod. Newly imported
fishes glitter with a most intense
golden luster. They are active, playful
fishes, and a small school of them in a
well planted tank is a delight to watch.
Unfortunately, all that glitters is not
gold, for in a few months, the golden
luster may gradually fade to a dull
silver color. It has been found that the
golden color is produced through some
harmless bacterial action in the skin
of the fish, and that aquarium conditions inhibit this process. Much research is needed to explain this phenomenon fully. Dr. Axelrod reported
that when he bred these golden fish,
all the offspring were silver.

The fishes, however, are very hardy
and have a wide tolerance for different water conditions. Feeds on all
types of dried, freeze-dried, frozen
and live foods.
Temperature, 75 to 80°F .

Hemigrammus caudovittatus
Ahl
Popular name: Buenos Aires Tetra
Meaning of name: Hemigrammus,
half-line; caudovittatus, with tail stripe
through middle
Length: 3½ inches
Argentina
This is the largest of the *Hemigrammus* known to aquarists. Although it has its defenders as a community tank fish, there are known
cases where it has been convicted of
fin-nipping, particularly after it grows
large. It devours many types of plants.
Breeds similarly to the Goldfish, the
male chases the female to thickets
where she drops rather adhesive eggs.

Hemigrammus armstrongi

Parents must be removed after spawning. Not difficult to spawn, but ought to have a tank of at least fifteen-gallon capacity. Breeding temperature should be in the neighborhood of 72° to 74°. The species is easily fed and cared for, as may be surmised from its wide temperature range. A golden and albino variety of this fish exists. The female is slightly the larger and is fuller in outline. Except at the moment of spawning she is the aggressor in chasing the male, sometimes killing him. Temperature range, 60° to 85°.

Hemigrammus erythrozonus
Durbin

Popular name: Glowlight Tetra

Meaning of name: Hemigrammus, half-line, in reference to the incomplete lateral line; erythrozonus, with a red zone (stripe). *Length:* 1¾ inches

Potaro and Mazaruni Rivers, Guyana

Hemigrammus caudovittatus

Hemigrammus erythrozonus

Glowlight Tetras distinguish themselves by a brilliant red line that runs from the eye to the peduncle. This marking and the white edging of their fins makes them highly attractive fishes, especially against a darkish background and a top electric light. Although they are well suited to life among other fishes of about the same size, they make a beautiful picture as a small school limited to their own kind. The original importation was discovered by chance in a temporary overflow pool bordering the Mazaruni River in Guyana. The fishes proved to be both hardy and prolific, resulting in a firmly established and well-distributed breeding stock.

Hemigrammus nanus

Their breeding action is a little different from most of the Characoids in that they quickly lock fins, embrace, and do a "barrel roll," while about a dozen eggs are extruded and fertilized. This is repeated. Eggs are slightly adhesive. A fairly large but loose bunch of *Myriophyllum*, other fine-leaf plants, or artificial spawning grass are ideal for catching them. They are being bred in large quantities. They will take ordinary foods, but love newly-hatched brine shrimp, live or frozen. Temperature, 70° to 80°F.

Hemigrammus nanus
(Luetken)
> *Popular name:* Silver Tip Tetra
> *Meaning of name:* Hemigrammus, half-line; nanus, dwarf
>> *Length:* 1¾ inches
>> Lagõa Santa, Minas Gerais, S.E. Brazil

This nice little fish, with its metallic bronze scaled body and complementing silver-tipped fins, is apt to be underrated unless seen against a dark background and preferably under top lighting. Otherwise, the effect of the fins is largely lost. Silver Tip Tetras are delightfully active and playful, but may frequently nip the fins of slower-moving fishes, such as Veiltail Guppies or Siamese Fighting Fish. The species occurs both with and without an adipose fin, which has led to some confusion and caused one of Europe's leading ichthyologists to classify it wrongly as *Hasemania marginata*, a name known only in the European trade. It was brought to Germany just prior to World War II, and to the U.S. in 1949.

The species has been freely bred by amateurs as well as professional wholesalers. The procedure is the same as for other small Characoids. The male has somewhat brighter tips on his fins. Temperature, 70° to 80°F.

Hemigrammus ocellifer
(Steindachner)
> *Popular name:* Head-and-Tail-Light Tetra
> *Meaning of name:* Hemigrammus, half-line; ocellifer, with eye-like spot
>> *Length:* 1¾ inches
>> Guyana

Hemigrammus ocellifer

Hemigrammus pulcher

"Head-and-Tail-Light,"is an appropriate name because the glitter in the eyes and at the base of the tail seems luminous. This is one of the more popular fishes in the trade. These fishes are rather easily bred for Characoids. Their temperature range is about 67° to 84°. They breed best at approximately 76°. They are not fussy about diet, but, like most fishes with teeth, they ought to have occasional meals of fresh animal substances.

Hemigrammus pulcher
Ladiges
Popular name: Pretty Tetra
Meaning of name: Hemigrammus, half-line; pulcher, pretty
Length: 1¼ inches
Upper Amazon
With so many small Characoids nearly alike to the amateur, it is always a relief when a new introduction has at least one clear identifying characteristic. So far among aquarists' fishes, we have seen none with which this one might be confused. The telltale marking is a broad wedge of black on the posterior part of the body, extending about one-third its length.

Body itself is also rather deep. In back of the gill plate will be seen two small light spots; also a light area just above the black wedge. All these markings have a light golden metallic glow; lower fins, lemon; dorsal, flecked red. Unfortunately, with increasing size the brillance of the black mark decreases. They breed like the other small Characoids but do not spawn often. A grown female throws a large number of eggs. Temperature, 72° to 82°.

Hemigrammus rhodostomus
Ahl
Popular name: Rummy Nose
Meaning of name: Hemigrammus, half-line; rhodostomus, rosy-red-mouthed
Length: 2 inches
Brazil
The reddish glow on the snout, extending over the top of the head, varies in intensity, sometimes barely showing. A small school of them in good color, preferably under a top light, makes a charming picture.
It is unaccountably strange that certain members of a family, out-

Hemigrammus rhodostomus

wardly similar, are so much more difficult to breed than some of their cousins. Temperature, 72° to 78°F.

A very similar species, *Petitella georgiae*, is often imported, and sold as a Rummy-nosed Tetra. This species grows just a bit larger, the red color of the mouth region does not extend beyond the gills, and the markings in the tail are not quite as distinct as in *H. rhodostomus*.

Pristella riddlei
(Meek)

 Popular name: Pristella

 Meaning of name: Pristella, a little saw, referring to the teeth; riddlei for Dr. Oscar Riddle, U.S. biologist, the collector

 Length: 1¾ inches

 N.E. South America

 Pristella stands out among small aquarium species for the distinct black-and-white contrast of the fins, particularly the dorsal. As the fish nearly always bears itself well, like a miniature yacht with sails spread, it can be depended upon to look its best. Without any loss to itself, it sets off some of the more colorful species. The uncommon white decorations of the fins can best be brought out by providing a dark background of abundant foliage, such as the leaves of *Sagittaria, Vallisneria* or *Cryptocoryne*. The fish looks most attractive when playing in and out of the shadows. When against lighter backgrounds, the black markings become prominent.

General comments regarding breeding habits, commercial supply, etc., are the same as for *Hemigrammus ocellifer*.

Temperature, 70°-80°.

Aphyocharax rubripinnis

Pristella riddlei

Aphyocharax rubripinnis
Pappenheim

Popular name: Bloodfin

Meaning of name: Aphyocharax, small Charax; rubripinnis, with red fins

Length: 1¼ inches

Argentina

Few of our more showy aquarium fishes either come from or can endure cold water, but the popular Bloodfin from Argentina is an outstanding exception. In situations where a temperature below 60°F is liable to occur, this is one of the safest fishes. Singly, or in a group especially, they always make a pleasing picture. They are well-mannered, easily fed, active, and long-lived. Although they breed like other Characoids, they seem to do best in certain districts where the water is alkaline. They are produced in quantity. Here some of the breeders successfully use a large breeding trap with screen bottoms. Eggs are non-adhesive. The sexes are hard to distinguish except by the full body of the female prior to spawning and the well-developed anal hook in the male, as in all Characoids. The red in the fins of the male is generally a little deeper, but since this is variable from time to time in both sexes, it is not a dependable guide. Temperature, 60°-78°F.

Prionobrama filigera
(Cope)

Popular name: Translucent Bloodfin

Meaning of name: Prion, saw tooth; brama, bream (a fish); filigera, bearing a filament on anal fin

Length: 2 inches

Amazon Basin

To the careless observer this fish might easily be mistaken for the much better-known *Aphyocharax rubripinnis*, but a closer examination will show it to have distinct, beautiful characteristics of its own. Its strikingly translucent body has a glass-like quality. The anal fin in adults is long and pointed, the first ray being opaque white. The red in the fins of the female is confined to the base of the tail, in the male this coloration extends well into the lower and partially into the upper lobe. The red of *P. filigera* is more vivid and the length is slightly greater than *A. ru-*

Anoptichthys jordani
Hubbs and Innes
   Popular name: Blind Cave Fish or Blind Characin
   Meaning of name: Anoptichthys, fish-without-eyes; jordani, after C. B. Jordan
   Length: 3 inches
   San Luis Potosi, Mexico
   In 1936 Mr. Basil Jordan, of Dallas,

Prionobrama filigera

bripinnis. As in many fishes with partially transparent bodies, the Translucent Bloodfin has a little heart-shaped design at the end of the lower spinal column. This is the fan-shaped end of the backbone, technically known as the hypural fin.

   Breeding habits are similar to *A. rubripinnis.* Temperature range, 72° to 85°F.

Texas, sent Innes an eyeless fish. Obviously, it was a Characoid, the only blind one. With the aid of Professor Carl L. Hubbs, the authority on cave fishes, it was found to be a new species, no doubt descended from *Astyanax mexicanus.* It was found in a Mexican cave and aroused such scientific interest that several expeditions were sent to study it in its native habitat.

Elaborate reports may be found in the publications of The New York Zoological Society and the New York Academy of Sciences, the latter for April 5, 1943. The fish is a whitish translucent with an underglow of pink. It has been commercially pushed as a "scavenger fish," and really is one. It finds bits of food at the bottom of the tank, either lost or spurned by other fishes. Gets along well in the aquar-

type, *Astyanax mexicanus*, with which they can be crossed, but with difficulty, for the actions of each breeding partner seem to irritate the other. Young from this cross have varying degrees of sight which is seldom, if ever, perfect. Adult *A. jordani* will devour inch-long fishes if, by chance, they get hold of them. They are ravenous eaters and will accept any type of food.

Anoptichthys jordani

ium, seldom bumps into anything (never with force), is perfectly peaceful and hardy. Most aquarists feel a needless pity for it at first, but they end by regarding it as a special pet.

Generations of influences that destroyed sight also changed breeding methods to an extent. They have trouble in keeping spawning contact, but in general they act like their proto-

Moenkhausia oligolepis
(Guenther)
   Popular name: Red-eye Tetra
   Meaning of name: Moenkhausia, after W. J. Moenkhaus; oligolepis, with few scales
   Length: 4 inches
   Brazil and Guyana
   A flashing red upper half of the eye contrasts with a leaden gray body to

Moenkhausia oligolepis

give this fish an individuality easily remembered. It has other features, too. The large, black spot at the tail root and the black edging of the scales, presenting a laced effect, are pleasing points. The front ray of the anal fin, as with so many of the Characoids, is white. There is a small golden spot in back of the adipose fin, just above the tail. The market for *Moenkhausia oligolepis* is mostly supplied by foreign breeders, who send quantities of them here at a size of about one and one-half inches. Purchasers are usually surprised to find how large and how rapidly they grow.

At a two-inch size, it makes a fairly good community-tank occupant, but as it reaches maturity it is not to be trusted among other fishes. The species is not easily spawned, but when it does breed, large numbers of fertile eggs are produced. Breeding habits similar to those of *Hemigrammus caudovittatus*. Temperature range, 70° to 85°. Breeds best at about 75°F. Should often be fed chopped worms or minced raw fish, but will take any food, especially frozen or freeze-dried. It accepts flake foods, but the heavy metals they contain affect their breeding.

Moenkhausia pittieri
Eigenmann
Meaning of name: Moenkhausia, for Dr. W. J. Moenkhaus, Indiana University; pittieri, for H. Pittier, a botanist of Venezuela
Length: 2½ inches
Venezuela (Lake Valencia)
The small iridescent sparkles of

green set upon a body of glistening silver give this fish its distinct beauty. These colors, together with the ventral area, which under certain lights displays a light shade of blue, are sharply contrasted by the fiery red of the eye, especially in the upper half of the iris. Less obvious, but no less distinctive, is this fish's boldly prominent dorsal fin with its unique contours and its equally handsome anal fin.

Gymnocorymbus ternetzi
Boulenger

Popular name: Black Tetra

Meaning of name: Gymnocorymbus, naked (unscaled) nape; ternetzi, after its collector, Carl Ternetz

Length: Up to 3 inches

Paraguay

While preserved specimens from nature come as long as three inches, aquarium specimens rarely reach two inches fortunately. After the fish at-

Moenkhausia pittieri

In adult specimens the sexes may be distinguished by the males having longer and more pointed dorsal and anal fins. The species has been bred by European aquarists, and its habits are the same as for similar Characoids. It is a good community tank fish.

Temperature range, 70° to 82°F.

tains a length of 1½ inches, its chic black markings progressively pale as the fish gets bigger. When swimming, they look like little black fans moving about, for the tail fin is so translucent that it is rarely seen. Black Tetras are pert-looking fishes that contrast well with other tankmates. They are not aggressive and are able to take care of

Gymnocorymbus ternetzi

Thayeria boehlki

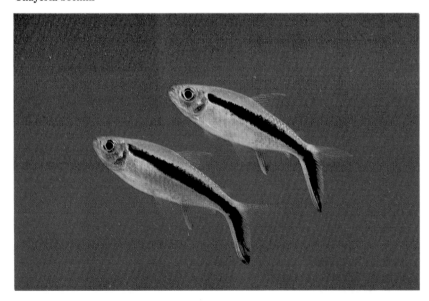

themselves. Though they have been bred at 1½ inches, the two-inch ones are more apt to produce. For breeding methods use the standard procedure described in the introduction to Characoids. Black Tetras are always available and in good supply. Temperature, 68° to 80°F.

Thayeria boehlkei
Weitzman
Popular name: Penguin Fish
Meaning of name: Thayeria, for Nathaniel Thayer; boehlkei, a personal name for Dr. James Boehlkei
Length: 2½ inches
Amazon Basin

This rather odd and attractive fish has recently become very popular in the United States and Europe. While in motion it maintains a horizontal position, but when relaxed it assumes an oblique, headup angle. The bold black stripe is edged above and below by iridescent pin-stripes. No other coloring. Sexes look very similar but, with experience, it is possible to differentiate the slightly slimmer shape of the male. They are easily bred and are now produced in large quantities by breeders in the Orient. A breeding pair drift about slowly in open water, then they do a spirited love dance, nudging each other on the sides prior to the actual spawning. Very small fry hatch in two days and require the smallest sizes of microscopic live foods.

Adult specimens accept a variety of foods. Peaceful, but expertly gobble baby fishes. Temperature, 70° to 78°F.

Megalamphodus megalopterus
(Eigenmann)
Popular name: Black Phantom Tetra
Meaning of name: Megalamphodus, with large tooth on both sides; megalopterus, large fin
Length: 1½ inches
Brazil and Colombia

The Black Phantom Tetras are among the loveliest of the small Characoids. They are pleasantly, if not brilliantly, colored and are very interesting to watch in a medium-sized, well-planted community tank. The water should be slightly acid and not too hard, *i.e.*, somewhat below 100 p.p.m. total hardness. Thickets of fine-leafed plants such as *Myriophyllum, Cabomba,* or *Ambulia* will greatly enhance the well-being of this species; the males establish territories and are a delight to watch as they defend them, spreading to the utmost their large, almost flowing dorsal and anal fins. They dance around one another, each one trying to gain an advantage over the other. When on a well-balanced diet, these little fish will even spawn in a community tank as long as it is not too crowded or no larger fishes are present to bully them. Of course, the chance of raising fry in such a situation is almost nil. The eggs, as well as any fry that might hatch, would, in ordinary circumstances, be greedily eaten by other fishes as well as by the parents themselves. They are easy fishes to breed, however, and are usually quite prolific. Fry are very tiny when first hatched and require infusoria as a first food, but soon graduate to newly hatched brine shrimp. Both of these

Megalamphodus megalopterus

foods should be on hand if raising the fry is contemplated. Sexes are easily distinguished at a fairly early age. Males are slightly larger, have larger dorsal and anal fins, and the adipose fin (the small fin between the dorsal and tail) is black in the males and a pretty red in the females. Temperature, 78° to 82°F.

Metynnis species
Popular name: Silver Dollar
Meaning of name: Metynnis, with a plough
Length: 4 inches
Throughout northern South America
Metynnis is a genus distinguished from *Colossoma* and *Mylossoma* by the long, low adipose fin. Several species have been imported, all sharing the appropriate name of Silver Dollar and all looking quite similar. The only apparent difference among them is the length of the adipose fin.

All *Metynnis* are silvery in color, sometimes with dark spots or bars that disappear with age. There is usually some orange or yellow in the tail and anal fin. All will take prepared foods, but in nature they feed on aquatic plants and fallen fruit. They will create havoc with aquarium plants. Plastic plants do well for such herbivores. Peaceful, attractive, and hardy. Almost never bred. They are said to scatter non-adhesive eggs. Temperature, 72° to 82°F.

Metynnis *spec.*

Mylossoma aureum
(Spix)

Meaning of name: Mylossoma, body shaped like a millstone; aureum, golden

Length: 3½ inches

Amazon

One of the most attractive and enduring of the disc-like Silver Dollars, as they are popularly called. *M. aureum* is so flat that it seems emaciated. The fact that it keeps living happily in what appears to be a thin condition reminds one of the old saying, "a lean horse for a long race."

The dark portion of the anal fin is a rich, golden brown, and the broadest part of the fin is up towards the tail. This is an exceptional feature. In life, it is difficult to tell just where the body edge ends and the anal fin begins. Imagine a continuation of the curve of

Mylossoma aureum

the lower belly line to approximate where one ends and the other begins. The scales are very small and very silvery. The soft vertical bars are gray and the back is light olive. A speck of color appears on the adipose fin. The eye is warm golden.

The ventral fins are incredibly small.

Sex differences are not distinct; the fish has rarely been bred.

Silver Dollars make good community fish, especially when kept with companions that are not diminutive. Comfortable between 72° and 85°F. Easily fed. They eat plants.

Colossoma nigripinnis
(Cope)

Popular name: Pacu

Meaning of name: Colossoma, huge body; nigripinnis, with black fins; pacu is the common Indian name for the fish in the jungles of Brazil

Length: 2 feet

Amazon Basin

In pet shops, very young, one-inch-long *Colossoma* are sometimes mistakenly sold as Piranhas, since they resemble them very closely in shape, color and fins. The aquarist who takes them home however, soon realizes that these "Piranhas" are the most gentle fishes he ever owned. Pacus consume enormous quantities of food of any kind, and grow at a phenomenal rate, but they never fight with any other fish. They make no demands on water conditions and become quite friendly with the owner who feeds them. They do demand space though, and an eight- to ten-inch specimen should have at least a 50-gallon tank. Temperature, 72° to 80°. They are a prime and delicious food fish along the Amazon. They are now protected by the Brazilian government and exportation is prohibited, but they often are found mixed with *Metynnis*.

Serrasalmus species

Popular name: Piranha

Meaning of name: Serrasalmus, salmon-like

Length: 10 inches

Colossoma nigripinnis

Serrassalmus spec.

A close-up of a head of a piranha.

Throughout most of South America

Tales of how swarms of blood-thirsty Piranhas skeletonize large wading or swimming animals in a matter of minutes have created a rather morbid public interest in them as aquarium fishes. These fishes have razor-sharp, triangular teeth that interlock between lower and upper jaws. They bite out chunks of flesh that are swallowed whole. The wound is said to be painless. They can cut nets and fishing lines. There are several species, varying in ferocity, some are even harmless. The most savage are those with the shortest, bulldog-like muzzles. Single specimens are shy and easily scared. When raised together they constantly attack each other. For this reason, they need a large and well-planted tank. They are fond of all types of live food and may be fed on raw meat, liver, and fish. Color varies with species, from lemon trimmings on silver to some with bright red bellies. There are several complete books just on Piranhas. These books detail the species and how they spawn. The books may be found at your local aquarium shop.

Chalceus macrolepidotus

Chalceus macrolepidotus

Popular name: Red-tailed Chalceus

Meaning of name: Chalceus, made of copper; macrolepidotus, with large scales

Length: To 12 inches

Guyana

Red-tailed Chalceus have to be handled with extreme care after they have arrived from the collecting grounds in Northern South America. They become extremely frightened, and at the slightest disturbance may jump out of the tank or smash against the glass sides. Fins, scales, and lips damage easily. It is best to purchase young, immature fishes of about two to four inches, since they adapt best to aquarium conditions at that size. As they adjust, they become more and more intolerant towards each other. It may become necessary to separate individuals. However, if they have settled down and adjusted to the tank, they are gorgeous creatures indeed. Their tails and fins are a subtle raspberry color while their handsome rows of large, rounded scales radiate a pearly luster.

Their food consists of most types of frozen and living foods with bloodworms (red mosquito larvae), black mosquito larvae, glass larvae, and brine shrimp either live, freeze-dried, or frozen as the first readily accepted. The fish grow at a fast rate if fed frequently and plentifully. Temperature, 75° to 80°F.

Triportheus elongatus

(Guenther)

Meaning of name: elongatus, elongated

Length: 5 inches

Triportheus elongatus

Guyana and Amazon Basin

This is a robust and reasonably hardy fish, which, unfortunately, is not too often seen. The young of this species look much different from the adults, having a tan body, black pectoral fins and a completely clear tailfin. They grow quickly on various types of food, but prefer to feed at the surface. An excellent jumper. Temperature, 70° to 80°F.

Micralestes interruptus
Boulenger

   Popular name: Congo Tetra

   Meaning of name: Micralestes: small fish which can escape quickly; interruptus: interrupted, referring to the incomplete lateral line

   Also known as *Phenacogrammus interruptus*

   Length: 3 inches

Congo River

This interesting tetra from Africa grows what look to be feathers on the tail. This happens only in the male, as the fish matures. The female, when adult, has shorter fins and never grows quite as large as her mate. This fish might be said to have many color phases, but more truly they are prismatic effects according to how the light strikes their scales, and the relative position of the observer. With a dark background and the light coming from in back of the observer, the brilliant prismatic colors follow each other in a seemingly endless variety, mostly blue, green and yellow. Held in the air in net, under flashlight, the color effect is startlingly gaudy. To enjoy its full beauty, the aquarium reflection should be put over the front of the tank.

Micralestes interruptus

The Congo Tetra is one of the larger tetras and should not be kept with much smaller species. It prefers soft, acid water and a temperature between 75° and 82°.

Arnoldichthys spilopterus
(Boulenger)
Popular names: African Red-eyed Tetra, Red-eyed Characin
Meaning of name: Arnoldichthys, after Johann P. Arnold, a German aquarist; spilopterus, with spot on fin
Length: Approximately 4 inches
Tropical West Africa, Lagos to Niger estuary
This is a somewhat delicate, easily frightened fish, which should be handled with extreme care until it becomes used to aquarium conditions.

Large, well-planted tanks are necessary to help them lose their nervousness. Water that has been used in an aquarium for some time is good, but such water should be slightly acid. Live foods such as *Daphnia*, brine shrimp, or bloodworms should be offered when specimens are first acquired, but later they will accept a good quality of dried and freeze-dried foods. They prefer to feed at the surface or in midwater. Temperature, 76° to 80°.

FAMILY ANOSTOMIDAE
This is a group of medium-sized Characoids that has become quite popular in recent years. Some swim in a very characteristic head down position and are popularly called Head-

Arnoldichthys spilopterus

Anostomus anostomus

standers. All come from South America. With the exception of *Chilodus punctatus*, none has been bred with regularity.

Anostomus anostomus
(Linnaeus)
Meaning of name: Anostomus, turned up mouth
Length: 4 inches
Common in Guyana, rare in the Amazon

In coloration this fish looks like a cousin of *Nannostomus trifasciatus*, though a large and rather sluggish one at that. The dark portions of the forked tail root are deep blood-red, as are the dark parts in the dorsal, the adipose, and the beginnings (at the body) of the ventral and anal fins. In addition to these strongly characteristic markings, there are three bold, broad, black stripes along the body. The fish is related to the genus *Leporinus* and swims in somewhat the same fashion. Although this species was described by one of our earliest great naturalists, it was not imported for aquarists until 1933. It is a generally peaceful fish, but some individuals become dangerous and aggressive in a community tank, mercilessly chasing and nipping their victims. It possesses an extremely upturned mouth and in an upside-down position frequently scrapes at algae-covered rocks. It will eat most foods, however, and even bits off the bottom, by turning its whole body sideways and pulling them in laterally. Temperature, 75° to 80°.

Leporinus fasciatus
(Bloch)
Meaning of name: Leporinus, with a snout like a rabbit; fasciatus, banded
Length: Up to 12 inches
Amazon and Guyana

Because this very striking fish is extremely difficult for collectors to gather in the wild and because it has not been bred in captivity, *Leporinus fasciatus* has never been commonplace. It is an enormous leaper and jumps over the nets of natives. To illustrate its acrobatics and toughness, one kept in a public aquarium jumped obliquely upward a distance of five feet, landing in a marine tank of a different temperature. After several hours it was returned undamaged to its own tropical freshwater tank. As this fish is rather sluggish in its movements, the aquarist is apt to become careless about keeping the tank covered. One should not forget, however, that the most able jumpers, such as *Pantodon* and the reedfishes, appear to be slow movers. The coloration of this fish consists of alternate bands of ivory yellow and black. The fish has and needs no other colors. An interesting feature is that with age the number of bands increases. The young have five, while fully grown adults show ten.

The species usually maintains a slightly head-down angle, common in the family. Eats anything, harmless, but quarrelsome among each other. Nibbles at plants. Temperature, 70° to 80°.

Leporinus fasciatus

Chilodus punctatus

Abramites microcephalus

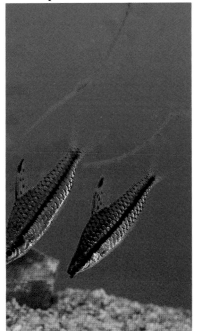

Chilodus punctatus
Mueller and Troschel
Popular name: Headstander
Meaning of name: Chilodus, with teeth on lips; punctatus, spotted
Length: 3 inches
Guyana

Some fishes, without possessing any actual brightness of color, are nevertheless brilliant. An arrangement of contrasts or of designs in blacks, grays, olive, or brown tints, combined with sparkles of silver can be very effective. Such a fish is *Chilodus punctatus*. The middle band is clear black while the spots on the scales and the markings in the dorsal fin are brownish. This is one of those species that maintains an oblique balance most of the time, head downward. Whether absorbed in thought or merely looking on the bottom for food is a question any aquarist can answer for himself without fear of contradiction.

The species has been bred in captivity. It is said to lay glass-clear eggs in fine-leaved plants near the bottom. Its mouth is rather small, but the fish is not fussy about diet. Peaceful and not very lively, but capable of lightning speed when pursued with a net. Temperature, 75° to 80°.

Abramites microcephalus
Norman
Meaning of name: Abramites, like Abramis, the bream; microcephalus, small headed
Length: Up to 5 inches
Lower Amazon

Distinctly a novelty. Its assortment of markings range from white through shades of gray to heavy black, thus it easily catches and holds the eye. The crescent in the tail fin is white. The other parts are mostly grays and blacks. Going about with the forepart of the body tilted downward is a characteristic pose; from this peculiarity one would expect them to be bottom feeders. While they do feed off the bottom, they feed equally well in mid-water, but dislike floating foods. They also nibble on live plants and usually select the most expensive ones.

The fish has been kept with other species and occasionally, fins of long-finned species were nipped. When among their own they tend to be belligerent toward each other. Happiest at an average temperature of 75°.

Carnegiella strigata

THE HATCHET FISHES
FAMILY GASTEROPELECIDAE

Strange little creatures, these Hatchet Fishes, with their bulging bellies, yet so thin from the front view. They seem to be built on some highly specialized plan, not unrelated to the principles employed in airplane contruction. They are indeed known as Dwarf Freshwater Flying Fishes, for in their native waters, when alarmed, they skim lightly over the surface for considerable distances. Although in the aquarium they will eat live brine shrimp, *Daphnia,* and even prepared food that floats, it seems to be their nature to catch insects on or near the surface of the water. They never pick up food from the bottom.

All Hatchet Fishes in petshops are imported from South America. Like all fish caught in the wild, they can be easily frightened and often dash against the glass cover or sides of the tank, causing serious injury. Specimens once well acclimatized live rather long, even when fed only on dry-prepared foods that float on the surface. Few have been bred in captivity. They are attractive novelties, well worth a place in a mixed aquarium, provided one does not hope to breed them.

They are not related to a well-known genus of marine Hatchet Fishes, nor to the famous Flying Fishes of the seas.

It has been pretty well established after centuries of argument that marine Flying Fishes, despite their amazing performances, do not voluntarily move their wing-like fins while sailing through the air. Our little Hatchet Fishes, however, are equipped with a deep, thin breast keel of bone, supporting relatively huge muscles attached to the "wings." It is known that this equipment enables them to vibrate their plane-like pectoral fins when in flight.

In the matter of temperature they seem, on the average, to prefer water in the neighborhood of 75°. Like most fishes that hang about the surface of the water, they are not very active, but can move fast enough when occasion demands.

Carnegiella strigata
(Guenther)

Popular name: Marble Hatchet Fish

Meaning of name: Carnegiella, named for Miss Margaret Carnegie; strigata, streaked

Length: 1 3/4 inches

N.E. South America

This Hatchet Fish is considerably smaller, more wisp-like, and colorful than *Gasteropelecus levis.* No adipose fin is present. While not hardy, it is often more durable than *Gasteropelecus levis.* Requirements are the same.

One breeder reports several large spawnings at a temperature of 83° to 87°F. The male courted by circling the female and dashing closely past her. The pair did much leaping out of the water, but the actual spawning took place in a side-to-side, head-to-tail position, the small transparent eggs being scattered among floating plants, such as *Riccia.* The species takes a variety of dry and living fish foods. The only way to distinguish the sexes is to take a top view of the fish and look for the broader body of the female.

Gasteropelecus levis

Gasteropelecus levis
(Eigenmann)
　　Popular name: Silver Hatchet Fish
　　Meaning of name: Gasteropelecus, axe-belly; levis, smooth
　　Length: 2¹/₄ inches
　　Amazon Basin and Guyana
　　This is the commonest of our Hatchet Fish importations. The lower part of the body is mirrored silver, while the top is olive. These colors are separated by a pleasing blue-black stripe which itself is enclosed between two narrow, pale silver lines. All fins are clear, including the long, arching, graceful pectorals or "wings."
　　These fishes like clear water at temperature of about 75°.
　　There is a similar species, *Gasteropelecus sternicla*, which is so similar that a count of fin-rays, teeth, and scales is needed to detect the differ-ence—a job for an ichthyologist. The aquarist may regard them as one fish. Like many of the fishes with marked ability at leaping, it spends almost all of its time near the surface of the water. It is probably looking for small insects which have either fallen on the surface or are flying near it. Since it feeds off the surface, it should be given floating foods such as freeze-dried brine shrimp. When frightened, they often smash against the tank walls and death can occur.

FAMILY HEMIODONTIDAE
　　This is another group of South American Characoids. They differ from the family Characidae by having no teeth in the lower jaw. Characidae have a full set of teeth. The family contains some of the most exquisitely colored Pencilfishes.

Nannostomus anomalus

Nannostomus trifasciatus

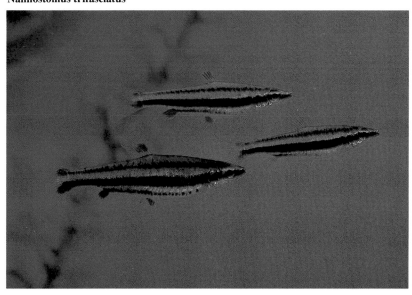

There are several species that are very common in the hobby. *Nannostomus beckfordi* is plentiful since many breeders of tropical fish have mastered the art of propagating this species.

Nannostomus anomalus

Steindachner

Popular name: Anomalus Pencilfish

Meaning of name: Nannostomus, little mouth; anomalus, abnormal, referring to lack of adipose fin; also known as *N. beckfordi*, a Guyana species which may be identical with this one.

Length: 1 ½ inches

Amazon and Rio Negro

The long dark body-band of this fish comes through with an intense black and is bordered above by a vividly glistening gold. The eye is light gold divided by the black line that extends to the tip of the mouth. There are red ornamentations in the dorsal, tail, and anal fins. The back is "fish olive," and the belly is bright white. The fish is sprightly in its movements, standing still momentarily and then moving forward briskly. They are stubborn spawners and breed like the average egg-dropper, depositing spawn among rootlets of floating plants and plant thickets. The babies adhere to plants and glass sides somewhat longer than most, taking about five days before they become free-swimming. Commercial breeders in Europe and the Orient are raising these Pencilfishes, so that we no longer depend on imported wild stock. Food for this species, living or prepared, should be small, for they have tiny mouths. Temperature range, 75° to 80°.

Nannostomus trifasciatus

Steindachner

Popular name: Trifasciatus or Three-lined Pencilfish

Meaning of name: Nannostomus, little-mouth; trifasciatus, with three bands

Length: 1¾ inches

Amazon

One of the most satisfactory and beautiful of fishes. They have a good aquarium temperament and are peaceful toward other fishes, except for an occasional nip at a long fin. They are, however, a bit unfriendly toward each other. The tank should therefore be well planted, especially with fine-leafed plants, so that smaller individuals can escape harassment. They are omnivorous, but prefer smaller types of live foods.

Spawning, which is rather rare, usually takes place among loose *Riccia*. The eggs hatch in three days at a temperature of 75°. The babies are long and narrow and do not resemble the parents for several weeks. They poise themselves at odd angles.

Unless very hungry, the parents do not eat the eggs. With good feeding and plenty of room the young become adults in seven months. The species went through a period of scarcity following its first introduction, but new importations have been made since 1945. It continues to be stubborn about spawning. Temperature range, 70° to 80°F.

Peocilobrycon espei
Meinken
Popular name: Barred Pencilfish
Meaning of name: Poecilobrycon, variable fish that can bite; espei, after a Mr. Espe

Amazon Basin

The Barred Pencilfish apparently is the only member of the family having a color pattern fundamentally different from that of all other Pencilfishes. While most of them are marked with more or less horizontal lines, *P. espei* exhibit five vertical bars on a tan body. Interestingly, many other Pencilfishes assume a similar pattern of horizontal lines.

Poecilobrycon espei

Barred Pencilfishes are not often imported nor bred commercially and are, therefore, quite a rare sight in the dealer's tank. They have been bred on occasion, however, but the young are said to be rather delicate and difficult to raise. Nevertheless, when free-swimming they can be started on newly hatched brine shrimp instead of the smaller infusoria. Temperature, 78° to 82°.

Peocilobrycon harrisoni
(Eigenmann)
Meaning of name: Poecilobrycon, variable fish that can bite; harrisoni, after Harrison
Length: 2 ¹/₂ inches
Guyana

These Pencilfishes have become quite plentiful in recent years. They are not bred commercially but are imported in large numbers since they are found in an area fairly accessible to collectors of tropical fishes in Guyana. They grow larger than most other members of the genus but require the same care. Adult specimens are a bit quarrelsome at times, but they do no harm to any but the most long-finned tank mates. Therefore, they should not be kept with Veiltail Guppies or such sluggish swimmers as Veiltail Angel Fish. Temperature, 75° to 82°F.

FAMILY CITHARINIDAE
This is an exclusively African group containing some brilliantly colored large fishes. We have included two of the most striking species.

Distichodus lusosso
Schilthuis
Meaning of name: Distichodus, with two rows of teeth; lusosso, probably a native name
-*Length:* About 15 inches
Central Africa

These fishes, as well as the slightly smaller but very similar *D. sexfasciatus,* are the most brilliantly colored species of the genus *Distichodus* that are imported. The pattern of the body,

Poecilobrycon harrisoni

bold black bands against a warm orange background, is sure to arrest even the most disinterested viewer. While they grow a bit large for most community tanks, they are comparatively peaceful until they reach maturity. At that time it is difficult to keep more than one of these scrappy specimens, unless the tank is large and thickly planted. Many plants, however, are eaten by these fishes, and only tough-leaved varieties such as *Sagittaria, Cryptocoryne* or *Ludwigia* are safe. Both species of *Distichodus* are sensitive to water conditions when first imported, doing best in soft and acid water. After they have become acclimated, their hardiness leaves nothing to be desired. They are not the least bit fussy about food, and all types are eagerly eaten, but, as usual, live and frozen foods, especially insect larvae, are preferred. Spawnings of these beautiful Characoids have not been reported, and secondary sex characteristics are not apparent. Temperature, 75° to 82°.

THE GYMNOTID EELS
FAMILY GYMNOTIDAE

The Knifefishes, as aquarists call the Gymnotid Eels, are not Eels at all, but close relatives of the Characoids, as has been determined by anatomical studies. From the Characoids, and, in fact, most other fishes, they differ in having the vent placed at the throat, and by their elongate body and long anal fin. All of them are from South America or southern Central America. Most aquarists confuse the Gymnotids with the African and Asiatic

Distichodus lusosso

Distichodus sexfasciatus

130   FISHES

"Knifefishes" (*Notopterus* and relatives), which are occasionally brought in as aquarium fishes. The notopterids have the vent in the normal position and do not even belong to the same order as the Gymnotids.

The Knifefishes, so-called on account of their blade-like appearance, are, in some species, entirely too large for the household aquarium, the adult size in nature being two feet or more. It is therefore only the smaller sorts we aquarists occasionally possess. There are many species looking closely alike, so that positive identification is not easy. However, they are so similar in their ways, that, so far as the aquarist is concerned, they may be treated as a group.

The most interesting thing about them is their ability to swim forwards or backwards, seemingly with equal ease. A graceful rippling of the long anal fin propels them in either direction, slowly or rapidly as occasion requires. The way in which they instantly reverse themselves in the aquarium when pursued by a net is most interesting.

Nothing is known of their breeding habits. We do know, though, that they are tough and can live in pretty bad conditions.

The best known member of the family is the "electric eel" (*Electrophorus electricus*) of South America, often seen in public aquaria, but too large (up to six feet) for a home aquarium. The family Gymnotidae is sometimes split up into several families by ichthyologists, but we prefer to keep it intact in this book.

Eigenmannia virescens
(Valenciennes)
Popular name: Glass Knifefish
Meaning of name: Eigenmannia, after Eigenmann, famous American ichthyologist; virescens, green
Length: To about 12 inches
South America (Guyana, Surinam, Northern Brazil)

Most Knifefishes, including this one, are rather secretive, becoming more active at dusk than during daylight hours. They are odd creatures, rightly bearing their most descriptive common name. They have only three fins: two pectorals and one anal, the latter extending almost the whole length of the body to nearly the very tip of the tail. Knifefishes are not advisable in the community tank, since they occasionally nip the fins of other fishes. Even though their eyesight appears to be poor, they are quite able to pursue other fishes (particularly their own kind), probably by means of the very weak electric field all Gymnotids are able to generate around their bodies. Disturbances in this field are then picked up by special receptor cells that are part of the lateral line system. These fishes locate food in this manner. Knifefishes are hardy creatures once acclimated to aquarium conditions, but they do prefer neutral to slightly acid water and lots of hiding places. A cover of floating plants will help greatly in overcoming their shyness. Their food consists mainly of worms and crustaceans which, to the hobbyist, means *Tubifex* worms, white worms, *Daphnia*, brine shrimp, and bloodworms, either live or frozen. Their

Eigenmannia virescens

Sternarchus albifrons

mode of reproduction is mostly un-known. Temperature, 72°-80°F.

Apteranotus albifrons
Linnaeus
  Popular names: Black Ghost Fish, Ghost Knifefish
  Meaning of name: albifrons, with white forehead, referring to white stripe on back
  Length: Up to 16 inches
  Amazon and tributaries
  This is, without doubt, the most agile of all Knifefishes. The acrobatic feats it can perform in trying to avoid the net are astonishing. It can take off instantly in any direction and swim several times around a rock or stump, tail first and with incredible speed, without bumping into other objects. And all this is accomplished with just the use of the two pectorals and the long waving anal fin, since its tail and one-rayed dorsal are of no use for locomotion. All South American Knifefishes are imported directly from their native waters. Secondary sex characteristics have not been observed. The Black Ghost is a long-lived fish; specimens already mature have been kept in captivity for over 5 years. Temperature, 75° to 82°F.

THE CYPRINIDS
FAMILY CYPRINIDAE
  The Cyprinids form the largest family of fishes known. Nearly all have scales, but none has teeth in the jaws. In place of jaw teeth, they have curved pharyngeal bones in the throat, which bear grinding teeth. Many Cyprinids have barbels (whisker-like structures about the mouth), but only a few rare ones have more than two pairs. No Cyprinid has an adipose fin, and no Cyprinid ever occurs naturally in South America or Australia.

  The Cyprinids vary in size from the giant Mahseer of India, which grows to six feet in length, to such tiny creatures as *Rasbora maculata*, of scarcely more than an inch. By far the greater number of species are small and minnow-like, and among these we find many of our best small aquarium fishes. The genera and species are most numerous and varied in Southeastern Asia, tropical Africa, and the United States, in the order given. Towards the north the species are fewer in number.

  Some of the minnow-like ones are among the most brilliantly colored of all fishes. This is particularly true of the minnows of the Southern Appalachians, the gorgeous colors of which, at times, equal or surpass the showiest of the exotics. Unfortunately most of the more gaudy American minnows live in swift-running water and would not be well suited to the ordinary still-water aquarium.

  The Barbs give gaiety and grace to an aquarium. Their large, mirror-like scales constantly catch the light and flash it back from many angles, for they are seldom still.

  A sparkling appearance is only one of their merits. They are peaceful, playful, most of them are easily bred, and they prosper at moderate temperatures, being quite happy within a range of 68° to 76°.

  The temperature requirements of the Barbs are simple. They are in-

Barbus arulius

cluded among exotic fishes that may
be bred in outdoor pools in summer-
like climates of areas where the nights
are not cold. If placed in a large, well-
planted space and constantly supplied
with live food, they will prosper and
breed without further attention. It might
be added that most of them are of
popular aquarium-sizes. Despite their
general similarity, it is not difficult to
detect the interesting differences in
the many species known to the aquarist.

Nearly, but not quite, all of them
have short whiskers or barbels about
the mouth, a characteristic for which
the genus is named.

In some books it will be noticed that
our small Barbs, for which we use the
generic name *Barbus*, are placed in the
genus *Puntius* (*Puntius conchonius*

Barbus conchonius

instead of *Barbus conchonius*, for example). The late Dr. George Myers
said this is an unimportant matter, and
that aquarists are justified in sticking
to *Barbus*. The reasons are several,
partly ichthyological and partly a matter of convenience.

A sunny situation not only suits them, but shows them off best. Aged water and plenty of plants should be provided.

They are rather long-lived, four to eight years under favorable conditions. Any kind of food is accepted. Another point of value is that they usually are not "scary" fishes.

Breeding *Barbus* is a simple matter. The female, naturally a little bigger than the male in many species, becomes noticeably larger as she fills with spawn. When this evidence is apparent, she should be placed with one or two males in an aquarium thickly planted with fine-leafed plants. The breeding is similar to that of the Goldfish, which is related to Barbs. The males chase the female and when she becomes sufficiently excited, she scatters or sprays adhesive eggs on the plants or wherever they may fall. As both sexes soon eat what eggs they can find, it is well to have the plants densely arranged to discourage this. The aquarist, of course, should promptly remove the fish when spawning is finished. The eggs hatch quite quickly, requiring only about 38 to 40 hours. The young are easily reared since most of them are able to take newly hatched brine shrimp as a first food.

Barbus arulius
(Jerdon)
Popular name: Arulius Barb
Meaning of name: Barbus, from the barbels present in some, but not all, species
Length: 4 to 5 inches
Southeast India

The color pattern of young Arulius Barbs strongly resembles that of *Barbus filamentosus*, except that the black bars are not quite clear cut. While growing up, these bars fade considerably, but not completely, as in B. filamentosus, and no black spot ever appears on the caudal peduncle. The body coloring at maturity is about the same for both with a slightly more intense greenish lustre for Arulius Barbs. The body outline is somewhat deeper, not quite as streamlined, and close examination reveals the presence of two barbels.

They exhibit the same secondary sex characteristics, i.e., the longer dorsal of the male. Spawning takes place mostly at dusk in fine-leaved plants such as *Myriophyllum*, Willow Moss (*Fontinalis*), *Ambulia*, or artificial spawning grass. As with some other Barbs, a partial embrace takes place at each spawning act. Temperature, 75° to 80°.

Barbus conchonius
Hamilton-Buchanan
Popular name: Rosy Barb
Meaning of name: Barbus, from the barbels present in most Barbs; conchonius, after a native name
Length: 2½ inches
India

For many years, the Rosy Barb has been, without doubt, the best known and most popular Barb among aquarists. This very familiar fish becomes brilliantly colored when breeding.

When love-making is over, the male lays aside his gay courting costume.

On average, the male is a little smaller.

Usually in good supply and is one of the hardiest of the Barbs. Temperature, 68° to 80°.

Barbus everetti
Boulenger

Popular name: Clown Barb

Meaning of name: Barbus, from the barbels present in some, but not all,

plenty of live food help put it in breeding condition.

The colors develop when the fish is about two inches long. At that size, or a little larger, the big blue-black spots are more clearly defined than in the fully mature fish. They have two pairs of barbels. They require a large, well-planted aquarium with a temperature range of 72° to 82°.

Barbus everetti

species; everetti, after the collector, Everett

Length: 5 inches

Malay Peninsula and Borneo

The Clown Barb, named for the conspicuous spots that decorate its body, is one of the bigger Barbs and one of the more difficult to spawn. The immature fish have four vertical bars against a tan body.

Aeration, a little fresh water, and

Barbus fasciatus
(Bleeker)

Popular name: Striped Barb

Meaning of name: Barbus, with barbels; fasciatus, striped

Length: Up to 5 inches

Borneo, Sumatra, Malay Peninsula

Instead of the vertical slashes we are more used to in Barbs, this brilliant, silvery fish has well-defined, blue-black stripes running horizon-

Barbus fasciatus

tally. It has been much favored by American aquarists ever since it was introduced in 1935. The fish also has a stripe along the middle of its back.

The sexes are easily distinguished: the female has a fuller form, less pronounced stripes, and a broader middle stripe. Temperature, 70° to 80°.

Barbus filamentosus
(Cuvier and Valenciennes)
Popular name: Filamentosus Barb
Meaning of name: Barbus, with barbels; filamentosus, with thread-like extension of dorsal fin
Length: 4 to 5 inches
Southern India and Sri Lanka (Ceylon)

Immature specimens of this fish look so different from their parents that it is easy to see why some aquarists in the past have mistook them for a separate species. When young, Filamentosus Barbs are adorned with four distinct black vertical bars. The body is silvery, and the fins are very often dark red. As the fish matures, the bars fade, leaving only a large black spot on the caudal peduncle; the sides

turn a mother-of-pearl luster with hints of green and blue. In the male, some dorsal fin rays become long and drawn out and reach almost as far back as the tail.

Filamentosus Barbs, like most barbs, are very active fishes and not easily frightened. They require medium to large tanks to reach full size and to mature properly. Water conditions are not very important as long as extremely hard and alkaline conditions are avoided. These barbs will eat prepared, frozen, freeze-dried, and live foods and they can be brought to breeding condition with the same foods if the supply is kept adequate. Males drive wildly at breeding time. Fairly large eggs are laid in fine-leaved plants. Temperature, 75° to 80°.

Barbus nigrofasciatus
Guenther
Popular name: Black Ruby Barb
Meaning of name: Barbus, with barbels; nigrofasciatus, black-banded
Length: 2¼ inches
Sri Lanka (Ceylon)

Although collectors of this interesting fish tell us of having to endure sultry equatorial heat, the fishes themselves do not seem to like it either, for they are captured while taking refuge under shady banks. When naturalized in the aquarium they are happy in comfortable room temperatures, although breeding is most successful at between 75° and 80°. They breed like the other Barbs already described.

If this species would appear in its best color at all times, we would not hesitate to rate it as one of the most

Barbus filamentosus

Young of B. filamentosus

beautiful Barbs now known to aquarists. The rich glow of ruby in the forward part of the body seems to force itself through a stubborn film of near-black and is simply stunning. Only the males assume this color, but not for long. A partial change of water or other stimulation may start the magic. The contrasting blackness of

the fins and body accompanies the glowing dark red; when one color goes, the other vanishes. Then we have a rather drab, barred Barb. Temperature, 70° to 80°.

Barbus oligolepis
(Bleeker)
   Popular name: Checkerboard Barb
   Meaning of name: Barbus, with barbels; oligolepis, having few scales
   Length: 1½ inches
   Sumatra
The beautiful black-bordered, orange dorsal instantly identifies this fish. No other known Barb has markings even slightly similar.
   Sexes are easily distinguished by the differences in color. The species has a small pair of barbels.
   At breeding time the orange in the dorsal of the male intensifies. His body

Barbus nigrofasciatus

Barbus oligolepis

Barbus orphoides

blackens and his scales sparkle blue and green. Breeding as per other Barbs. There are about 200 eggs to a spawning. The young hatch in sixty hours at 78° and are very small and translucent. They require the finest sizes of live food. When several females are ripe at the same time, they may be bred together with an equal or a greater number of males.

In contrast to other Barbs, *B. oligolepis* is somewhat less playful and spends most of its time in the lower half of the tank. Temperature, 72°-82°.

Barbus orphoides
(Cuvier and Valenciennes)
   Popular name: Red-cheeked Barb
   Meaning of name: Barbus, with barbels

Length: 7 to 8 inches
Indonesia, Thailand, probably Malaysia

Fast-growing, handsome, hardy, and robust best describes these fish. They are somewhat plump, quite strong, very agile, and are capable of swimming at great speed. One can witness their strength by the struggle they put up when netted. They grow quite large on practically any type of food, provided it is abundant and the fish are given plenty of room.

It should not be too difficult to get them to spawn in an aquarium, since they often reach maturity at a rather young age and at half their full size. Water conditions for rearing Red-cheeked Barbs are not critical. They do equally well in slightly acid as well as mildly alkaline water. Females are

Barbus schwanenfeldi

much more rounded in the outline of the ventral region.

Temperature, 70° to 80°.

Barbus schwanenfeldi
(Bleeker)

Popular name: Tinfoil Barb

Meaning of name: Barbus, with barbels; schwanenfeldi, after a personal name

Length: 12 to 14 inches

Thailand, Malaysia, parts of Indonesia

This is a large deep-bodied Barb suitable only for very large tanks sparsely planted with strong, tough-leafed plants. They will eat all tender plants and by their vehement motions uproot any which are not well established. Even though Tinfoil Barbs are generally peaceful toward other fishes,

it is not a good idea to keep them with fishes much smaller than themselves. At feeding time, their gluttonous appetite will seldom permit small or shy fishes to get their share of food.

Secondary sex characteristics are not apparent. Certain variations in the intensity of the markings of the median fins, i.e. dorsal, anal, and caudal fins, are sometimes thought to represent sexual differences, but this has not been verified. Temperature, 70°-80°.

Gold Barbs

(Probably a mutant of *Barbus semifasciolatus*)

Length: 2¹/₂ inches

This fish has been kept for years in our tanks, but we are still not certain of its ancestry. In the trade it is known as

Gold Barb

Gold Barbs (Albino Form)

Barbus tetrazona

Barbus schuberti, but that is not a valid scientific name. It is said to have been developed by a Mr. Thomas Schubert of Camden, N.J., hence the trade name.

Whatever the name, the fish is beautiful, peaceful, and easily cared for. It breeds readily in typical Barb fashion and is very prolific. Between 400 and 500 eggs per spawning are normal for a full grown female. Temperature, 68° to 82°.

Barbus tetrazona
Bleeker
Popular name: Tiger Barb
Meaning of name: Barbus, with barbels; tetrazona, four-banded
Length: 2 inches
Malaysia to Borneo
Tiger Barbs are unusually high-spirited fishes. This trait has both ad-

vantages and disadvantages: it provides liveliness to the aquarium and stimulation to other fishes, but when *B. tetrazona* become too exuberant, they nip the flowing fins of slower-moving fishes, such as Bettas, Angelfish, and Veiltail Guppies. From our experience, it is best to keep this fish only with its own kind; even then, the tank should be a rather large one, say ten or preferably fifteen gallons. A

Male Albino **B. tetrazona**

twenty-nine gallon tank containing about fifty of these beauties makes a strikingly lively and colorful sight.

Females can usually be distinguished by their fuller outline. They also show less red in the ventral fins as well as in the nose.

Breeding is typical, with the exception that they are keen spawn-eaters. Males are liable to nip anal fins of females prior to spawning, even to the extent of killing them. Temperature, 70°-80°.

eating. The young are very small, but in a large, established tank they get enough natural infusoria to give them a good start. The parents, of course, should be promptly removed after spawning. To rear fifty is considered good. A school of about that number is a pleasant sight.

This species in spawning will sometimes jump out of the water or possibly even out of an uncovered aquarium.

Temperature, 70°-80°.

Barbus titteya

Barbus viviparus

Barbus titteya
Deraniyagala
Popular name: Cherry Barb
Meaning of name: Barbus, with barbels; titteya, native name
Length: 1⅞ inches
Sri Lanka (Ceylon)

Due to the considerable changes in color that this fish goes through, no single picture does it justice. Some strains of the fish show more color intensity than others.

The species is best bred in pairs in the usual Barb manner, but they are avid egg-eaters. Shallow water and plenty of plants help prevent this egg

Barbus viviparus
(Weber)
Popular name: Zig-Zag Barb
Meaning of name: Barbus, with barbels; viviparus, having live young
Length: Up to 3 inches
Southeast Africa

Its curious body markings distinguish this Barb from other species of this large genus. The second horizontal line does not run parallel to the first which is rather unusual for fishes of this type. Both lines meet just beyond the gills and at the caudal peduncle, a marking that has given this fish its common name, which, however, is not a very exact description. Zig-Zag Barbs are otherwise not a very colorful species, the fins are clear and the body is drab olive above and silvery below. On the other hand, they are very hardy and seem very resistant to disease.

Weber, the ichthyologist who first described these fishes in 1897, found well-developed young inside a specimen. He concluded that they were live-bearing fishes, hence the name "viviparus." Later, after Weber's preserved material was reexamined, it turned out that he had opened the gut of the fish and that the "young" were some type of baby cichlid which had been swallowed as food. This does not mean, however, that Zig-Zag Barbs are carnivorous—they readily eat all kinds of prepared foods. This simply shows that they, like most other fishes, will not reject any wiggling morsel, fish or not, as long as it is small enough. Zig-Zag Barbs are, without doubt, egg-laying fishes and spawn like most other Barbs in fine-leaved plants. Mature males are easily recognized by their slimmer body. Temperature, 70° to 80°.

Tanichthys albonubes
Lin

Popular name: White Cloud Mountain Fish or White Cloud

Meaning of name: Tanichthys, for Tan, a Chinese boy scout who found the fish, ichthys, fish (Tan's fish); albonubes, White Cloud

Length: 1 1/4 inches

Tanichthys albonubes

White Cloud Mountain near Canton, China

Seldom does a fish have so many good points. In addition to being attractive, peaceful, active, and easily bred, it also stands a great range of temperature: 40° to 90°. It eats anything, but prefers small food given often. Breeds best at 68° to 75°. The male, distinguished by a longer and more colorful dorsal fin, chases the female as she scatters eggs freely. White Clouds have been successfully bred both with and without the use of plants. It is entirely possible to raise many young in the presence of their parents, since cannibalism is not a well-developed trait in these fishes. But, if large numbers of fry are desired, it is safer to use plants and remove the breeders after spawning occurs.

At ages from two to ten weeks the babies are extremely beautiful, looking like young Neon Tetras, *Paracheirodon innesi*, with a dazzling streak of electric blue-green from eye to tail.

A very similar fish, *Aphyocypris pooni*, has been imported and become established in our tanks. It requires the same care as *Tanichthys albonubes*.

Temperature, 65°-80°.

THE RASBORAS

Of the approximately forty-five species of *Rasbora* known to science, only some have been tried in aquariums. Space does not permit a listing of all the species; those listed here are long-time favorites of aquarists.

Wing Commander Marsack, an experienced aquarist, made personal field studies of the Malaysian region and the conditions under which most Rasboras live and breed. The waters are generally acid, going as low as 5.5 on the pH scale. This is very likely produced by humic acid generated by the decomposition of leaves and dead wood as the streams pass through dense jungles before emerging into the open, where these fishes mostly live.

Broad-leaved *Cryptocorynes* grow in such profusion that their roots creep out of the soil and form mats over the bottom, making a perfect refuge for newly hatched fishes. The eggs of *Rasbora heteromorpha* (and probably others) are spawned against the underside of the leaves, where they adhere until hatched.

The fact that most of the species are observed in large schools in nature leads one to suspect that they are "community breeders," spawning in such large numbers that liberal space is required. In aquariums we get them into seemingly perfect condition, loaded with spawn, yet nothing happens. This also applies to the hard-to-spawn Characoids. Certainly we have missed some trick, for in natural conditions both of them are tremendous breeders. What makes it all the more puzzling is that they both take kindly to aquarium life and live for years in splendid health.

Except for a very few little-known species from Africa, all the *Rasboras* are native to southeastern Asia, from India to Borneo.

Rasbora elegans

Rasbora elegans
Volz

Meaning of name: Rasbora, a native name; elegans, elegant

Length: 5 inches

Malaysia and eastern parts of Indonesia

A central black body spot below the first dorsal ray, more or less oblong in shape and varying in intensity, roughly distinguishes this species. In addition to the ocellated dot at the tail base, there is a horizontal, narrow, dark line just above the anal fin. The fish does not have the glittering appearance of burnished silver common to such individuals as *Mylossoma aureum* but instead has more of a leaden gray with a touch of warmth.

The central body spot in the female is paler, and she is also more aggressive than the male. The anal fin of the female is clear; it is yellow in the male. *R. elegans* seldom breeds in captivity. In the aquarium it spawns on fine plants.

This species grows rather large, and when it reaches maturity at five inches it makes an especially attractive show fish. Edged in dark gray, the large scales show like a sleek coat of armor, which, of course, is what they are.

In its native habitat it can be found in small streams where it reaches great numbers.

R. elegans enjoys a mixed diet, will live peacefully in a community tank and will do well in a temperature of from 70° to 80°.

Rasbora heteromorpha

Rasbora heteromorpha
Duncker

Popular names: Rasbora, Red Ras-bora, or Harlequin

Meaning of name: Rasbora, a native name; heteromorpha, differing in shape from most members of the genus

Length: $1^3/_4$ inches

Malaysia and Sumatra

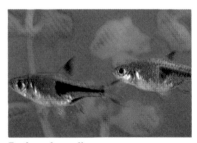
Rasbora hengeli

For many years *R. heteromorpha* has occupied a prominent place in the minds of all advanced fish fanciers. It has been the open or secret ambition of many to own this unique, beautiful fish which stands in such relief to its paler cousins. Today, the trade name "Rasbora" is taken for granted to mean *R. heteromorpha,* as if no other species existed.

The lure of financial returns has spurred collectors and importers to such elaborate efforts in bringing them alive from Asia that they now arrive by the thousands; previously dozens were considered an event. They ship well and are a leader in sales volume. Many experts have tried to breed them, but few have had success. Reports of spawnings vary somewhat in detail but, for the most part, they agree. The successful temperature is from 78° to 82°. The action takes place within a day or two after a ripe pair has been placed in a planted tank containing water that has aged only a few days. The male swims over the female for a time. She assumes an upside-down position, contacting to her belly the underside of leaves, such as *Cryptocoryne* or large *Sagittaria*. She is apparently searching for a suitable place on which to spawn. She is possibly preparing a place to which her eggs can adhere. On the other hand, she may be coaxing the male, for presently, but not immediately, he joins her under a leaf. He quickly clasps her in the crescent he makes of his body; the female continues in an upside-down position. During the momentary, trembling embrace, several small, crystal-clear eggs appear and are attached to the underside of the leaf. The action is repeated at intervals under different leaves for about two hours by which time thirty to eighty eggs have been ejected. Kept at a temperature of 80°, the eggs hatch in eighteen hours.

It is probable that clean, new leaves best serve the purpose. If they are coated with algae, the eggs are apt to fall and be eaten. One successful breeder uses water at pH 6.5, has *Bacopa* as a spawning plant, and conditions his breeders on brine shrimp and white worms.

The surest method of telling the sex in breeding-sized fish is the golden line along the top edge of the black triangle. By overhead artificial light, the line of the male will be found to be more brilliant and deeply colored. A less dependable indication is the ventral points forward along the belly in the male.

Rasbora heteromorpha moves about the aquarium easily and without nervousness. It is adaptable in diet and temperature, a range from 68° to 88° produces no ill effects. It lives for about five years.

A very similar, if somewhat smaller species, *Rasbora hengeli*, has been imported from the same general region in large numbers in recent years. The black triangular spot is narrower, often only indicated by a line somewhat broadened at the front end. Care and maintenance appear to be the same as that given for *R. heteromorpha*.

Rasbora trilineata
Steindachner
Popular name: Scissor-Tail
Meaning of name: Rasbora, a native name; trilineata, three-lined
Length: Up to 3 inches
Johore in Malay Peninsula

Although a number of the Rasboras are difficult for the amateur ichthyologist to distinguish from one another, the distinctive markings on the tail fins should end any confusion about this species. Each lobe is whitish towards the outer part, then tipped black. Many fishes partially close the tail fin when starting to move. The markings of the Scissor-Tail make it apparent that it uses a sort of clipping action when it starts to move, hence its popular name. The body is somewhat translucent.

They are frequently bred by commercial breeders at a length of two to three inches and are always available. The young are easily raised on newly hatched brine shrimp. Temperature, 70°-80°.

Rasbora trilineata

THE DANIOS

This group of lively and spirited little fishes has been popular with hobbyists practically since the early beginnings. They are beautiful, hardy, and among the easiest-to-breed egg laying fishes. The name Danio, which is the generic name under which they were first described, has stuck with them as the popular name, much like the name Tetra has stuck with the many popular small Characoids.

Alb. **R. trilineata**

Breeding the Danios

The spawning of the Danios is interesting because it challenges our ingenuity and resourcefulness in overcoming the strong tendency of these active fishes to eat their own eggs as they fall. The scheme is (1) to have the water so shallow that the fishes have no chance to spear them as they sink, and (2) to have the eggs fall into a trap where the fishes cannot follow. The trap consists simply of small marbles or pebbles to a depth of about an inch. The eggs are non-adhesive and drop between the marbles to the bottom. One danger with marbles is that the fishes are liable to wriggle among them in fright and be unable to get out. In that respect, quarter-inch rounded stones are better.

As spawning time approaches, separate any promising-looking female, and feed her for a week on choice food. Have the aquarium prepared and seasoned: ready for her and two or three lively males. Place the

which to produce fine, large specimens, and they are well worth the pleasant effort. While it is possible to raise them entirely on prepared foods, graded according to size, the result does not produce a robust fish. They

Brachydanio albolineatus

Brachydanio frankei

aquarium where it will get good light, introduce the female a day ahead of the males. If there is no spawn in three or four days, separate and try again. The spawning action is easily recognized. It is a wild chase, similar to that indulged in by Goldfish. If a glass-bottom tank is used, the aquarist can look up through the base to see whether eggs are scattered among the marbles. To a practiced eye, the shape of the female is sufficient indication of a spawning.

The fishes, of course, are removed after spawning. At this time an infusoria culture should be started for the young, which will hatch in about two days. They adhere, at first, in odd positions in their beginning efforts to move about, but in two more days they act like fish and have appetites. As the spawns average about 200 eggs, it is desirable to give the babies plenty of room. They should be continuously pushed in growth. It is the only way in

are apt to be small and even deformed. Live food is better, newly hatched brine shrimp being ideal. The best age for breeders is about one year. At two years, they are old. They seldom live beyond an age of three years.

Brachydanio albolineatus
(Blyth)

Popular name: Pearl Danio

Meaning of name: Brachydanio, short Danio; albolineatus, white lined, an erroneous designation due to description from a preserved specimen that had changed color

Length: 2¹/₂ inches

Burma

To be seen at their best, many fishes should be viewed by reflected light, that is, with the light coming from the observer towards the fish. This is especially true of *Brachydanio albolineatus,* whose exquisite mother-of-pearl colors can be appreciated only under those conditions. Particularly interesting are the colors in the anal fin, which ordinarily pass unnoticed. Some aquarists claim that this fin shows colors in the male only, but this is not in accordance with the observations of other hobbyists who find that both sexes possess it. Possibly, it is a little stronger in the male. The ruddy glow about the lower rear part of the body is deeper in the male.

Another strain available on the market has a golden body and faint markings.

Temperature, 68° to 78°.

Brachydanio frankei
Meinken
  Popular name: Leopard Danio
  Meaning of name: Brachydanio, short Danio; frankei, after Franke
  Length: About 2 inches
  Precise location unknown

This little Danio has been the object of much controversy since it was first imported and given its Latin name in 1963. We do not know at the present time exactly where the fish comes from. It first appeared in hobbyists' tanks in Czechoslovakia and from there was brought to Germany, Holland, and the United States, but its natural habitat remains a mystery at the present writing. Some aquarists call it a mutant, while others regard it as a subspecies of the old favorite, the Zebra Danio (*Brachydanio rerio*). It is said to produce fertile offspring when crossed with B. *rerio*, which is not the case with crosses between other species of *Brachydanio*.

Good-sized, vigorous specimens should be chosen when breeding the Leopard Danio, as there is a tendency in this species for successive generations to mature at smaller sizes. Sexes are easily distinguished. Mature males are much more slender than the females and exhibit a distinct golden glow over the entire body. Females, on the other hand, are silvery.

On occasion, a curious disease crops up among these Danios. The males, particularly, become thin and emaciated, refuse food, and then die within a week or two. It is probably caused by intestinal parasites, but much research is needed to establish the real cause and to suggest ways of treating sick individuals.

Nevertheless, we can consider the Leopard Danio a very hardy fish, not at all demanding in water conditions, food and temperature, which makes it a perfect fish for the beginning aquarist. Temperature, 70° to 75°.

Brachydanio rerio
(Hamilton-Buchanan)
  Popular name: Zebra Fish, Zebra Danio
  Meaning of name: Brachydanio, short Danio; rerio, a native name
  Length: 1³/₄ inches
  Bengal, India

Of the various small egg-layers, this fish is, no doubt, the most permanently popular and with good reason. In an exceptional degree, it has all the points that make an ideal aquarium occupant. It is unusually active without being nervously annoying. It is a fish to show to advantage when moving in schools. In fact its beautiful horizontal stripes—repeated in each

Brachydanio rerio

fish—give a streamlined effect that might be the envy of our best automobile designers.

The sexes can be distinguished, but not at a glance. As is usual in many species, the females are noticeably fuller as spawning time approaches. This is particularly true of all of the *Brachydanios*, but it is possible to tell the sex of adult *B. rerios* by the fact that there is a more bluish cast over the female, particularly in the tail fin. In adult males, the horizontal stripes tend to acquire a more golden hue.

Zebra Danio is a misfit name, since the stripes on Zebras are mainly vertical. The fish has extraordinary temperature tolerance, from a low of 60° to a high of 110°, but it breeds at 72° to 77°. Takes any food.

Danio malabaricus
(Jerdon)
Popular name: Giant Danio
Meaning of name: Danio, a native name; malabaricus, from Malabar
Length: 4 inches
India
Giant Danios are admirable fish, always on the move, easily fed and bred, rather long-lived, ordinarily peaceful, and a standard member of a "happy family" tank. We have heard of their eating much smaller fishes, but this is liable to occur with many species when the difference in size is great. *D. malabaricus* is the largest of the imported Danios.

Distinguishing the sexes is not easy, except at breeding time when the female is fuller in her belly outline. The ruddy hue in the fins and anal region of the male is a breeding color and ordinarily does not appear. The same breeding color in the female is less pronounced. In mature fish, the gold vertical and horizontal bars and stripes are more broken in the female. In addition, she is usually slightly larger than the male. Unlike the other popular Danio, the Zebra Fish, *D. malabaricus* has adhesive eggs and breeds like Barbs. Temperature, 68° to 80°.

Labeo bicolor
Popular name: Red-tailed Shark
Meaning of name: Labeo, lips; bicolor, two colors
Length: 4³/₄ inches
Thailand
The position of the triangular dorsal fin, occurring anteriorly to the ventral fins and the ventral mouth, has led aquarists to dub this fish, as well as some other species, shark. Nothing in the disposition or personality of these fishes warrants the designation. The elongated and somewhat compressed body, as well as the fins, of *L. bicolor* are black; the forked tail is a contrasting bright red. A velvet black and brilliant red are indications that the fish is in good condition. Inferior

Danio malabaricus

Labeo bicolor

color occurs when conditions are faulty. The point of the dorsal fin is edged in white. There are two sets of barbels.

It likes slightly alkaline water, pH 7.1 to 7.3, and prefers a temperature in the high seventies. Algae that have grown on leaves or aquarium walls are good news to this species.

They are omnivores and not choosey about food. They play rather roughly among themselves but do not harm one another seriously, as long as the tank is thickly planted and enough hiding places are provided. They have bred in captivity.

Labeo variegatus
Pellegrin
Popular name: Variegated Shark
Meaning of name: Labeo, lips; variegatus, variegated
Length: 6 inches
Central Africa

Adults of this species are a dark gray color, with numerous, but faint, red spots. The fishes feed on algae and other vegetable matter but seem to prefer other foods in the aquarium. All live and frozen foods are relished, but floating dry foods are only reluctantly taken. They are peaceful towards other fishes but among themselves very quarrelsome. It is best to keep only one in a community tank. Temperature, 72° to 82°.

Morulius chrysophekadion
(Bleeker)
Popular name: Black Shark
Meaning of name: Morulius, black; chrysophekadion, chryso, golden

Length: 12 inches
Sumatra, Java, Borneo

This species, when first introduced to the aquarium scene, caused considerable excitement. Its black shark-like appearance set it apart, and its high price indicated rarity. As it became more available, the price became less formidable and when the Red-tailed Shark (*Labeo bicolor*) was introduced sometime later, *M. chrysophekadion* lost its popularity. It is an excellent species, however, for a large aquarium, and its hardiness and willingness to accept all types of aquarium fare make it a fish worthy of consideration. It is a bottom feeder and is somewhat shy. Although it feeds on algae, it does not remove it from leaves. We have found no reports of its breeding in captivity. It is apt to be aggressive with its own kind.

Balantiocheilus melanopterus
(Bleeker)
Popular names: Tricolor Shark, Bala Shark, Burnt Tail Fish
Meaning of name: Balantiocheilus, with pouch-like mouth; melanopterus, with black fins
Length: 14 inches, usually 7-8
Western Indonesia, Malaysia, Thailand

All Tricolor Sharks offered for sale at the time of this writing are imported, because all attempts at breeding them have so far been unsuccessful. Their mode of reproduction, even in their natural habitat, is largely unknown, and sexes cannot be determined. They are somewhat delicate when first acquired and an occasional

Labeo variegatus

Morulius chrysophekadeon

Balantiocheilus megalopterus

individual may refuse to accept food for several weeks. Offering live foods, such as *Daphnia*, brine shrimp, or bloodworms, plus applying the standard procedure of temporarily raising the temperature a few degrees above the normal range are the best means of persuading these strikingly beautiful, graceful fishes to become established in the aquarium. Once this has been successfully done, they are hardy and long-lived, fairly peaceful towards other fishes but somewhat quarrelsome among themselves. Tricolor Sharks are avid jumpers and capable of lightning speed. They should, therefore, be kept in spacious, well-covered tanks.

The unfortunate, but popular, name "shark" has been applied to this and a number of very unsharklike fishes, probably because the dorsal fin of these fishes is shaped somewhat similarly to a true shark's dorsal and is, particularly in this species, always held erect. But in other respects, they do not resemble true sharks in either appearance, manner, size, or ferociousness.

Temperature, 75° to 80°.

THE LOACHES
FAMILY COBITIDAE

The Loaches are much like the Cyprinids, but they differ from them in having three or more pairs of barbels. They never have jaw teeth. Most of them have a movable spine just below the eye, with which they can inflict a painful wound when handled carelessly. They are bottom-dwelling fishes, often rather secretive, and should be given rocks or pieces of driftwood for hiding places.

Misgurnus anguillicaudatus
(Cantor)

Popular name: Japanese Weatherfish

Meaning of name: Misgurnus, from Misgurn, old English name for Loach; anguillicaudatus, with an eel-like tail

Length: Up to 8 inches

Japan, China

This fish differs from *Botia* and *Acanthophthalmus* by the absence of the movable spine below the eye. It is light gray with irregular blotches of darker gray, while the European form, *Cobitis fossilis*, is light brown with several dark stripes along the body. They are virtually the same fish both from the scientist's and the aquarist's viewpoints.

Before the merits of *Corydoras* as aquarium scavengers were so well known, the "Weatherfish," as well as other forms of Loaches, were much used for this purpose. Some aquarists still utilize them, but seldom in sizes over four inches in length. Their movements are wild and unpredictable, somewhat like a "chicken with its head cut off." When these fishes are fully grown, their strange, lashing actions are intolerable to the aquarist, for the sediment is whipped into a state of suspension and sand is shifted without regard to scenic effect. However, it would be incorrect to give the impression that this fish is always on the rampage. It is quiet for periods, often buried in the sand with its head looking out cutely. Then it will emerge and begin a peculiar, interesting action of "combing" the sand surface in search of food. Sand and dirt are taken into the mouth and rapidly expelled through the gills.

This fish stands temperatures from 40° to 80° and has seldom been bred. They spawn on the bottom and the young bury themselves for a long period, no doubt feeding on microscopic life and vegetal decomposition.

Botia macracantha
Bleeker

Popular name: Clown Loach

Meaning of name: Botia, not known; macracantha, big spine, from the spine on the face below the eye

Length: 5 inches or more

Borneo

Loaches are usually thought of as long and eel-like, such as the Weatherfish, but there are others of more usual fish form, like our present subject.

The hinged spine, which lies in a groove beneath the eye, is a vicious weapon that makes other fishes keep their distance.

By nature a shy fish, largely nocturnal, but by association with other sorts it can be "reformed," as it were, especially if there are no places where it can completely hide. The Clown Loach has a quaint habit that is alarming when first seen. When any fish lies on its side at the bottom, it usually means *finis*. Clown Loaches love to rest this way and do so frequently, especially under the shallow shelter of an overhanging stone. Lives eight years or more.

Eats most aquarium fare and is a good, long-lived "scavenger." Efforts

Misgurnus auguillicauda

Botia macracantha

Botia lucas-bahi

to breed it have all met with failure. Temperature range, 68° to 82°.

Botia lucas-bahi
(Fowler)
> *Popular name:* Tiger Loach
> *Meaning of name:* Botia, unknown; lucas-bahi, personal name
> *Length:* Up to 6 inches
> Thailand, Malaysia, Indonesia

Like most other members of the family, Tiger Loaches are bottom-dwellers, inhabiting streams and rivers with sandy or gravelly bottoms. They are extremely swift swimmers and are equally good at digging and undermining stones. They do this most efficiently, and the tank should be set up accordingly to make them feel at home. They use anal and tail fins to fan the sand away. Occasionally, with wide-open mouths, they "push" gravel from underneath stones to make hiding places, where they spend much time. At times, for lack of space, the fishes lie on their sides, giving the impression of being sick. This, however, is quite normal behavior and no cause for concern.

The fishes are omnivorous, eating prepared as well as live and frozen foods. They are quite efficient in extracting *Tubifex* worms from gravel, as well as eradicating pond and ramshorn snails.

Temperature, 72° to 80°.

Botia sidthimunki
Klausewitz
> *Popular name:* Dwarf Checkered Loach
> *Length:* About 1½ inches

Thailand

This is probably the smallest of all Loaches, usually reaching only an inch or a little more in length. It is pleasantly marked with a somewhat variable checkered pattern above the horizontal black line running the entire length of the body. Though a bottom dweller, this Loach spends more time than other members of the family foraging among plants in the middle reaches of the tank.

There is a strange similarity between this species and the Pigmy Catfish of South America, *Corydoras hastatus*. Both are the smallest members of their respective, but widely different, families and the only ones not exclusively feeding on the bottom. This is possibly another case of convergent evolution where two geographically separated species have evolved in the same way, resulting in amazingly close similarities in form and behavior. Dwarf Checkered Loaches are fair "scavengers," accepting almost any kind of food.

Because of their small size and hardiness, attempts at breeding them might be more successful than with the large species, but raising the fry will probably be more difficult. Hints on how to set up a tank for spawning cannot be given, however, since nothing is known about the reproductive habits of the genus *Botia*. But success with one species will certainly contribute to our knowledge of Loaches in general and might lead the way to successful spawnings of other species.

Temperature, 72° to 80°.

Acanthophthalmus semicinctus
Fraser-Brunner

Popular names: Kuhli Loach, Coolie Loach

Meaning of name: Acanthophthalmus, with spine near eyes; semicinctus, half-banded

Length: 2³/₄ inches

Malaysia and parts of Indonesia

An odd little Loach and rather pretty. It is also an active, durable fish. The bands across the back and sides are black on the edges and shade into dark gray in the middle. The eye, occurring in one of the dark patches, is not easily seen. A rather comical set of bushy barbels, looking like an obstinate little moustache, adorns the mouth.

The fish is a fair scavenger of rather limited capacity. Although nocturnal by nature, it readily learns to eat in daytime. Unlike other aquarium Loaches, it never grows too large. It should be provided with rocks and crevices for hiding. Other similar species have been imported and although distinct differences can be found in their markings, for the aquarist's purposes, the popular name of "Coolie" may be applied to all of them. A few spawnings have been recorded. They almost certainly breed in the mulm at the bottom of the aquarium.

Temperature, 70°-80°.

Acanthopsis choirorhynchus
Bleeker

Popular name: Horse-faced Loach

Length: 5 inches, seldom up to 8 inches

Botia sidthimunki

Acanthophthalmus semicinctus

Acanthopsis choirorhynchus

Burma, Thailand, Malaysia, Indonesia

This Loach is certainly not the most colorful of the family, but its shape and amusing antics make it worthwhile keeping. The fish spends a considerable amount of time buried in the gravel with only the eyes and mouth showing, ready to disappear at the slightest sign of danger. While searching for food, however, it becomes extremely active and, from an aquarist's point of view, it is very useful in maintaining a clean tank. Sifting the gravel through its mouth and gills, much like some of the South American "earth-eating" Cichlids of the genus *Geophagus*, the fish leaves no corner of the tank untouched. When disturbed at this activity, it dives head first into the gravel. It disappears with lightning speed and most amazingly, literally seems to be able to swim through the gravel only to emerge safely on the other side of the tank. This is standard behavior of most of the Mastacembelids, the spiny eels, but unusual for Loaches. Of course, only well-rooted plants can withstand such activity and new plants should be protected from uprooting by means of rocks or flowerpots.

These Loaches are very enduring and peaceful. They usually outlast other tank mates. They can be offered almost any kind of food as long as it sinks to the bottom. Sex differences have not been observed and their means of reproduction are unknown. Temperature, 75° to 80°.

FAMILY GYRINOCHEILIDAE

This family contains but one genus and probably only one species. The peculiar structure of the mouth allows these fish to attach themselves to smooth stones by suction, even in swiftly running water, and continue to breathe. They inhale water through an opening with a valve-like flap, and pass it over their gills without releasing the suction of the mouth.

Gyrinocheilus aymonieri
(Tirant)
Popular names: Indian Sucker, Chinese Algae-eater
Meaning of name: Gyrinocheilus, with lips arranged in circle; aymonieri, after a personal name
Length: Usually up to 4 or 5 inches, larger in nature
Reportedly from Northern Malaysia and Thailand

These suckermouth fish have not been reported from India, but the strong possibility exists that their range includes Burma and even Southern China. Their importation came just at the time when the previously plentiful South American *Plecostomus* species became scarcer due to government-ordered seasonal embargos, chiefly by

Gyrinocheilus aymonieri

Trinidad. Indian Algae-eaters consequently became popular and are now being imported on a large scale.

Young *G. aymonieri* are perfectly peaceful and can do a fair job in keeping plants and rocks free of algae, but older ones frequently attack large, deep-bodied fishes, such as Angelfish, Discus, or larger Gouramis. They seem to be fond of the slime produced by these fishes and are often seen scraping away at the sides of these poor creatures, sometimes injuring these fishes to such an extent that a serious wound develops. This seems to attract *Gyrinocheilus* even more, since they often return to the same spot. This may cause death to the victim once bacterial or fungus infections take hold. Temperature, 70° to 80°.

THE CATFISHES

The Catfishes, made up of many different families that do not even resemble each other, nevertheless have distinguishing features only Catfishes possess. For example, no Catfish ever has scales, though some are more or less covered with bony plates. Many of them have very conspicuous barbels. Most people recognize a Catfish when they see one, but few know that not every Catfish is a scavenger. Most Catfishes are more or less nocturnal fishes. They hide or are quiet during the daytime but move about very actively at night. This often terrorizes the other fishes in an aquarium, who like to rest or sleep at night. The Smooth Armored Catfishes, such as *Corydoras*, seem to be an exception to this rule.

THE SILURID CATFISHES
FAMILY SILURIDAE

These Catfishes are easily identified by the extremely long anal fin and by the dorsal fin which is either very small and far forward or altogether absent. All Silurids are from Europe or Asia.

Kryptopterus bicirrhus
(Cuvier and Valenciennes)
  Popular name: Glass Catfish
  Native name: "Limpok"
  Meaning of name: Kryptopterus, hidden fin, an allusion to the almost invisible one-rayed dorsal fin; bicirrhus, with two hairs (whiskers)
    Aquarium size: 2½ inches
    Java, Borneo, Sumatra, Thailand
As one of the most nearly transparent fishes kept by aquarists, the Glass Catfish lives up to its popular name with the truly glass-like flesh of its long tail section. But when a light is held to shine through the body, it displays a wealth of prismatic colors. The skeleton is fairly visible. The internal organs are set in an extraordinarily forward position as is the barely perceptible, hair-like dorsal fin just above the body cavity. The fish maintains a constant rippling motion with its long anal fin, even when it is standing still in midwater.

Were it not for the opaque, silvery sac containing the internal organs, it would be difficult to see this fish at all.

Brine shrimp, *Daphnia, Tubifex,* glass worms, and Enchytraeids are eagerly (although at first shyly) eaten. Harmless. Not bred. Temperature, 72° to 82°.

THE MOCHOKID CATFISHES
FAMILY MOCHOKIDAE

The Mochokid Catfishes form a small family confined to the fresh waters of tropical Africa. Most of them have the barbels on the lower lip fringed or branched, like some (but not all) of the South American Doradidae. Many Mochokids swim upside down.

Synodontis nigriventris
(David)
  Popular name: Upside-down Catfish
    Meaning of name: Synodontis, with fused tooth plates; nigriventris, black belly
    Recorded length: 3¾ inches
    Lower Congo River, Africa

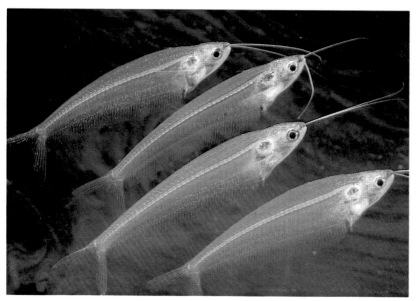

Kryptopterus bicirrhus

Synodontis nigriventris

This entertaining little character, completely unconcerned as to whether it swims top-up or top-down, was introduced to aquarists in 1950.

Markings are in shades of gray and black on a changing background, ranging from olive to light yellow.

They have proved peaceful and interesting.

As with many Catfishes, they tend to be nocturnal. They have a keen sense of ownership of a favorite location. The underside of an elevated flat stone, if provided, is a favorite perching spot. Easily fed. Temperature, 74° to 80°.

THE BAGRID CATFISHES
FAMILY BAGRIDAE

The Bagrids are "ordinary"-looking Catfishes with dorsal fin present and of usual place and size, anal fin of moderate length, no "armor" on the body, and the "whiskers" usually long. All are from Africa or Asia. The differences between the Bagrids and the South American Pimelodids are small and internal, so that, for the aquarist, the best distinguishing feature is the habitat.

Mystus tengara
(Hamilton-Buchanan)

Meaning of name: Mystus, derived from mystax, meaning whiskers; tangara, the native name in the Punjab is "ting ga rah"

Length: 4 inches

N. India, the Punjab, and Assam

This species, to be correct, should have eight barbels, two of them nasal. It is an interesting, attractive aquarium

Mystus tengara

Etropiella debauwi

fish. Easily fed and cared for. Harmless. Seems happy at a temperature ranging at about 72° to 80°.

THE SCHILBEID CATFISHES
FAMILY SCHILBEIDAE

Representatives of this family are found in Africa and Southeast Asia. Most of them are schoolfishes, more active at dusk than during the day. None have been bred in aquaria. Some have been nicknamed "sharks," for their erect dorsal fin, their silver-gray color, and their sharklike movements. They are not at all aggressive fishes.

Etropiella debauwi
(Boulenger)

Meaning of name: Etropiella, small Etropier (another genus); debauwi, after a personal name)

Pimelodus clarias

Length: 3 inches
Central Africa

This is one of the few Catfishes that spends most of its time in mid-water, not near the bottom. It is also a typical schoolfish and becomes very shy when kept alone. There are no external sex differences, and we have had no report of their breeding habits. Temperature, 75° to 80°.

THE PIMELODID CATFISHES
FAMILY PIMELODIDAE

The Pimelodids are Catfishes very similar in most features to another family (Bagridae) but come from South and Central America.

Pimelodus clarias
(Bloch)

Meaning of name: Pimelodus, fat-toothed; clarias, like the Indian Catfish, Clarias

Length: To 12 inches

All of South America east of the Andes from Panama to Buenos Aires

This is one of those fishes that is most attractive when small, but when fully grown, it is neither good-looking nor suited to the aquarium. Adults not only lose those stunning big spots, but reach a length of ten to twelve inches. Varieties from different locales of South America are spotted differently; some are altogether unspotted. Only smaller specimens are imported and, in an ordinary-sized aquarium, they retain decorative dots, which are dark brown placed on a golden background. They are harmless, moderately active fishes having the novel characteristics

Pimelodus pictus

of the South American Catfishes, including that of being difficult to breed. We know nothing of their reproductive habits. They are occasionally imported and, thus, are sometimes found in the stocks of dealers. Easily fed.
Temperature, 70°-80°.

Pimelodus pictus
Popular name: Polka Dot Pimelodus
Meaning of name: Pimelodus, with wide teeth.
  Length: 4 inches
  Northern South America
  Fast moving catfish, and like many similar species, a gluttonous feeder. It does not require special water conditions, but seems to be more comfortable at a higher temperature. 78° to 82° is a good range. They are rather

susceptible to "ich" (*lchthyophthirius*) and, once afflicted, difficult to cure. Hiding places should be provided, but the fish uses them only intermittently.

Sorubim lima
  (Bloch and Schneider)
  Popular name: Shovel-nosed Catfish
  Length: Up to 20 inches
  Brazil
  A rather strange-looking Catfish with a mouth resembling a duck's bill. The Shovel-nosed Catfish is not a scavenger, as most Catfishes are thought to be, but a predator, especially when large. For this reason, it is not suited for a community tank containing fishes of up to Swordtail size. It is a nocturnal fish and should be provided with hiding places.

Sorubim lima

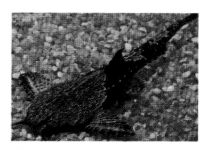

Bunocephalus *spec.*

THE BANJO CATFISHES
FAMILY BUNOCEPHALIDAE

The Bunocephalids are small unarmored Catfishes with very wide, flat heads. They are similar in appearance and difficult to tell apart; for this reason, they are rarely identified correctly by aquarium dealers. All Bunocephalids are from South America.

Bunocephalus species
Popular name: Banjo Catfish
Meaning of name: Bunocephalus, with hills (bumps) on the head
Length: 5 inches
Amazon

This is one of several very similar species of Banjo Cats that are imported from time to time. The colors are dark and mottled above and light beneath. They have very small, beady

This fish prefers to feed near the bottom and should not be given dried food. Occasional specimens, however, learn to take lumps of freeze-dried brine shrimp at the surface. In large tanks they often "cruise" or glide just above the bottom, with outspread barbles, much in the manner of true sharks. Capable of considerable speed when alarmed. Temperature, 75° to 82°.

eyes. When the tail fin is spread, which is seldom, it shows a rounded form.

Seldom bred. In the past, catfishes of this family were reported to carry their eggs adhering to the abdomen. Though this has been observed in the aquarium with one species of Banjo Cat, others have been found to lay their eggs in sand.

They are very sluggish fishes but able to bury themselves in gravel by powerful and slow lashing movements. When held in the water or even lifted out of the tank they play "possum." Temperature, 70°-80°.

THE ARMORED CATFISHES
FAMILY CALLICHTHYIDAE

This is a large group of mostly South American Catfishes which, instead of having ordinary scales, are covered with two main rows of overlapping, bony laminations or plates.

They share with all other Catfishes the needle-sharp, often serrated first spines of the dorsal and pectoral fins. Being pricked by one of those spines when trying to extricate them from a net is a rather painful experience.

They occasionally dash to the surface for a gulp of air. This neither indicates distress, nor that they are full-fledged air-breathers.

The most important group of the armored Catfishes, at least from the aquarist's point of view, are the various members of the genus *Corydoras*.

Although many of us like these fishes for their own marked individualities and their contrast to other aquarium species, it is as scavengers that they have permanently established

themselves in popular favor, largely replacing snails for that purpose.

They are droll, gnome-like little beings going about their business of life in what seems to us a serio-comic fashion. This business, as far as the aquarist is concerned, is that of scavenging. It would hardly be going too far to give them the title of health officers, for their self-appointed task is going about the bottom of the aquarium seeking bits of food that other fishes have overlooked and which would soon contaminate the water. They go further than this as they consume dead leaves, dead snails, and even dead *Daphnia*. True, they will not work on the side glasses as will snails, for they are strictly bottom-feeders. The important point is that few fish attack a *Corydoras* of moderate size, whereas many of our exotic fishes make short work of snails. Then again, snails eat fish eggs. Finally, once established, they are difficult to get rid of. This is not true of our little scavenger fish. However, under suitable circumstances, snails should be used as auxiliary cleaners, that is, in association with such fishes as will not kill them.

Unfortunately, many *Corydoras* in home aquaria lead a very meager existence. Especially since the advent of flake and freeze-dried foods, which tend to float much longer than other foods, our little scavengers often remain hungry at feeding time. Some of them, of course, soon learn to turn upside down and feed at the surface, but they really prefer to eat in a more normal position. Furthermore, many

Corydoras aeneus

new hobbyists even expect them to feed on the sediment which accumulates on the bottom of the aquarium, since the clerk at the pet store had sold the fishes with the promise that they would "keep the bottom clean."

This is a rather unfortunate state of affairs, since *Corydoras*, as well as the much larger *Hoplosternum*, make very interesting pets when properly cared for.

As should be observed by now, care must be taken that these Catfishes receive enough food where they most easily find it: on the bottom. By foraging for food on the bottom, they do stir up much of the settled dirt, which then is picked up by the filter. This alone is a valuable service. Armored Catfishes will eagerly eat all types of food, but in order to raise extra fine specimens, or

to breed them, frequent feedings of live and frozen foods are almost indispensable.

We have good accounts of the breeding habits of *Hoplosternum thoracatum*, the Hoplo Catfish, and of *Corydoras aeneus*, the Bronze Catfish. *C. aeneus*, which is probably representative of the whole genus, exercises no parental care. *H. thoracatum* builds a nest that it guards with utmost vigor.

Corydoras aeneus
(Gill)
Popular name: Bronze Cat
Meaning of name: Corydoras, spiny fish with helmet; *aeneus*, bronzy
Length: 2³/₄ inches
Trinidad
A very good scavenger fish intro-

duced in 1933, it is easily distinguished from other members of the genus by the absence of any pattern markings on either body or fins. Now perhaps our commonest *Corydoras*, as well as the hardiest. Temperature, 70°-80°.

In mature fish in good condition, the sexes are rather easily told apart. If viewed from above, the much wider girth of the female becomes quite obvious. At spawning time, the female—and occasionally the male as well—will clean either leaves of aquatic plants, the glass sides of the aquarium, or some other smooth object which she considers suitable for depositing eggs. Having prepared the site, the pair will go through an embrace of sorts, during which it is quite obvious that the female tries to bring her mouth as close as possible to the vent of the male. Through locking of pectoral fins, the pair holds this position for a few seconds. When they break apart, the female is seen resting with a few, usually four to five, rather large eggs in her cupped ventral fins. Presently she will swim up to the previously cleaned spot and deposit the extremely sticky eggs. This process is repeated until up to about one hundred eggs are laid. During this time, the male never goes near the eggs, and the question as to how and when the eggs are fertilized is still the subject of some debate. However, repeated close observation of the spawning process seems to leave no doubt that sperm is released by the male during the partial embrace. At the same time, the female picks it up with her mouth and then releases it while she deposits the eggs. After spawning, both fishes will resume their normal activity, and that includes eating Catfish eggs if they come across any. Therefore, the parents should be removed. The eggs hatch in about four days and fall to the bottom of the tank. In another four or five days, they will have absorbed their yolk sac and start foraging for food on their own.

Newly hatched brine shrimp is the best first food, but a finely powdered prepared food that sinks will do in a pinch.

Corydoras agassizi
Popular name: Agassiz Corydoras
Meaning of name: Corydoras, spiny fish with helmet; agassizi, after Louis Agassiz, zoologist
Length: 2 inches
Northern South America
Like all other Corydoras, this is a very peaceful fish, and a busy bottom feeder. With proper lighting, the color of the body is a pleasing metallic green. Care is the same as for all other Corydoras. Has rarely been bred. Temperature, 70° to 80°.

Corydoras arcuatus
Elwin
Popular names: Bowline Cat, Tabatinga
Meaning of name: Corydoras, helmeted Doras; arcuatus, arched like a bow, with reference to the stripe
Length: 2¹/₂ inches
Upper Amazon
A very distinctive *Corydoras* with a bright pearly body traversed by a

Corydoras aeneus, *Albino form*

Corydoras agassizi

clear, arching black line. No need to confuse this with any other species. It was described and named by the English ichthyologist Margery Elwin, and since its importation by the noted collector Rabaut in 1939 has rarely been bred. For lack of an established scientific name when first imported, dealers called it "Tabatinga," after the name of a tributary of the far reaches of the Amazon where it was collected. That name stuck and is still the popular designation.

Like the other *Corydoras*, it does not seem to have an atom of fighting spirit. Its defense, as with most other Catfish, consists in stiff fin spines. Always spread when caught or in danger, these make a nasty wound in the throat of any fish trying to swallow it. Temperature, 72°-80°.

Corydoras hastatus
Eigenmann and Eigenmann
   Popular name: Pigmy Catfish
   Meaning of name: Corydoras, helmeted Doras; hastatus, with a spear, in reference to the spearhead-like spot on tail root
   Length: 1¼ inches
   The Amazon
   Though delicate-looking, this fish

Corydoras arcuatus

is really quite hardy. Its movements are unlike those of other Catfishes, possibly excepting the Glass Catfish, *Kryptopterus bicirrhus*. Instead of grubbing about the bottom, it balances itself by rapid motion of the pectoral and caudal fins, ready to dart quickly in any direction.

The body is translucent olive, with a dark stripe on the sides.

A few large, single eggs are deposited on the sides of the glass. Neither eggs nor young are eaten by the parents. The babies are about ⅛-inch long when hatched and are easily reared on brine shrimp nauplii.

These fish do best when kept in small schools. They take ordinary food and breed at about 75°.

Corydoras hastatus

Corydoras julii

Corydoras julii
Steindachner

Popular name: Leopard Corydoras
Meaning of name: Corydoras, helmeted Doras; julii, it is not known for
what Julius this species was named.
Formerly known as *Corydoras leopar-
dus*
 Length: 2 inches
 East and Northeast Brazil
A distinctive importation of 1933.
They arrived in large numbers and
promptly gained many friends, who,
for the most part, consider them to be
the best of the *Corydoras.* They are
prettily marked, very active, hardy,
and not too large. They can be roughly
recognized by the triple stripe on the
sides, the black spot above the center
of the dorsal fin, and the spots extending over the nose. Temperature, 72° to
82°.

Corydoras schwartzi
 Meaning of name: Corydoras, spiny
fish with helmet; schwartzi, after the
name of the collector
 Length: 2¼ inches
 Northern Brazil
 · A strikingly patterned Corydoras.
The fish are hardy, active, and some-
what less shy than other newly ac-

quired Catfishes. They have not been
bred in captivity, but there is no reason
to believe that they spawn in a much
different manner than *C. aeneus.* Temperature, 72° to 82°.

Brochis coeruleus
Cope
 Popular name: Hump-backed Catfish
 Meaning of name: Coeruleus, blue
 Length: 3 inches
 Amazon Basin
This species is the largest of the
Corydoras type of Catfishes. The
young specimen might be confused
with *C. aeneus,* but its body is chunk-
ier, its dorsal fin is higher (like a sail),
and its head is more pointed. The
Hump-backed Catfish is very useful
for cleaning out *Tubifex* worms that
have become established in gravel. It
is very hardy, fast growing, peaceful,
and good for larger community tanks.
Very little is known about its breeding
habits, but most likely it spawns similarly to species of *Corydoras.* Temperature, 75° to 80°.

Corydoras schwartzi

Brochis coeruleus

Hoplosternum thoracatum

Hoplosternum thoracatum
(Cuvier and Valenciennes)
Popular name: Hoplo Cat
Meaning of name: Hoplosternum,
armed sternum, thoracatum, refers to
the thorax
Length: 6 inches
Panama to Brazil
Often wrongly known as a spotted
Callichthys. Callichthys callichthys, a
bubble-nest builder, has been bred repeatedly. *Hoplosternum thoracatum*
is a close relative that also builds a
bubble-nest, but should not be confused with *Callichthys,* as there are
certain differences in bony structure.
In 1955, still another closely related
fish appeared on the market: *Dianema
urostriata.* It has a very deeply forked
tail.
Hoplo Catfishes are very active
scavengers, well suited for large tanks.

Their vigorous rooting leaves no section of the aquarium untouched, and
only deep-rooted plants can withstand
such activity. No *Tubifex* worms will
ever become established in tanks containing a Hoplo Cat.
Mature males can be readily distinguished from females by their generally larger size and the thickened, orange colored spines of the pectoral
fins. When breeding, male Hoplo Catfish build large nests of froth at the
surface, usually underneath a floating
lily pad. In the aquarium, they readily
accept substitutes. A piece of glass or
plastic, suspended horizontally from
the frame of the aquarium and touching the surface, or a floating but se-
curely anchored plastic dish with a
smooth bottom will do nicely. The
nest-building is accompanied by much
noise, caused by the slurping of air and

the expelling of bubbles through the gills. Spawning usually begins during the nest-building period. In fact, the male enlarges the nest considerably after spawning is completed.

The spawning act itself is one of the strangest in the world of fishes. The pair will circle each other a few times under the nest in mid-water, while the female is trying to gain a position to the side of the male. He then stops and quick thrusts of her body glues the eggs to the underside of the lily pad. This process is repeated from twenty to thirty times, resulting in an average spawn of two hundred fifty eggs. Large spawns can consist of almost five hundred eggs.

After all eggs have been deposited, it is best to remove the female.

The male busily enlarges the nest and, taking a position in mid-water

Dianema urostriata

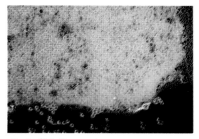

Nest of **H. thoracatum**

slightly tilts his body, turning his ventral side toward the female. Hanging from his vent, a thin, thread-like structure can be observed now, about one-half inch long. This appears to be a very elongated genital papilla. The female takes the papilla into her mouth, and at that very moment releases from three to ten eggs into her tightly cupped ventral fins. At the same time, the male releases sperm, which the female apparently stores in her mouth until she deposits the eggs she is now holding between her ventral fins into the nest. After resting on the bottom for a few seconds, she swims up to the nest, turns upside down, blows a few bubbles, (and, presumably, deposits the sperm at this time) and with a few below the nest, guards the eggs with utmost vigor. Keeping the sharp, serrated pectoral spines fully spread and locked in position, he drives off even the largest intruder with powerful whip-like movements of his body.

The eggs hatch in three to four days and helplessly sink to the bottom. The male, whose guardianship instinct is much diminished by now, should be removed. In another four to five days, the fry are ready to take food. They can consume copious amounts of newly hatched brine sprimp.

It is possible to let the eggs hatch artifically. Since they stick so tenaciously to whatever was used in nest-building, the whole "nest" can be removed and submerged in a separate

Plecostomus *spec.*

tank for hatching and rearing. This tank should be well aerated. A word of caution: a guarding male will attack the hand removing the nest!

THE SUCKERMOUTH CATFISHES
FAMILY LORICARIIDAE

The Suckermouth Cats are elongated, flattened Catfishes with a full coating (except on the abdomen) of bony plates that are rough with a thick coating of fine prickles. The mouth forms a sucking disk under the head. The adipose fin, if present, is supported by a bony spine covered with fine prickles. The Suckermouth Cats inhabit South America as well as Central America to Nicaragua.

Plecostomus species
Popular name: Suckermouth Catfish

Meaning of name: Plecostomus: folded mouth

Length: Up to 10 inches

Nearly all of South America East of Andes

There are many species of this genus and several have been imported. With their peculiar mouths, they can cling tenaciously to any smooth surface. They are well equipped for eating algae, which they do industriously, even going up and down *Sagittaria* leaves without injuring them. They are most active at night.

Color: gray with brown markings. Eats anything. They have a keen sense

Loricaria *species*

of property rights and bully or kill other scavenger fish, even their own smaller brethren. One to a tank is best. Temperature, 62° to 80°.

Loricaria species
Popular name: Whiptail Loricaria
Meaning of name: Loricaria, armored one
Length: 3-5 inches
Tropical South America
Many species of *Loricaria* have been imported but few identified. Purchasers of this species need not suspect damaged goods because there is no thread on the lower half of the tail. The "whip" is on the upper part only. Body markings are olive grays and near blacks. Body quite shallow and rather broad. Not a very active fish, but good algae eater.

Few people have bred Whiptails. Forty very large amber-colored adhesive eggs were placed in the form of a narrow triangle on top of a clean rock. Male sits over eggs, crudely fanning them for the incubation period of eight days. He cleans them with his mouth, removing any fungus. Ignores the babies.
Temperature, 78°.

Farlowella species
Popular name: Twig Catfish
Length: 8 to 10 inches
Southern Guyana
These are highly specialized fishes whose diet consists almost exclusively of algae. Very few individuals accept other foods. They should not be kept together with other algae eaters, such as *Plecostomus* or *Gyrinocheilus*, the

Farlowella *species*

Mouth of **Farlowella**

Indian Algae Eater, since they cannot compete with such active species.

The mature males develop bristles

on side of head. Rarely bred in captivity. Temperature, 72° to 80°.

Otocinclus species

Popular name: Dwarf Suckermouth Catfish

Meaning of name: Otocinclus, sieve-ear, in allusion to the holes in the skull in the ear region

Length: 1¾ inches

Tropical South America East of the Andes

Many of these species have been imported but few identified. One of the more remarkable members of this species is *Otocinclus affinis*. An interesting little "scavenger fish," it goes over leaves more thoroughly, from top to bottom, than any other fish. When tired, it seems to take a nap, perched in some odd posture, usually atop a leaf. Peculiarly, the fish sometimes swims upside down, clinging to the water surface as snails do and apparently clearing it with its sucker mouth.

Otocinclus has seldom been bred. A well-known American wholesale breeder who has been successful with the fish writes: "On the glass side of an aquarium, much in the manner of *Corydoras aeneus*, they lay single eggs the size of a small pinhead. They hatch in about forty-eight hours, the transparent young sticking to the glass for two days before venturing to the bottom to look for food."

This species causes the large wholesaler much financial grief, for when newly received, crowded in bare containers, and lacking plant life, they die off like flies. Under the better condi-

Otocinclus affinis

tions supplied by the retailer and the aquarist, they are more at home and live satisfactorily.

A most inoffensive fish, which once acclimated, seems fairly hardy. Temperature range, 68° to 82°.

THE KILLIFISHES
FAMILY CYPRINODONTIDAE
The Killifishes, or Egg-laying Tooth-carps, belong to the order Cyprinodontiformes along with their live-bearing relatives, the Guppies, Swordtails, Platies and Mollies. The Killies are well distinguished from the Live-bearers by the absence of the external sex organ or gonopodium (the modified anal fin) of the males.

There are over 200 species of Cyprinodontidae known, most of them inhabiting Africa and America. Southern Asia has only a few species.

In the culture of the Killifishes are several specific features in which they differ from most other families. For one thing, few or none give one big spawning all at one time. Pairs usually spawn a few eggs a day over a more or less extended period. The eggs are tough-shelled, usually with some long thin filaments or "hairs" attached to

them and are more often placed singly among dense, bushy plant growths (such as *Riccia*), or (in certain genera) placed in the mud of the bottom. Finally the eggs take longer to hatch than those of most other small aquarium fishes. The shortest time is about one week, the average is about two weeks, while with some of the annual species, the eggs may take several months to hatch. With the tropical species, spawning often takes place in an aquarium for several extended periods throughout the year. Few of the North American species have been spawned extensively by aquarists.

After the sexes have been separated for one or two weeks and well fed with nourishing food, spawning will usually commence as soon as they are placed together in a well lighted, healthy aquarium containing the necessary bushy plants (see "Annual Killifishes" for the mud spawners). Nylon spawning mops may be used instead of the plants. As the spawning goes on day after day, the easiest method of handling the eggs is to remove the bushy plants (or spawning mops) containing the eggs about once a week and place them in a rearing tank. The rearing tank should be large enough and well enough planted to enable smaller, more recently hatched young to escape their older brethren. Eggs laid over two or three weeks apart should not be placed in one rearing tank.

Spawning behavior is almost always the same throughout the family. The male comes up alongside the female and pushes her broadside against the plant growth. There, with fluttering fins and trembling bodies, a single egg is laid and fertilized. Then the process is repeated. Only one pair spawns together at one time. Extra males should not be present, but one male may spawn with several females. The eggs are about the size of a pin head, which is considered fairly large, and consequently produce fry of good size. Newly-hatched brine shrimp can be used as the first food. Growth is rather rapid.

The large babies sometimes eat the small ones. While the dwarfs of any large hatching of fishes may as well be disposed of in that way, it must be remembered that there is usually a week's difference in age of a lot of Killifish young and it would not be fair to assume that the small ones are runts. To save the little fellows through their infancy, they should be occasionally sorted for size. A female may produce 400 eggs during a breeding season.

The species of *Aplocheilus* and *Epiplatys* have flat heads and large mouths. With some others more or less similar in appearance, they are sometimes spoken of as "the *Panchax* group," but this grouping has no basis in classification. The eggs of these genera take about two weeks to hatch at 75°F.

Some Killies, such as the larger species of *Aplocheilus, Epiplatys,* and *Aphyosemion,* and all or nearly all the annuals, possess a somewhat combative temperament, and males often attack and sometimes kill other Killies and occasionally even members of other groups. Spawning females should always have a place to retire from the attentions of overly ardent or combative males. Species of such disposition are better left out of a community aquarium.

Many of the Killies are great jumpers and will leap through very small openings left in the tank cover.

Killifishes are the favorites of many hobbyists, but unfortunately, very few species are offered for sale in petshops. But an organization devoted to the study, propagation, and maintenance of these fishes was formed many years ago. Members of this organization—the American Killifish Association—trade in fish and eggs of many species and publish information in monthly bulletins. Membership is available to anyone interested in Killies, and details about the organization can be found in current hobbyist magazines.

Fundulus chrysotus
Holbrook
Popular name: Goldear Killifish
Meaning of name: Fundulus, bottom fish; chrysotus, golden-ear, with reference to golden gill plates
Length: 3 inches
Southeast United States

Although this handsome fish is very variable, it is easily recognized. On its olive sides are a few spangles of green gold, usually mixed, on the male, with round red dots. Sometimes added to these are irregular islands of black. Extremely beautiful specimens are sometimes seen in which the red dots strongly predominate, while a deep reddish hue extends into all of the fins,

Fundulus chrysotus

Aplocheilus lineatus

even with the female, which in the ordinary form has them clear. The light spot on the gill plate is green to gold. Eyes, usually yellow. There is another strain that is spotted heavily with black.

The species is a typical egg-dropper, preferring such plants as *Myriophyllum* for spawning purposes. The eggs at 75° hatch in about 12 days, and the young are easily reared. The female is less colorful.

The fish is highly regarded by European aquarists and even by some Americans. A snail-killer, it sometimes rips fins of other fishes.

Temperature, 60° to 80°.

Aplocheilus lineatus
(Cuvier and Valenciennes)

Meaning of name: Aplocheilus, simple lip; lineatus, striped

Formerly known as *Panchax lineatus*

Length: 3¹/₂ to 4 inches

India

The colors of this species vary so much according to the light in which it is placed that one picture can show a composite of the truth. At times the lines of metallic scales seem like rows of tiny mirrors of burnished gold. Both sexes may be of a uniform, pale green color, but the female always has more and stronger vertical bars and very few red dots. The black spot at the base of the dorsal also identifies her.

This is the best known of the *Aplocheilus* species, as well as the easiest to breed. It has a mouth of considerable capacity, and in its larger sizes the fish can suddenly dispose of a half-grown Guppy.

The eggs are laid singly in fine-leaved plants or spawning mops and hatch in about two weeks. The fry are large enough to handle brine shrimp nauplii.

Epiplatys dageti
Popular name: Firemouth Killifish
Meaning of name: Epiplatys, very flat above, with reference to the head; dageti, after the French ichthyologist Daget. Formerly known as *E. chaperi*

Length: 2 inches

Gabon, W. Africa

One of the true old favorites. While of recent years it has been crowded by more showy species, it holds a place in many collections. It is fairly hardy and of a popular size.

Epiplatys dageti

A small but very individual color characteristic of the male is the fiery appearance of the lower lip and sometimes also the throat, best seen from the front view. Another peculiarity of the species that makes it easy to recognize, and at the same time tell the sex, is the pointed extension, in the male, of the lower part of the tail fin. This is a peculiarity that clearly sets the species apart from any of its relatives, near or far.

Though a free breeder, its eggs and fry are considerably smaller than those of *Aplocheilus lineatus*. Infusoria are recommended as a first food. Temperature, 65° to 90°.

Aphyosemion australe
(Rachow)
Popular name: Lyretail
Meaning of name: Aphyosemion, a fish with a banner; australe, southern

Length: 2¹/₂ inches
Cape Lopex, Africa

When not kept in conditions to its liking, it "folds up," becomes narrower, does not spread its fins and is apt to resign from life altogether. In a favorable environment, it is not a delicate fish.

Considering that it comes from tropical Africa, it stands water of moderate temperature very well, 68 to 70 degrees suiting it admirably, although for breeding it should be kept warmer, say 72 to 74 degrees. However, it is very particular about *aged* water, preferably a little acid, about pH 6.8. This is important in breeding.

Eggs are deposited, a few at a time, among such plants as *Riccia*, or on artificial, floating, spawning mops. They are rather easily seen, and parents do not touch them. There is no advantage, however, in keeping the

Aphyosemion australe, *2 Males*

breeders with the eggs, once they are through the spawning period, which is likely to last several weeks. Hatching period, about 10 to 12 days. The fry grow rapidly if fed plenty of newly hatched brine shrimp.

The coloration of the male is a rich brown. Females are tan colored and have unmarked fins.

Aphyosemion bivittatum, *Male*

Aphyosemion bivittatum
(Loennberg)

Meaning of name: Aphyosemion, a fish with a banner; bivittatum, two-striped

Length: 2½ inches
Tropical W. Africa

The fish itself varies considerably in color, only showing its best in aged water in a well-planted aquarium, and in not too much light. Live food is important to it.

It moves about the aquarium dart-

Aphyosemion bivittatum, *Female*

ing and then standing still, balanced by a continuous movement of the pectoral fins.

Aphyosemion gardneri

By nature, the species is suited to living with other fishes, but special care should be taken to keep it only in old water. On the whole, it is one of the "touchy" species, requiring skilled handling.

Like other members of the family, it deposits eggs among plant thickets. These hatch in about 12 days, at a temperature of 72 degrees. The young vary much in size and should be graded to prevent cannibalism.

Aphyosemion gardneri

Meaning of name: Aphyosemion, a small fish with a flag (referring to the fins); gardneri, after a personal name
Length: 2¹/₂ inches
Nigeria

A beautiful and hardy Killifish, but, as is the case with so many of them, males do not tolerate each other's company very well. On occasion, males of this species will attack fishes of different species.

They are prolific breeders, depositing eggs in fine-leaved plants or artificial spawning mops near the surface of the water. It takes approximately 10 to 12 days for hatching, and the youngsters are large enough for feeding on newly hatched brine shrimp nauplii.

Temperature, 70° to 78°.

Roloffia occidentalis
(Loennberg)

Popular name: Golden Pheasant
Meaning of name: Roloffia, of the ichthyologist, E. Roloff; occidentalis, from the west
Length: 3 inches
Tropical West Africa

Not often imported, this striking Killifish may be considered in the "select" class among aquarium fishes.

It likes aged water and a rather subdued light and does best on live foods. Should not be placed with fishes much smaller than itself. Capable of jumping over an aquarium edge that is several inches above water level. Keep closely covered at all times.

As with most of the Killifishes, the sexes are easy to tell by the pronounced differences between the fins of the male and female. In this instance, the male has a pattern in the tail fin, while the female has none. As might 'be expected, his coloring is much the brighter.

The fish is rather slender up to two years of age, at which time it becomes heavier. The colors continue to intensify, especially the indigo. The odd, lower extension of the anal fin also appears in late maturity. Single large

Roloffia occidentalis

eggs, deposited on the bottom, hatch in about sixty days. Temperature range 70° to 80°.

Jordanella floridae
Goode and Bean
Popular name: American Flag Fish
Names for David Starr Jordan and the State of Florida
Length: 2 inches
Florida

Jordanella floridae

Aquarists have not always been as successful with this beautiful and interesting species as they could have been had the food requirements been better understood. Apparently *Jordanella* has been mistaken for a sunfish, a strictly carnivorous fish, and has been denied algae, an important part of its diet.

As the male is a strenuous courter, the breeding aquarium should be thickly planted, including, if possible, some *Riccia*. A well-established 5-to-10-gallon tank containing soft algae is best. For several days eggs are deposited in depressions or among rootlets at the bottom and are cared for by the male, who fans them and then protects the babies. The young are easily raised.

The species is rather combative, and is a heavy eater. In absence of algae, some boiled spinach should be alternated with other foods. Florida dealers supply this attractive, interesting fish. It prefers alkaline water. Temperature, 65° to 80°.

THE ANNUAL KILLIFISHES

MUD SPAWNERS

The remaining Killifishes differ from the preceding ones in the fact that they do not deposit the eggs on plants but place them in the mud or very fine sand at the bottom of the aquarium. Even more remarkable is that most of the species, including more especially the South American *Cynolebias* and *Pterolebias* and the African *Nothobranchius*, are annual fishes, completing the life span in less than one year. Whether they are completely annual or not, all of the fishes in this division are short-lived. We know of no specimen that has lived to be two years old. On the other hand, these annuals include the most brilliantly colored of all Killifishes, and the males of some of them are among the most gorgeously colored of all fishes.

The discovery that some of these Killies are annuals became known to aquarists in Germany as early as 1920, but the fact that there is a large group of annual species, all belonging to a group of closely related genera, was not generally known until Dr. George S. Myers presented the evidence in two papers published in 1942 (in Stanford Ichthyological Bulletin) and 1952 (in the Aquarium Journal). It was he who first called them "annuals."

In their native habitats, these fishes live in mud-bottomed ponds and sloughs, sometimes connected with a permanent body of water, but more often not. Towards the end of the rainy season, they spawn in the mud, and the adults then mostly wither and die, usually because the pond simply dries up. The eggs, however, survive, buried in the damp mud under the surface crust. There they remain, for a month and a half to several months. The heat of the sun apparently slows up the development of the eggs, for it has been noticed that eggs kept in water hatch sooner in cooler water than in warmer.

When the rains again begin to fill the pool, hatching occurs almost at once, and a new generation of fishes, born of parents long dead, grows very rapidly. However, the same sort of life cycle transpires even if the body of water in which the fish live does not dry up completely.

Although several species come from tropical Africa and South America, it is well to remember that they naturally inhabit well-shaded, still pools where the temperature does not

Spawning **N. guentheri**

Nothobranchius guentheri

rise excessively. Many capable aquarists have failed with these fishes because of the fixed idea that all exotic fishes must be kept at a high temperature; this is an error caused by a too inflexible interpretation of the word "tropical" as applied to aquarium fishes.

While these fishes are among the more tedious to breed and difficult to handle, their great beauty makes the effort worthwhile and challenges our

ability as aquarists.

Breeding tanks need not be large; even two-gallon bowls can be used for the smaller species. As a bottom layer to receive the spawn, peat moss that has been soaked in water for a few weeks works best.

Nothobranchius guentheri
(Pfeffer)

Meaning of name: Nothobranchius, with pseudo gills; guentheir, after A.

Guenther, ichthyologist
Length: 2 inches
This is one of the most brilliantly colored of the annual Killifishes. They should be kept in fairly soft, slightly acid water and frequently fed with a variety of live and frozen foods. *Tubifex* worms, however, should be fed sparingly, if at all. Adult males are

Pterolebias peruensis

rather belligerent toward each other, and it is best to keep just one male per tank.

In nature, this species is found in very small bodies of water, which often dry out completely during the dry season. This, of course, kills the fish, but their eggs survive the dry spell buried in the mud on the bottom. Within a few hours after the next rain has filled the pond again, the young fish will hatch. Their growth rate is phenomenally fast, and in about six weeks the young fishes are already spawning.

In the aquarium, we can imitate the conditions in nature by keeping these Killies in a small aquarium with a layer of well-soaked peat moss on the bottom. Temperatures in the seventies are best.

Mature fish in good condition will spawn daily, laying one egg at a time

into the peat moss. After about two weeks, the peat containing the eggs should be taken out with a fine net, gently squeezed to remove excess water, air-dried until it is just damp to the touch and then stored for about six weeks in a closed plastic bag or other container at a temperature of 70° to 75°. After the incubation period, the damp peat moss can be placed into a tank containing freshly aged water and presto, within an hour or so, tiny young will appear. They are ready to feed immediately, but require infusoria for a day or two before they can tackle freshly hatched brine shrimp.

Pterolebias peruensis
(Myers)
Popular name: Peruvian Longfin
Meaning of name: Pterolebias, Lebias (type of fish) with wings; peruensis, from Peru
Length: 3 inches
Peru
This is a South American species of annual Killifish, but the conditions for life are the same as for the African *Nothobranchius* species. They also deposit their eggs in the mud on the bottom, but in doing so they dive head first, side by side into it. Therefore, in the aquarium the layer of peat should be sufficiently high (at least 2 inches) whereas for *Nothobranchius* a one-inch layer is more than enough. The egg-drying process is the same as for *Nothobranchius*, but eight weeks of dryness usually gives better results. Fry are also larger and can handle newly hatched shrimp the first day. Growth is extremely rapid, but an

almost constant supply of food is needed.
Temperature 68° to 76°.

THE LIVE-BEARERS
FAMILY POECILIIDAE

The live-bearers are easily distinguished from the Killies by the elongated gonopodium or intromittent anal fin of the male. It is largely by differences in the structure of this organ that the various genera are classified. All the Poeciliids are from the New World, the greatest number of genera in the species occurring in Central America and the West Indies.

There are several groups of viviparous or live-bearing fishes, but many of them are not yet known to aquarists. However, the family includes most of the live-bearers kept in home aquaria, and we interrupt the sequence at this point to give a general account of live-bearer breeding.

Breeding the Live-bearers

Not many years ago, specialists of exotic fishes were often in receipt of letters, usually to "settle a bet," asking whether fishes really have their young born alive. The popularity of exotic fishes has become so general that the public now accepts the phenomenon of viviparous or live-bearing fishes without surprise. No more letters on that point are received. However, there is some basis of truth in the idea that only mammals give birth to their young, for, while many of our aquarium fishes do indeed present developed young to the world, apparently without going through the egg period, this is not precisely true. Fully formed eggs are in the egg duct of the female, where they become fertilized, are hatched and grown to the same point of maturity as the young of egg-laying fishes that have absorbed their yolk-sacs, and are ready to swim freely. In other words, the eggs of viviparous fishes have the protective advantage of hatching within the body of the female, and of entering the world well equipped to meet life on a competitive basis.

While it is true that an egg is the medium through which every live-bearing animal (whether warm- or cold-blooded) transmits the spark of life, there is a great difference between the internal process in mammals and fishes. In mammals, the ovum or egg after fertilization becomes attached to and is part of the mother. Its life stream proceeds from her. Except for the mother's supplying oxygen to the eggs and young, no such relationship exists between ordinary viviparous fishes and their babies.

Period of Development

Females have no definite period of gestation as do warm-blooded animals. The young develop according to temperature and after maturity are delivered at somewhat variable times, dependent upon conditions. Possibly the urge of the mother is a factor, for we know that if one fish is selected from a number of apparently "ripe" females and placed in fresh water, she is liable, through stimulation or excitement, to deliver within an hour. The babies are likely to be just as perfect as those coming from the other females several days later, indicating that they have been well formed for some time. In the mother they lie folded once, with head and tail meeting, and are delivered in this form, one at a time, or occasionally two. Soon they straighten out and swim for the best refuge they can find. The young, when first introduced to the world, are about a quarter-inch long, which is considerably larger than those from most species whose eggs hatch externally.

As has been stated, temperature has a bearing on the period of incubation, but to give the reader an approximate idea of what to expect from average conditions, it may be said that at 75 degrees the time from fertilization to delivery is about four to five weeks. The time may be greatly protracted by a few lesser degrees of temperature. At 67 degrees it may be as long as 12 weeks. As with the egg-layers, however, it is believed that fairly rapid incubation produces the stronger young.

Maturity Age

Different species vary considerably in this respect, and all species vary according to the conditions under which they are reared. A young Guppy, male or female, raised at an average temperature of 75 to 80, given plenty of room and live food, will be ready for breeding in six to eight weeks. Platies are almost as rapid, while the minimum time for the maturity of Mollies is approximately twice as long. Early breeding of females does not affect final size.

Fertilization

Interesting as are the facts already related regarding the live-bearers, they would be incomplete without an account of the fertilization itself. Those not already acquainted with the process will find it instructive. Many aquarist friends have found the theme of reproduction of live-bearing fishes to be an easy and natural medium for preparing young people for the "facts of life." To outward appearances, the sexes are the same at birth. In a few weeks the anal fin of the male fish becomes just a trifle more pointed. As time for maturity approaches, it rapidly lengthens into a straight, rodlike projection, carried backward and parallel to the body, and usually close to it, although capable of being quickly moved at any angle, forward or sideways. All appearances of a fin have disappeared. This is now called the *gonopodium*. In form and length it varies with different fishes. In Platies it is small and not always easily seen. In Guppies and *Gambusia* it is unmistakable, while in such genera as *Phallichthys* and *Poecilistes* it is quite obvious. The tip of the gonopodium varies in shape in different species.

The male in courting grandly spreads all fins and excitedly approaches the female, usually parallel to her and a little from the rear. He may circle her, all the while on the *qui vive*, ready to make a quick thrust from a position of vantage. The act is over in a second. The female never seems to be flattered by these attentions. Nevertheless, "love finds a way," and live-bearing fishes continue to multiply even faster than the rapidly increasing ranks of aquarists.

The live-bearers do not mate in the sense that the Cichlids do, nor the Gouramis. They are not even polygamous, but strictly promiscuous. Reproduction with them is conducted on a basis of what might be termed impersonal opportunism.

Subsequent Fertilization

A female is able to store sperm from one mating for fertilization of four or five successive broods of young. These will be about the same distance apart in time as the time between fertilization and the first delivery. Immediately after a female has delivered her young, the males are intensely attracted to her and double their attentions. Although she is able to deliver another brood without further male contact, the question is whether such subsequent contact would result in part or all of the young inheriting the characteristics of the last male mate. This is brought up for the reason that if a fish breeder wishes to establish the characteristics of a certain male in its descendants, such as, for instance, particularly attractive markings in a Guppy, he would not be safe in assuming that the first four or five broods are necessarily fertilized by the chosen male if the female has, prior to the fifth delivery, been exposed to another male. That presents an interesting subject for research. It is, of course, also a possibility that a second male contact any time after the first delivery of young, but before the fifth, would have no influence on the first 5 broods, but might fertilize later ones.

When Is a Female "Ripe"?

Except with those few live-bearers that are black, or nearly so, there is a contrasting dark area on the female's body, close to the vent. It varies in shape and clearness in different species, but tends towards a crescent form, or sometimes a triangle. This is called the "gravid spot," caused by the dark portions of the internal organs showing through the stretched abdominal walls. This, however, is by no means a sure sign of pregnancy. In some color varieties of Swordtails and Platies, no black spot develops. In others, a male might have it as well. Occasionally, in a light-colored variety, the abdominal wall is so thin and transparent that little heads with eyes can be seen inside, peeping into the outside world. In that case, of course, there can be no doubt about the state of affairs. Most important, however, the sides of the fish bulge when seen from a top or side view. A little experience will give an idea of how far matters have progressed. With fishes, we do not have all the guiding facts that help our own medicos to make their computations in timing human births, but sometimes our guess is just as good!

Frequency

Frequent breeding does not seem to shorten the life nor affect the final growth of either egg-layers or live-bearers. Interference with nature is more questionable.

194   FISHES

Number of Young
Broods may be as few as 3 in number, or well over 100. A fair average for a grown fish to deliver is 40 to 50. Anything over 100 is considered unusual. Some species have fewer and larger young than others. As previously stated, while the size of the female greatly influences the number of young she delivers, it has no effect on the size of the babies. Twins, attached belly-to-belly, are occasionally delivered. They usually die within weeks.

Saving the Young
With all prolific animals, nature seems to set up some barrier so they do not overrun the world. With live-bearing fishes in the aquarium, it is cannibalism on the part of parents. Aquarists can easily circumvent this tendency and save the babies. First of all, the fewer fishes present at the time of delivery, the better. This includes the male, his function having been completed weeks or months previously.

There are two general methods of saving the young. One is by providing them with hiding places, such as plant thickets, and the other is by the use of some mechanical contrivance that prevents the mother from getting at her babies.

Many such mechanical devices have been developed for the preservation of newly-delivered baby fishes. They have their points of merit. The central idea of them is to confine the ripe female in a space where she can live and which provides a small opening (or openings) through which the

young fall or swim, and through which they cannot easily return.

V-shaped arrangements of sheets of glass in aquaria, with the bottom of the V slightly open, can be used in a large way for a number of ripe females at one time. Also a single sheet of sloping glass with the lower edge nearly against one side of the aquarium glass is another variation. Special "breeding traps" can be purchased.

These various mechanical devices have their uses, especially if the aquarist is not in a position to place the expectant mother in a thickly planted tank. It will be found, however, that in well-equipped establishments, where the breeding of live-bearers is conducted on a large scale, traps are seldom used. Preference is given to the other method utilizing thickets of plants as hiding places. The ideal aquarium for the purpose is an oblong one of from 5- to 10-gallon capacity, one-half of which is thickly planted. At the surface should be some floating aquatics such as *Riccia* or Hornwort. Any planting that provides a thicket is satisfactory, such, for instance, as masses of *Anacharis, Myriophyllum* or *Nitella*.

The planted side of the aquarium should be *towards the light*, as this is the natural direction for the young to take. The parent will not give chase among the plants or will do so only feebly. The young sense their danger and are pretty cute at dodging.

There are several advantages to this plan of delivery. The female can be placed alone in the aquarium well in advance of expected appearance of young, thereby avoiding a certain amount of danger in handling her at a later time, which might cause injury, and more probably, premature birth. In such an aquarium she can be well fed and kept in fine condition. With the aid of the open space, she can easily be caught and removed after the completion of her duty to her species—and to her owner. By this scheme, practically no young are lost, and they grow well when left in the planted aquarium.

Shallow water seems best adapted to the needs of the young of the live-bearing species, although this is not an absolute requirement. From birth to two weeks old they seem safer in depths of seven inches or less.

Premature Births

As has already been stated, the handling of a live-bearing female shortly prior to her time for delivery is liable to result in premature births, even with gentle care. Some kinds of fishes are more sensitive than others. Guppies are seldom affected, while Mollies are touchy. The invariable sign of a premature delivery is when the yolk-sac is not fully absorbed and is to be seen attached to the belly of the baby. Such young are heavy, and unable to rise from the bottom without effort. Few of them survive. If the sac is small, it is advisable to salt the water, one full teaspoon to the gallon.

Feeding Young Live-bearers

Unlike many egg-layers, young live-bearers spare the aquarist the fuss of providing live microscopic food.

Being born of good size, they can manage newly-hatched brine shrimp at once or will do fairly well on finely powdered fish food of almost any kind. Manufacturers have grades especially for them, but this is only a matter of size. Any granular food can be pulverized for the purpose. Size of food can be increased as the babies grow. They like microworms.

At a reasonably high temperature, say about 75 degrees, they should be fed from 2 to 4 times daily. Whether the food be prepared or living, there should be only enough of it to last a quarter hour. Excess prepared food fouls the water. Too many *Daphnia* reduce the oxygen content. Snails dispose of prepared food the fishes have not taken. For this reason it is advisable to have plenty of them with young fishes of all kinds that are being raised on prepared foods. As the fishes grow, some species will kill the snails. If there is evidence of this, the snails may as well be removed and *Corydoras* substituted.

Sometimes beginner aquarists write that their baby fishes have not grown much in several months. This state of affairs is likely to end in permanently stunting them, even though better conditions are later provided. Some causes of retarded growth are: too small aquariums, too many fishes, too low temperature, too little food, too little live food, infrequent feedings.

When May Young Be Placed with Adults?

The answer to this question depends much on the size of the parents.

Large parents of a given species do not have larger young than small parents, but they can swallow bigger fishes. The offspring of average parents are safe to place with the parents when the young have tripled their length, which should be in a month, with correct feeding. When placing *any* small fish in *any* aquarium, consider what the largest fish in that aquarium might be able to do to the little stranger. Can the big fish swallow the little fish?

posed victim are the only considerations.

Generally, the live-bearers will not eat young fishes if they have a good supply of choice live food for themselves. And, generally speaking, it should be said that any fish introduced into an aquarium is apt to fare better if its hosts and future companions are in that mellow humor that is produced by having had a good meal, particularly if the new arrival happens to be small!

Blue Veiltail Guppy

Female Guppy

Half-Black Guppy

Live-bearers seem to be quite impersonal toward their own particular young or the young of their own species. They are neither more nor less liable to eat them than the young of other parents or of other species. Their own appetites and the size of the pro-

Keeping Species Separate

As a matter of avoiding later confusion, it is best to keep the young of all similar species separate. This is particularly true of the live-bearers. Many of them not only look alike before maturity, but they are liable to breed much earlier than would be expected. Hybridization between different species is not very likely to occur in an aquarium of mixed fishes, but undesired crosses are quite liable to happen between different color strains of the same species, such, for instance, as between red and blue Platies. This causes a degeneracy of pure types. When crosses are wanted, they should be deliberate.

Red Veiltail Guppy

Poecilia reticulata
Peters
Popular name: Guppy
Meaning of name: Poecilia, variable fish; reticulata, net marked, or mottled. Formerly known as Lebistes reticulatus
Length: male, 1¹/₈ inches; female, 2¹/₄ inches
Trinidad, Guyana and Venezuela
Artificially introduced into many other locations.

"Missionary Fish" would be a fitting name for this little beauty, for it far exceeds any other species in the number of convert aquarists it has made. And many of these converts who branched out and became aquarists in a big way still keep Guppies, and still feel that, with their infinite variety of colors, they are the most interesting of all aquarium fishes. Each male is as individual as a thumbprint.

Besides its beauty, the Guppy has other great merits. Scarcely any other fish combines so many cardinal points in such degree. It is a live-bearer, the most popular type of fish. It is an extremely fertile as well as a dependable breeder. It is unusually active. It will thrive in close confinement. It can stand foul water. It has an extreme temperature range of 40 degrees, from 60 to 100. It will take any kind of food. It does not fight. It is not timid. It matures rapidly, an important point for those aquarists breeding for special points. It is subject to few diseases. It can be had everywhere at prices available to everybody.

The activity of the male is extraordinary. Whether flashing about in pure joy of living, or paying court to a female, he is ever the embodiment of intensity. He might well be termed "the playboy of the aquarium."

In highly developed stocks, some of the females appear not only showing some traces of color in the tail fin but also shiny highlights in it. Any color in the female adds value to a show pair.

Many beautiful strains of long-finned Guppies have been developed in the U.S., and breeders in the Orient are mass-producing a fantastic number of colorful Guppies for shipments all over the world.

No fancy breed can long be maintained without tireless vigilance in quickly discarding imperfect males and in the early isolation of virgin line-bred females. Maturity takes place very early, and a female once fertilized by an inferior male is "ruined" as a select breeder until she has dropped all his young—a matter of some 6 months—without attention from another male. Her previous misalliance then has no bad effects on offspring by a later and better mate.

Breeding all sorts of animals for certain qualities, whether done on scientific Mendelian principles, or by "rule of thumb," involves the continual mating of the best close relatives. Unrelated breeders, of just as high a grade, will not give as good results. As before stated regarding fishes, this can be carried on for generations without apparent physical deterioration, but breeders having both quality and good size should be chosen.

Excessive fin development does not occur in the young. Half-grown males of promise are best to use as breeders. The act of fertilizing requires more agility than that commonly possessed by fin-laden males. Besides, Guppies are old at two years.

We do not agree with those who theorize that color inheritance is carried only through the male line. According to sound principles, the female, showing little or no colors, still transmits the influence of her ancestry.

At several points, we have suggested that certain fishes appear to best advantage with the light striking directly on the side we see. That is, from the back of the observer toward the tank. This is especially true of male Guppies. With most aquariums the light comes from the wrong direction for that, but it is a rewarding effort to even temporarily place them in a viewing jar with the sun playing on them.

The Guppy seems to be the only exotic fish species with enough variety of fixable points to establish it as a basis for fish fanciers. Guppy societies exist and have set show standards for judging points.

Most Guppy diseases yield to "salt treatment." This may be carried far, as they can easily stand enough salt to kill most external enemies (and other fishes). The fatal "hollow-belly" can usually be avoided by feeding several times daily on varying foods; live, fresh and prepared. A good average temperature for Guppies is 70° to 88°. They are apt to worry snails to death by nipping at them.

Poecilia sphenops
Cuvier and Valenciennes
Popular name: Liberty Molly
Meaning of name: Poecilia, variable fish; sphenops, wedgeface
Length: 2 to 4 inches
Gulf Coast of Texas to Venezuela
Coming unheralded from Yucatan and imported by Wm. A. Sternke of Opalocka, Florida, in 1935, this color variety of *P. sphenops* created quite a stir and was soon widely distributed, as it proved to be a good breeder. The fish turned out to have so much exuberance (to put it politely) that it became something of a pest in chasing other fishes. This caused its popularity to wane, and possibly the strain lost some of its intense coloring through inter-breeding with other varieties of P. *sphenops*, which could readily be expected. For many years it was impossible to procure specimens showing the original bright coloring. Then, new stocks were imported, and fish farms have made them available.

Kept by themselves in a large aquarium, they make a lively living picture. As they are jumpers, their tanks should be covered with either screen or glass. Temperature; 68° to 80°.

P. sphenops is the most widely distributed species of the genus, so it is not surprising that it is also the most variable as to size and color, and, to some extent, in disposition.

A black strain has been developed by professional breeders and marketed under the name Yucatan Molly. They are easier to keep than the common Black Molly, less prone to diseases, and less selective in diet.

Poecilia sphenops *(Liberty Molly)*

Some Yucatan Mollies have a strong orange crescent at the end of the tail fin, and some have beautiful dorsal fins as shown on "Liberties." None of these colors, nor their variations or combinations, has much bearing on the identification of the species. Even the ordinary color, an olive gray with darker markings, means little. The aquarist's usual problem is to tell *sphenops* from *latipinna*. Fortunately this is not difficult. In *latipinna* the first ray of the dorsal fin starts in *front* of the highest point of the back. With *sphenops* it starts in *back* of the *hump*. The males are the more easily classified.

Mollies are particularly subject to injury in shipment, resulting in mouth fungus, ich, and shimmies. Early salt baths are effective.

Poecilia latipinna
Le Sueur
Popular name: Sail-fin Molly
Meaning of name: Poecilia, variable fish; latipinna, broad-fin
Length: 3³/₄ inches
Coast of North Carolina to Florida; Gulf Coast and N. E. Mexico
This is the usual "Molly" of commerce. Coming from a considerable

Black Yucatan Mollies

Female Speckled Molly of the
"Yucatan" type

Male Black Lyretail Molly
("Yucatan" Form)

geographic range, it varies correspondingly in appearance, especially in that point of importance—the dorsal fin. This varies so greatly that it may class the individual either as a super-fish or as simply "another Molly." In a highly developed specimen, his resplendent dorsal fin is truly a crown of glory. To witness this "sail" fully exhibited in its royal splendor is to see something unforgettable—at least to an apprecia-

tive fish fancier or ichthyologist. Naturally his best display is put on either in a sham battle with another male (they seldom come to blows) or before what might be called his lady of the moment. With all sails set he comes alongside her with insinuating motions and then takes a position across her path as if, with a flurry of quivering fins, to prevent her escape. The colors displayed in these rapid and tense actions

Poecilia latipinna, *Male*

do not seem to be produced by excitement. It is merely an unfolding of the hidden tints, which are always present but displayed only on occasions. The dorsal shows a gentle blue iridescence, but it is in the tail fin that the real color display takes place. The upper and lower thirds become a flashing, light metallic blue, while the center is a beautiful golden yellow. Yellow also covers the forward part of the belly.

The body of the fish is olive, with five narrow brown stripes, separated by rows of a lighter, sawtooth pattern.

Mollies require more care in breeding than most of the live-bearing species, but that extra attention bears fruit. They must have plenty of room, a temperature close to 78 degrees and plenty of the right kind of food. Mildly alkaline or slightly salted water is de-

sirable. By nature, they are largely vegetarian and, being active, eat often. They almost constantly nibble at algae. For this reason alone the fish should be in a large, well-lighted aquarium, which is conducive to the growth of algae. If there is insufficient growth for the purpose, a flake food which contains much vegetable matter should be used. Live brine shrimp, *Daphnia,* or mosquito larvae should be given frequently but not constantly. Feeding 4 to 6 times in 24 hours is desirable, provided each meal is entirely consumed within 10 minutes. This frequent feeding is important, both to breeding stock and the growing young.

At the first sign that a female is ripening, she should be removed to a well-planted delivery tank of about 10 or more gallons in capacity. Gravid females of all Mollies are adversely affected by handling, and the results are reflected in the young being born dead or defective in some respect, usually too heavy to leave the bottom. In fact, Mollies in general and *P. latipinna* in particular had best be handled and moved from one aquar-

Albino Lyretail Molly, Female

Marble Sailfin Molly, Male

ium to another as little as possible. If things are going well with them, a good motto is "Let good enough alone." If only a single pair is being bred, it is preferable to keep the expectant female where she is and remove the male as a matter of precaution, although in the majority of cases, *P. latipinna* does not eat its young.

No female Molly should ever be placed in a small breeding trap. They need room and plenty of greens. All Mollies fail if crowded.

Xiphophorus maculatus
Guenther
    Popular names: Moonfish, Platy
    Meaning of name: Xiphophorus, sword-carrier; maculatus, spotted
    Length: male, 1 ¹/₂ inches; female, 2 inches
    Rio Papaloapan, S. Mexico

Red Wagtail Platies

Beyond doubt, the crest of public interest in exotic aquarium fishes is due in large measure to the outstanding characteristics of a few species. The Platy Fish was one of the true early leaders, and one, through its many good points, that has retained favor while others have come and gone. The Platy, in addition to being one of the most attractive and generally satisfactory fishes in its own right, has contributed to the aquarium a most interesting assortment of hybrids. It may be safely stated that few other fish have made possible such elaborate studies in the inheritance of characteristics. This valuable quality, however, can overwhelm us with complications and many finely-drawn distinctions.

It should be remembered that all color strains or varieties of the species *Xiphophorus maculatus* are still the same species, and that they themselves in breeding pay no attention whatever to the colors of their mates. In practical application this means that if the aquarist is interested in maintaining pure strains, he should keep all breeders of each variety in an aquarium containing only their own kind.

Platies are bred very much the same as Guppies, except that they are a little less likely to eat their young. Also, they do not take very kindly to the breeding trap but should be placed in thickly planted aquaria and fed liberally when young are expected. They have a temperature range from 65 to 90, but do best at about 74 degrees. They are among those fishes that like to pick at algae, and it should be supplied them if possible.

Gold Crescent Platy

Gold Wagtail Platies

Bleeding Heart Platies

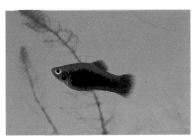

Red Tuxedo Platy

Xiphophorus helleri
Heckel

Popular names: Swordtail and Helleri

Meaning of name: Xiphophorus, sword-carrier; helleri, after the collector, Carl Heller

Eastern Mexico

One of the most important of aquarium fishes. Its striking appearance, interesting habits, and lively ways have made many an aquarium convert of those who saw it by chance. Its variable colors, combined with the fact that it is a good breeder, have made it useful in studying certain laws of inheritance. We have been able to create new strains and new hybrids of great beauty.

The original imported stock was strongly overcast with iridescent green and had metallic green in the tail spike. The saw-tooth line along the center of the body was red and distinctly formed. The tail spikes were straight and long. Only a small proportion of the stock now available has these original characteristics in full measure. That variable quality, which has made the Swordtail a good subject for experimentation, has also made it difficult as to stability, so that clearly-drawn lines in varieties for purposes of competition in aquarium shows are hard to maintain.

The several Swordtails, in addition to being showy, are good aquarium fishes, but a few special characteristics should be remembered. They are wonderful jumpers, especially the

Red Velvet Swordtail

Albino Swordtail

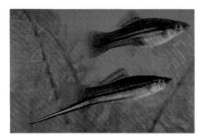

Green Swordtails

Red Wag Swordtail

males. Males are apt to bully one another, so it is best policy to have but one male in an aquarium. Like Mollies, they enjoy eating algae. It should be furnished them, if possible, even if it has to be scraped off another tank. In its absence, a little finely chopped lettuce or boiled spinach is desirable. It is a species that feels the effect of a single chilling for a long time and may never recover from the shimmies (resulting from that cause). They should have an average temperature of 72° to 80° and frequent small meals.

Otherwise, breeding and care as per standard description. The sexes, at first, look alike, but as the male develops to maturity, not only does his anal fin change into an organ of sex, but the lower rays of the tail fin elongate into the well-known spike. If this change occurs while the fish is still small, it will never grow much more. Good-sized males are secured only by growing them rapidly while young. This calls for plenty of room (aquarium of 10 gallons or more), no overcrowding, a warm temperature and plenty of live food. The species likes a flood of light, and shows best in it.

A large female is liable to deliver more than 100 young.

Xiphophorus variatus
Meek
Popular name: Variatus
Meaning of name: Xiphophorus, sword carrier; variatus, varied or variable
Length: 2 inches

Black Lyretail Sword

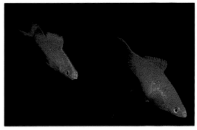

Marigold Swordtails

Brick-Red Lyretail Swords

Red-Tailed Variatus

Black Variatus

Rio Panuco to Rio Cazones, E. Mexico

The specific name of this fish, *variatus*, is surely appropriate. In coloration, it is one of the most variable of aquarium fishes. For this reason it offers aquarists interesting problems in fixing colors.

The males carry the colors, which begin to show at about four months, and are fully developed in a year.

This species is quite hardy and for short periods can stand a temperature as low as 50 degrees. The *X. variatus* is a prolific live-bearer. If well-fed, the parents are not likely to eat their young.

Gambusia affinis holbrooki
Girard

Meaning of name: Gambusia, worthless; affinis, related; holbrooki, after J. E. Holbrook

Length: male, 1½ inches; female, 2½ inches

Atlantic Coast States, Delaware to Florida

To many aquarists, at least in the United States, *Gambusia affinis* represents the beginning of an epoch. It was our first live-bearer. The species was advertised by dealers as the eighth

Marigold Variatus

Gambusia affinis

wonder of the world. Hobbyists were eager to prove or disprove for themselves all claims for this strange fish. All placed them in with fancy lace-tail Goldfish. Soon the beautiful fins of the Goldfish were in shreds, and the Gambusias were banished. But they were kept long enough to prove that they have their young born alive and to demonstrate that they bred faster than purchasers could be found. This is not surprising, for in appearance they have no merit sufficient to offset the disadvantage of their destructive natures. Like other efficient fighters, they give no notice of attack.

G. affinis is a justly famed fish, for it has saved many human lives by eating mosquito larvae. It has been introduced into many parts of the world for this purpose, and its chief service to man has been in destroying the larvae of the mosquito which carries the germs of malarial and yellow fevers. In tropical countries, in situations where the draining of mosquito ditches is impossible or too expensive, the little fish has been successfully brought into service. Its practical value is enhanced because it can live in good or bad water, and will stand a temperature range from 40 to 100 degrees. Success in building and maintaining the Panama Canal depended partly on the solution of the fever problem. *G. affinis* was and still is largely responsible for making Panama habitable to the white man.

There is much confusion in the minds of aquarists about the differences between the two common forms of *Gambusia* in our southern states.

The worst error, and the hardest to eradicate, is the idea that the black-spotted *Gambusias* form a distinct species, *holbrooki*. The black spotting has nothing whatsoever to do with separating the two forms! The facts of the case are these: In the southern United States (excluding Texas for the moment), there are two forms of *Gambusia*, an eastern and a western, practically identical in color, form, size and habits. The eastern form (*holbrooki*), which is found in lowland streams of the eastern seaboard from Delaware to Florida and Alabama, has eight rays in the dorsal fin, and the third ray of the gonopodium shows a deep split when examined under the microscope. The western form (*affinis*) occurs in lowland streams from Alabama to southern Illinois and south in the Texas coastal region to Tampico, Mexico. It has only seven rays in the dorsal fin, and the microscopic split in the third ray of the gonopodium is absent. In Alabama the eastern and western forms meet and merge their distinctive features so that certain individuals from this area cannot be placed definitely as one or the other form. Hence they are not nowadays regarded as distinct species, the western one being known as *G. affinis* and the eastern one as a race of it, *G. affinis holbrooki*.

Both sexes of both *affinis* and *holbrooki* are ordinarily pale gray fishes, often with faint bluish metallic reflections. The dorsal and tail are usually marked with rows of tiny dark dots. The dots in the tail easily distinguish the plain females from female

Guppies. Otherwise, they look much alike.

The velvet black spotting or blotching, which is prized in aquarium specimens, may be present in either *affinis* or *holbrooki*. Dr. George Myers, who collected *affinis* wild in North Carolina, said: "Schools of several hundred *Gambusias* were to be seen swimming in shallow water near shore. In every second or third school a single, or at most two, black males were observed; they were very conspicuous among their pale brothers. The original collectors who sent *Gambusias* north used to catch out these colored 'freaks' with a dip net, pair them with any large females caught in the schools, and ship them as a different species, the so-called '*G. holbrooki.*' These black freaks seem in many cases to breed true, and at least some of our southern dealers seem to have developed strains which breed consistently. Wild black-blotched females are extremely rare, but in the course of man's selective breeding for black fish, a proportion of fairly dark females appear. So far as available data go, the black blotching of either sex occurs about as frequently in the western *affinis* as in the eastern *holbrooki*, but the black color, as can be seen from the foregoing, no more indicates specific difference than does the black color of the black Molly."

For breeding in the aquarium, it prefers a temperature of about 75°. It conforms to the usual type of breeding described for "live-bearers," but is one of the species that is particularly likely to eat its young if given the opportunity. Since they multiply with such tremendous rapidity when in the wild state, it must be that the young very quickly take themselves off to good hiding places. With plenty of natural food, they soon develop to a size which is too large to be swallowed by the parents.

In the matter of food, they are easily suited. While preferring animal substance, they will take any of the prepared articles.

The species is very seldom attacked by any kind of disease.

In some of the streams of southern and western Texas, there are three or four other, very different species of *Gambusia*, at least one of which, the golden Gambusia (*G. nobilis*), has found its way into aquariums.

Belonesox belizanus
Kner

Popular name: Pike Livebearer

Meaning of name: Belonesox, after the garfish, Belone, and the pike, Esox; belizanus, from Belize, Honduras

Length: To 6 inches; females somewhat larger

Central America

Anyone attempting to maintain and possibly breed this species will have to first solve a very fundamental problem: how to supply a sufficient amount of food in the form of live fishes. Nothing short of live fishes will do, although a few individuals will sometimes take live brine shrimp, bloodworms, earthworms, and the like. The fishes are live-bearers but are not very likely to breed if not fed abundantly.

Since their native waters are often slightly brackish—they are mostly

Belonesox belizanus

found near the mouth of rivers—the addition of a little salt to their tank water will be beneficial. About two teaspoonsful of salt per gallon of water is not too much, and the hardier plants can withstand that amount.

Newborn young are already three-quarters of an inch long and nearly complete replicas of their parents. On their very first day of life, they are able to swallow fish of the size of newborn guppies, but will also do well for a while on live adult brine shrimp, live bloodworms, mosquito larvae, glass larvae, and large *Daphnia*. Youngsters grow at different rates, and if left together, larger ones will soon prefer their siblings over other foods. With good care, they will reach adolescence in about four months and full maturity at about six. Full size is attained in about one year.

FOUR-EYED FISHES
FAMILY ANABLEPIDAE

This family contains but one genus: *Anableps*. They are highly specialized fishes, found only in Central America and the Northern Coast of South America. Few are imported and, when available, command a fairly high price.

Anableps anableps
Linnaeus
  Popular name: Four-eyed Fish
  Meaning of name: Unknown
  Length: 8 to 10 inches
  Coast Sections of Northern South America

Four-eyed Fishes are strange creatures, and if the name alone does not arouse the curiosity of the hobbyist, a look at a live specimen definitely will. Their eyes are divided into an upper part for vision above the water sur-

Anableps anableps

face, and a lower part for underwater vision—hence their common name, Four-eyed Fish. They are surface dwelling fishes with positive buoyancy, which helps them float effortlessly just below the surface. In this position, the upper part of the eye is held above the water, but the fish regularly wets that part of the eye by dipping its head every few seconds. Four-eyed Fishes prefer brackish water, since their habitat is the lower reaches of rivers and streams, close to the sea.

Their food consists mainly of insects that have fallen into the water, but in captivity, they learn very quickly to accept other foods, preferably the floating kinds. Although the fish will pick food particles off the bottom, they can only do so with great difficulty.

Shallow water is best for two reasons: one can observe the fish much better when the water level in the aquarium is low, and the fish have less trouble in feeding off the bottom.

Anableps need a fairly roomy tank. It should be arranged with rocks, draftwood and/or plants which reach or protrude above the surface of the water. They are rather scrappy fish, at least among themselves, and should be able to get out of each other's way. Otherwise, the largest one will invariably take command and chase every other one to the point of exhaustion and eventual death.

They are live-bearers. Interestingly, the gonopodium of adult males is movable to one side only, either to the right or to the left. In females, the genital orifice is also located either to the left or to the right, and right-sided males can mate only with left-sided females and vice versa. Up to five large, one-inch babies are born at one time, and the period of gestation might last as long as five months. The fish are most comfortable at a temperature of 78° to 82°.

Meaning of name: Melanotaenia, with a black band; fluviatilis, of the river
Length: 5-6 inches
Northern Australia
Of the three species of Australian Rainbow fishes that have been im-

Melanotaenia fluviatilis

THE SILVERSIDES
FAMILY ATHERINIDAE

The Silversides are common salt-water fishes found on nearly all tropical and temperate coasts. A few permanently inhabit fresh water. The separate spiny dorsal fin and the Cyprino-dont-like mouth will identify fishes of this family.

Melanotaenia fluviatilis
Popular name: Red-tailed Rainbow fish

ported from that continent, this is certainly the most handsome as well as the largest. Thus it requires a slightly bigger tank. This is the species most often offered by petshops today. Red-tailed Rainbows are content with a variety of dried foods, but grow larger and develop more color on a diet of live, frozen, and freeze-dried foods. Water conditions are not very important as long as the water is not too soft or too acid.

They breed like other members of

the Silversides. After a short courtship dance in which the male circles the female with his fins fully spread, the female deposits single, hard-shelled eggs among the fine leaves of plants such as M*yriophyllum* (Foxtail), *Ambulia*, Hornwort, *Cabomba* or on the roots of floating Water Sprite and Water Fern. Artificial spawning mops

Melanotaenia maccullochi
Ahl
Popular name: Australian Rainbow fish
Meaning of name: Melanotaenia, with a black band; maccullochi, named for the late Alan Riverstone Mac-Culloch, ichthyologist at the Australian Museum, Sydney, Australia

Melanotaenia maccullochi

are also accepted. Fry hatch in about one week and immediately become free-swimming. They are very small, requiring infusoria for a couple of days before they can handle newly hatched brine shrimp.

Contrary to most fishes of this shape, the male is usually larger and more deep-bodied. His colors are more intense.

Temperature, 75° to 80°.

Length: 2 ³/₄ inches
Australia
Australian Rainbow fishes attain their beautiful coloration only when mature. Sexes are not too difficult to determine as long as the fish are in good condition. The male is usually a bit more brilliant.

Rainbow fishes readily spawn in fine-leaved plants over a period of several days. The very small eggs hatch in about a week. Fry are tiny and require infusoria as a first food. Temperature, 68° to 80°.

Telmatherina ladigesi
Ahl
   Popular name: Celebes Rainbow fish
   Meaning of name: Telmatherina, bony fish found in puddles; ladigesi, after Dr. Ladiges, ichthyologist in Germany
   Length: 2 to 2 ¹/₂ inches
   Celebes (Indonesia)
   For a fish coming from Indonesia, as this beautiful Rainbow fish does, one would expect it to thrive best in the same soft and acid water as do small species of *Barbus* and *Rasbora* and most other fishes from that area. Quite to the contrary, all Rainbow fishes—and this one is no exception—prefer water that is neutral to slightly alkaline in pH and medium hard. This is the quality of many tap waters, and all one needs to do to make it suitable for these fishes is to age it a few days. If only soft water is available, the addition of salt, about one teaspoonful per gallon, will improve it considerably.
   These Rainbows are schoolfishes, preferring the upper half of the tank where they swim about tirelessly. Because they live in swift-flowing streams, their tank should be well-aerated; they are uncomfortable in water of low oxygen content. Dried foods are readily taken, but preference is definitely given to *Daphnia*, brine shrimp, and mosquito larvae. Of the two dorsal fins, the second is the larger

and more striking, a unique characteristic of all Rainbow fishes. In this case it is lemon yellow, and in males the first rays are separated, much elongated, and jet-black in color. Spawning habits are similar to other members of the family. Single eggs are deposited in fine-leaved plants or roots of floating plants near the surface. Hatching time is approximately eight to ten days at a temperature of 78°. The fry become free-swimming immediately, but seem to grow rather slowly. A fairly high percentage of them never reach the free-swimming state, but become what the literature calls "belly-sliders." This failing is assumed to be caused by keeping the temperature too high, but no definite proof seems to be available. Temperature, 72° to 78°.

THE CHANDIDS
FAMILY CENTROPOMIDAE
   The Chandids are small, brackish and salt-water fishes of the Indian Ocean and Western Pacific. They are very much like the salt-water Cardinal Fishes but differ in having the spiny and soft dorsals connected at the base. Most of the species are translucent.

Chanda wolffi
   Popular name: Wolff's Glassfish
   Meaning of name: Chanda, a native name; wolffi, after a personal name
   Length: 1³/₄ inches
   Southeast Asia
   These are calm and peaceful fish, unhappy in tanks containing many fast-moving fishes. They should only be kept with fishes having the same tem-

Telmatherina ladigesi

Chanda wolffi

perament, or, better yet, entirely by themselves. Although an occasional specimen will take prepared foods, such fare is ignored by most of them. Live food must be offered to keep Glassfish in good health. In this species, there are no obvious secondary sex characteristics.

Chanda wolffi has replaced *Chanda lala*, the old favorite, in popularity with hobbyists, although it lacks the metallic sheen of *Chanda lala*. Apparently, it is more readily available to collectors in Southeast Asia. In addition, it is much more hardy. Temperature, 75° to 82°.

Therapon jarbua

Monodactylus argenteus

THE THERAPONIDS
FAMILY THERAPONIDAE

The Theraponids are spiny-rayed, saltwater fishes of the East Indies that frequently ascend rivers into fresh water. They have two nostrils on each side but differ from most related families in the absence of the small scale-like flap located at the base of the ventral fins.

Therapon jarbua
(Forskal)

Meaning of name: Therapon, shield-bearer; jarbua, a native name

Length in nature: 10 inches; usually much smaller in an aquarium

Red Sea, E. Coast Africa to China, N. Coast Australia

The drooping concentric lines on a ground of shining silver are dark gray to black. The large spot in the dorsal is particularly intense and adds to the already strange aspect of the fish.

Like the Chandids, to which it is closely related, it is a marine fish that enters fresh water; unlike the Chandids, it is an extremely active fish and will accept dried foods. It is very quarrelsome. Seldom imported and has never been bred in captivity.

Although a marine fish, it is easily kept in fresh water at a temperature of about 73° to 78°.

THE BUTTERFLY FISHES
FAMILY CHAETODONTIDAE

Almost all members of this family are marine fishes. Only *Monodactylus* enters freshwater. The deep forms and the scaly fins distinguish them from other aquarium fishes.

Monodactylus argenteus
Lacepede

Meaning of name: Monodactylus, with one finger, referring to appearance of dorsal and anal fins; *argenteus*, silvery one

Length: 4 inches

Indian Ocean

Not knowing that this is a marine fish, one would hardly suspect it. It is beautiful but not with that gaudy display we have come to expect of marine tropicals.

The fish is extremely silvery, while the dark portions of the upper and lower fins represent a beautiful, rich yellow. Preference in purchase should be given to the younger specimens. They will grow rapidly in a large aquarium, *but should not be unnecessarily disturbed or moved about.* Salt water unnecessary. Never bred. Temperature, 75 degrees.

Monodactylus sebae

Monodactylus sebae
Cuvier and Valenciennes

Meaning of name: Monodactylus, with one finger, referring to appearance of anal fin; sebae, personal name

Length: to about 7 inches

Western coast of Africa

Monodactylus are mostly marine fish, but do enter fresh water. They can be kept in either fresh or salt water, or anything in between. These are more quarrelsome than M. *argenteus* and are voracious feeders, needing plenty of live and frozen foods. They will also take freeze-dried and other prepared foods. This fish has been bred and will spawn in brackish water. Temperature, 75° to 82°.

THE ARCHER FISHES
FAMILY TOXOTIDAE

The Archer Fishes are a small family of four or five species from India, Southeastern Asia, and northern Australia. The head is flat above and pointed, the dorsal is set far back, and the soft dorsal and anal fins are scaly.

Natives in Asia have long known that the Archer Fishes shoot water at insects above the surface, but ichthyologists long doubted it, even ascribing the habit to a different fish *(Chelmon)*. Early in the 1900s, European aquarists first saw captive, imported Archers shoot, but it was not until the experiments of the late Dr. Hugh M. Smith in Thailand during the

Toxotes jaculator

1920s that the shooting was fully proved. In 1934, Dr. George S. Myers, while collaborating with Dr. Smith, worked out the structure of the shooting apparatus in the Archer's mouth. Long, colorful articles by Dr. Smith on this extraordinary fish appeared in "The Aquarium" (July, 1939 and August, 1944), and by Commander Alfred Marsack in January, 1952. Extinguishing distant lighted cigarettes at night by a pellet of water is one of their famous acts.

Toxotes jaculator
Pallas

    Popular name: Archer Fish
    Meaning of name: Toxotes, archer; jaculator, hurler
       Length: 5 inches
       Indonesia
       Here is one of the unique showmen

among aquarium fishes, and with the correct properties and settings supplied, it can be depended upon to do its act.

    That a fish could accurately aim a mouthful of water as a missile and bring down a fly seems to strain one's credibility. Aside from the mechanical difficulties of such a feat, anyone with a slight knowledge of optics knows that, due to surface refraction, objects do not appear in their true positions when one is looking into or out of the water, unless, as might rarely happen, the object is directly above or below the observer. A bullet from a rifle aimed at an angle to the water and pointed at a small object below the surface could not hit it unless allowances were made for the optical "blend." The same is true from the underside of the surface, looking out.

The Archer Fish has actually learned to compensate for this and will accurately splatter its prey from a distance of a foot or more and usually bring it down.

It shoots a few drops at a high speed, capable of reaching a distance of ten feet. If the first shot does not bring down the prey, it is followed by a rapid series until the insect falls. Few escape. The Archer's mouth is quite large, and the shooting is done while the lips are just above the surface of the water.

We are told that T*oxotes* varies considerably in color. Dorsal and anal fins are edged black. The six dark bars are a gorgeous black, making the fish easy to remember by its striking appearance, as well as its original way of obtaining its food. It will eat live food that it has not knocked into the water. Meal worms seem to be particularly relished. It will also eat live, adult brine shrimp and will readily learn to take lumps of freeze-dried brine shrimp.

Nothing is known as to sex distinctions or breeding habits. A temperature of 75° proves satisfactory. This is one of those species coming from salt, brackish, and fresh waters; we believe a mixture of sea water is advisable. These fish get along well together and even prove themselves sports by not quarreling when the shooter's victim is gobbled by another fish!

Like the various electric and walking fishes, the Archer Fish is a star attraction at a public fish show, for it will "knock off" live flies as long as the spectators choose to supply them.

THE SCATS
FAMILY SCATOPHAGIDAE

The Scats differ from the salt-water Butterflyfishes to which they are most closely allied in various technical internal features. They cannot be confused with any of the other groups of freshwater aquarium fishes. Most Scats are imported from brackish or fresh water in Indonesia. They do enter the sea.

Scatophagus argus
(Pallas)

Meaning of name: Scatophagus, offal eater; argus, thousand eyed (from the spots)

Popular name: Scat

Length: 10 inches

Indonesia

Although we are told that in nature the fish comes in 10-inch and even 12-inch lengths, the usual size seen in the aquarium is from 2 inches to 4 inches.

The fish is rather flat in form, or "laterally compressed," as it is called. In markings, it is so variable that one would easily get the impression that the different patterns indicate various species. There are two principal types.

One type is known as the Tiger, or Red Scat. Some aquarists believe the markings denote the male fish. While we believe this to be a mistake, we can offer no other evidence of sex.

The second type or variety has numerous round black spots on a greenish silvery body. It is often described as Green Scat.

Of the two varieties, the Tiger Scat has the most striking appearance and brings the best prices. Neither species is cheap.

A growing interest in marine aquariums finds a considerable number of Scats doing well in ocean water at full strength.

There has been much discussion as to whether or not the species can be successfully kept in fresh water. The answer is that it can, although the addition of a moderate amount of sea water or sea salt is advisable. If this is not done, the water should at least be kept in an alkaline condition—say a pH reading of 7.4 or a little higher. This is a good fish to be kept in localities where the water is hard.

fond of *Riccia* and *Nitella*, plants entirely strange to its native brackish and marine waters. Temperature, 70° to 78°.

Owners are usually very fond of this active fish, for it has "personality." It is a heavy feeder and always has a hopeful eye open for the appearance of the master. Quite a pet.

Selenotoca papuensis
Fraser-Brunner
Popular name: Silver Scat
Meaning of name: Selenotoca, selene: the moon; tocus, offspring—born

Scatophagus argus

In nature, the fish is one of the real scavengers of the sea, inhabiting the mouths of rivers and the docks of various tropical seaports. It is, therefore, not surprising to find that it will eat anything, although it is hard to account for the fact that it is extremely

of the moon; papuensis living in Papua (N. Guinea)
Length: 4 inches
A few aquarium fishes can live in either fresh or salt water. This is one that can. If a change is made from one to the other, it should be gradual.

Selenotoca papuensis

The lightly colored portions of this fish are brilliant, mirror-like silver, showing to especial advantage under strong light. The darker portions of the fish are black. No bright colors, nor even tints. Body flat, like that of a Scalare. Another species, *Scatophagus multifasciata*, occurs in Australia.

Altogether, it is a very satisfactory aquarium fish, certainly a showy one.

Scatophagus *spec.*

Eats anything. Never bred. Suited to living with other fishes of about its own size. Swims about the aquarium industriously, always on the move. There is no known method of distinguishing the sexes. Temperature range, 70° to 80°.

THE CICHLIDS
FAMILY CICHLIDAE

The Cichlids are spiny-rayed, basslike fishes found only in Africa, Mada-gascar, and tropical America, south of the Rio Grande in Texas. The sole exception to this is *Etroplus*, three species of which inhabit southern India.

In general the Cichlids are the big fishes of the aquarium. They are well represented by such species as the Oscar (*Astronotus*), Jack Dempsey (*Cichlasoma octofasciatum*), and the Jewel Fish (*Hemichromis bimacula-*

tus). Rather long fishes with slightly flattened, moderately deep bodies. The head, generally of good size, is armed with a strong, jutting lower jaw and small but sharp teeth, well suited not only to battle, but to the requirements of their remarkable habits in breeding, as we shall shortly see.

While a few of the Cichlids are peaceable citizens, most of them fight, especially with members of their own species, and more especially with those of the opposite sex. These battles mostly occur during courtship—terrific lovers' quarrels, as it were. Occasionally it is between mated pairs.

No doubt feeling confident of taking care of themselves in open battle, most of the larger species tear out plants, especially at breeding time.

Breeding Cichlids

With the unique exception of the mouthbrooders (whose habits will be described under their own headings), the Cichlids breed so nearly alike that a general description will fit nearly all of them. The few traits that may be peculiar to a species will be noted under its own special text. For example, that popular favorite, *Pterophyllum scalare* (Angel Fish), requires separate consideration.

The typical breeding actions of Cichlids are certainly the most interesting and highly organized of any known aquarium fishes, especially when the habits of mouthbrooders are added to that which now follows.

Mating itself is, with them, no hit-or-miss affair. At the very beginning, the ancient law of the survival of the fittest is put into practical operation. If raised from youngsters and left to themselves in a large group, pairs will mate themselves at maturity by natural affinity, which is one of the best ways of discovering pairs. Naturally, one needs adequate room and sound stock to carry out this plan. The usual procedure in trying to mate adult fishes that have not been raised together with a minimum of risk is to place them in a large aquarium with a glass partition between. That is their formal introduction. One fish is usually ready to mate before the other, and as flirtation through windows is nothing new in the world, one of them makes the opening advances. As again in our world, it may be either the male or the female to make the first move. This consists of a wagging of the body, spreading of the fins, and a variety of changes in coloring. When the "party of the second part" returns these salutations and shows signs of approval, it is time to take out the partition and note what happens. Usually the courtship continues, and it is not long before the "kissing" stage develops. This is where one of the uses of strong jaws comes in. They grasp each other by interlocking the lips and then begins the first real test. Each tugs and twists the other, apparently in a test of strength. They may go through the performance several times. If they do this repeatedly without either losing their "nerve," they may be considered to be as well mated as though they have a marriage certificate. But it often happens that one of them takes fright and beats a retreat after one of those vigorous kisses. Fear is fatal, and the victim of it is liable to get killed unless a safe retreat is found, or a kind fate in the person of the owner separates them.

Sometimes a subsequent trial will prove more successful, but it is advisable to try some other pairing, if substitutes are on hand. Certain fishes will reject or kill several proposed mates before meeting an agreeable affinity.

Owing to the physical tussle which takes place, an effort is usually made by the aquarist to match the candidates in size, but there are many instances of happy unions between fishes where disparity in this respect is great. Whether or not both fishes are ready to mate is the important thing. Their courtship promotes the elimination of the unfit.

To return to the actual business of breeding—let us consider the proper conditions which should be provided. Success is more likely in large aquaria. Among the larger species, 3 inches is about minimum breeding size. Some fishes should be bred in an aquarium of not less than 10 gallons. Twenty would be better. As size of the pair increases, follow with proportionate room. It will pay.

Water should be old and at a temperature between 75 and 80 degrees. The best bottom covering is approximately 2 inches of well-washed sand. Any moderately good light is satisfactory. Omit plants for most species. Exceptions in this respect will be noted.

For a few days prior to breeding, the fishes dig holes in the sand. They also start cleaning a surface which they regard as suitable to the reception of their adhesive eggs. This spot may be the side of the aquarium, a large stone, inside or outside of a flower-pot laid on its side, or even a spot on the bottom of the aquarium from which the sand has been fanned away. It has been observed that a light-colored surface is preferred to dark. For this reason some of our fish breeders place a piece of marble or other light-colored stone in the aquarium with mated Cichlids.

The breeding pair takes nothing for granted as to cleanliness. Regardless whether they select a mossy side of the aquarium or a piece of marble fresh from the quarry, the sacred spot to receive their eggs must be painstakingly gone over to insure its absolute cleanliness. They bite, scrape and polish it with their teeth until no flaw can be found.

A day or two prior to the actual spawning, both fish develop from the vent a breeding tube, or ovipositor. It first appears as a very small point or nipple. Whether it is a Cichlid or certain other species which deposit their eggs in a like manner, the appearance of the nipple is regarded as a sure sign that the fish is ripe for breeding. The tube shortly before spawning increases in length. In large specimens it may be as long as a quarter inch. It disappears within a week after spawning.

In general it is not easy telling the sexes. In older specimens the males often have longer pointed dorsal and anal fins. Where there is any distinctive difference in markings, this will be described in connection with the species. When the females are ripe, they are slightly fuller, but not in a pronounced way. It will be found that the breeding tube of the female is slightly blunt, whereas in the male it is pointed.

All things now being in readiness, the female approaches the prepared spawning spot and touches it lightly with the breeding tube, depositing one or more eggs. The male immediately follows, and with like action sprays the eggs with his fertilizing fluid. This is repeated many times over a period of perhaps 2 hours, when finally there may be from 100 to 2000 eggs laid in close formation. As this whole operation is carried on by a sense of touch and the eggs adhere very lightly, it is quite remarkable how few are lost or knocked off.

The spawning operation being completed, each fish takes turns fanning the eggs with the pectoral fins or tail. They relieve each other every few minutes. It is a popular idea that this fanning is to supply oxygen to the embryo within the egg. We know that bird eggs need oxygen, but with fish eggs there is also another consideration. As fungus is the great enemy of the eggs and the parents go to no end of trouble to have everything immaculate, presumably to avoid this danger, it seems quite likely they are preventing fungus-bearing particles of dirt from settling on the spawn. Sometimes, despite care, fungus develops on a few eggs. It attacks all infertile eggs. Apparently sensing the danger of its spread, the fishes eat the affected eggs. This sometimes ends in all the eggs, good and bad, being eaten.

At a temperature of 80 degrees the eggs hatch in about 4 days. Now begins the next of the several remarkable stages in the breeding habits of these fishes. The parents scrape the eggs off and the fry are carried in the mouth of either of the parents and deposited in a depression in the sand. It may be newly dug or one left from the home-building connected with the early part of mating. The parents alternate in making the trips between the hatching place and the depression until all are transferred. In some instances the fishes set up a stream so that neither end of the line is left unguarded. Each stands guard at one end, and as everything is in readiness for the transfer of young, a signal is given in fish language, and they dash past each other to the opposite terminus.

The young in the depression look like a vibrating, jelly-like mass (not very easy to see). For several days they are moved from one depression to another, gently carried in the mouths of the parents. While it is generally conceded that the lower animals do not reason things out, the result is often the same as though they do. What they do "by instinct" is often wiser than our actions guided by reason. Whether the apparent reasoning in the actions of animals is of their own creation or is a reflection of the master mind in nature makes little difference. Reasons for everything exist. It is interesting to speculate on them, and if we attribute higher thinking powers to our friends the fishes than they actually possess, we are only giving them the benefit of the doubt.

Cichlids have not only the most highly developed breeding habits from the social standpoint, but combine with them a seeming understanding of certain scientific principles which, as far as man is concerned, were discovered but yesterday. These are the recognition of the dangers from bacteria, and of their control through cleanliness. Reference has already been made to the scrupulous care in cleansing the spawning surface and to the eating of such eggs as have been attacked by fungus. Various interpretations may be placed on the practice of moving the young from one hole to another. As this is begun before the babies are old enough to eat anything, it cannot be to provide new pastures. One hole would be as safe from enemies as any other. Besides, in the open places where these fishes breed, they are absolutely fearless in the defense of their young, so the theory of safety may be dismissed. The theory which is in line with their other actions points to cleanliness, if you will. The babies are picked up in the mouth, a few at a time, and apparently chewed. They are only rolled around harmlessly and discharged into the next depression. Every last one is so treated. It is the fish's baby bath. Each one emerges perfectly cleansed of any particles. By using a series of depressions for the purpose, the parents are absolutely certain that all babies were "scrubbed," of which they could not be sure if they were kept in one place.

After four to ten days the yolk-sacs of the young have been absorbed, and they swim up in a cloud with the parents, usually in formation, headed one way. Stragglers are gathered up in the mouths of the parents and shot back into the school. This family unit is very beautiful to see and gives the aquarist one of his biggest and most lasting thrills. How long the parents and young should be left together is a question largely of sentiment. In the wild, the parents undoubtedly can be of much use to the young by protecting them after they are swimming about, but in the aquarium their usefulness ends at the point. The pleasure of seeing the parents and young together is the only reason for not separating them promptly. No hen could be more solicitous for her brood than are these devoted fish-parents for their fry. In their defense they are the very embodiment of savage fury, no matter what or how large the real or imaginary enemy. The owner himself had better not poke his nose too close to the water when peering into the domestic affairs of a large pair of Cichlids unless he wishes to have it shortened.

The young of the larger Cichlids are a fair size by the time the yolk-sac is absorbed and for the most part can get along without infusoria if newly hatched brine shrimp or finely-sifted *Daphnia* are to be had.

Theoretically these interesting pairs divide every domestic duty equally. It sometimes turns out that one is a better parent than the other, but resentment is clearly shown by the mate on whom the heavier part of the burden is shifted. An effort is made to drive the negligent parent to its duty. This failing, open warfare is liable to occur, resulting in the breaking up of matrimonial arrangments, the eating of eggs or young, and the death of the principal at fault. In other words, these fishes seem to have and to carry out a sense of justice. Otherwise we may look at it as the elimination both of the unfit parent and of its progeny. The eating of the eggs by either fish is, for the same cause, liable to end in the same way. Here, as elsewhere in animal life, defective individuals are eliminated by normal ones.

With many Cichlids it is possible and even advisable to hatch and rear the young away from the parents. This method is described under the heading of *Pterophyllum scalare.*

Some tact should be shown in approaching an aquarium containing eggs or young, as the parents are liable to misinterpret the intentions of the interested owner and eat their young to thwart the imagined enemy.

When the young and parents are finally separated, it is well to keep an eye on the old couple, as each may suspect the other of being responsible for the disappearance of the babies, and open an attack in reprisal.

Cichlids all tend towards carnivorous appetites, but few of them insist upon a diet exclusively of meats. While they do very well on live adult brine shrimp, live worms, flies, mosquitolarvae, scraped meat, shrimp or fish (cooked or uncooked), *Daphnia*, etc., they will take various frozen and freeze-dried foods as well. In a warm temperature—75 to 85 degrees—the

fishes are heavy eaters, and should be fed not less than twice daily.

Most of them will stand a reasonably wide range of temperature, about 65 to 90 degrees, although with valued specimens it might be unwise to risk anything below 68 degrees.

Cichlid parents, except Mouthbrooders, should be fed while caring for young. Live *Daphnia* have the double advantage that they drop young for the baby fishes and are themselves eaten by the breeders.

Large Cichlids live long. It is not uncommon for them to reach ten years, although after five years they are likely to develop certain signs of age not connected with feebleness. There are three such points that may be noted. The mouth does not close completely in breathing; a spinal hump forms just in back of the head; the colors become more fixed and permanent and do not change so readily under excitement.

Cichlids are commonly not good community fishes, although a number of big ones in a very large tank get along without trouble.

Aequidens portalegrensis
(Hensel)
Meaning of name: Aequidens, with teeth of same length; portalegrensis, for Porto Alegre, Brazil
Popular name: "Port"
Length: 4 to 5 inches
Southeast Brazil
Usually considered to be the most kindly of this general type and size of fish. Quite easily bred, even in aquaria that are too small. That is, it will manage in a ten-gallon aquarium, when it

Aequidens portalegrensis

ought to have a fifteen-gallon or larger.

The sexes are not easily told, but the male has more spangles, especially in the tail fin. The species is easily recognized by its blunt face and the peculiar pattern in the tail.

Apistogramma ramirezi
Myers and Harry
   Popular name: Ram
   Meaning of name: Apistogramma, in reference to peculiar lateral line; ramirezi, after Sr. Manuel Vicente Ramirez of Caracas, Venezuela
   Length: 2 inches
   Western Venezuela
One of the outstanding importations of 1947, this strongly individual little fish with a saddle-shaped dorsal has attained permanent popularity. It is not only beautiful but also easily

bred. It is free of that aggressiveness which marks most Dwarf Cichlids. While courting, males challenge and chase each other, but no harm is done.

The strong violet hue seen in adults is variable. It shows best in direct sunlight. Female shows rosy spot on sides when ready to spawn. She takes the lead in breeding and care of young. A tall spike at the front of dorsal fin indicates the male. A gold-colored form of A. *ramirezi*, sometimes called Albino Ram, is available. However, it is not a true albino, since it retains many of the iridescent spots of the wild form and also lacks the characteristic pink eye of true albinos.

Eggs are usually placed on a flat stone. Both parents fan the eggs, but the female takes a more active part in guarding the nest and young. Eggs can

Apistogramma ramirezi

also be hatched in a separate container as described for Angel Fish. Soft slightly acid water preferred. Temperature, 70° to 80°.

Astronotus ocellatus
(Agassiz)
  Popular name: Oscar
  Meaning of name: Astronotus, marked with stars; ocellatus, with eye spot
  Length: up to 10 inches
  Guyana, the Amazon, and Paraguay
  Allow us to present a strange Cichlid of such odd appearance and ways that one could well believe it to belong in another family. The scales are not very visible, the fish seeming more to be clothed in a sort of olive suede leather, handsomely decorated by a few fiery orange markings. Several color varieties have been developed.

When alarmed they have a peculiar habit of assuming a close head-to-tail position and doing a sort of slow roll.
  When young, *A. ocellatus* will feed on live food of the usual kind; when adult, they feed on one- to two-inch fishes. However, they can be raised just as well on lumps of freeze-dried brine shrimp, washed canned shrimp or small pieces of lean raw beef. Given a large tank, 55- to 100-gallon capacity, they spawn readily. They are excellent parents. Temperatures 70° to 80°.

Cichlasoma festivum
(Heckel)
  Meaning of name: Cichlasoma, thrush-body; festivum, gaily attractive, festive
  Length: 5 to 6 inches
  Amazon
  The magnificent oblique bar, trav-

Astronotus ocellatus

Astronotus ocellatus, *"Red Oscar"*

Cichlasoma festivum

ersing the body from the mouth to the upper tip of the dorsal fin, gives *C. festivum* a unique standing among aquarium fishes. The thread-like extensions or "feelers" seen on the ventral fins are a little longer than we commonly see among Cichlids. These increase with age, but nothing to compare with those on *Scalare*. The general color of the body is silvery with a green cast. The fins have none of the color markings common to many species of the genus. This fish is at its best in a size of about three inches. When it gets larger the markings are apt to become less distinct. Breeding temperature, about 82°.

The fish is fairly hardy, especially as it becomes older and larger. It is difficult to mate. Although not a timid fish, it seems to prefer privacy when mating and caring for its young.

Cichlasoma meeki
(Brind)
Popular name: Firemouth
Meaning of name: Cichlasoma,
thrush-body; meeki, for Professor Seth
Meek
Length: 4 to 5 inches
Yucatan

Not every fish has a pronounced individual characteristic marking. *C. meeki* has two: the green-edged spot at the base of the gill plate and a fiery red color along the lower mouth which often extends into the belly. This color is present at all times and is brighter in the male, but becomes most vivid during mating, especially in the female.

Up to a size of three inches, there are no external sex differences, except the belly coloring on the male may be a shade brighter. With another inch the male develops the usual long point on the dorsal fin, common to most male Cichlids.

It has been successfully bred many times. The breeding habits are the same as with the other Cichlids. It is surely worthy of a place in any collection of fishes of this type. Breeding temperature, about 80°.

Cichlasoma nigrofasciatum
(Guenther)
Popular name: Convict Cichlid
Meaning of name: Cichlasoma,
thrush-body; nigrofasciatum, black-banded
Length: 4 inches
San Salvador

For years this fish was considered to be the "Jack Dempsey" fish until the true "Dempsey" was found to be *C. octofasciatum.* While they breed like other Cichlids, it is more necessary to give breeding pairs an aquarium liberally supplied with hiding places, such as flowerpots, or large stones arranged in arches. The female assumes most of the care of the eggs.

C. nigrofasciatum is one of the high-strung Cichlids that changes its colors rapidly. They are often very quarrelsome, but usually very devoted parents. Oddly enough, the female has most of the color. Her irregular pattern of dull orange scales on the posterior part of her body extends into the lower fins.

The species not only fights its own kind, but is unsafe among other fishes. Its attacks are swift and with little warning.

Temperature 70°-80°.

Cichlasoma octofasciatum
Popular name: Jack Dempsey
Meaning of name: Cichlasoma,
thrush-body; octofasciatum, with eight bands. Formerly known as C. biocellatum
Length: Up to 8 inches
South America, probably Brazil

Before the reign of the Scalare, this fish, popularly and affectionately known as "Jack Dempsey," was the most popular of the Cichlids. Of its own type, with a long body and strong head, it is still the leader, for it has dazzling beauty, is hardy, is a good breeder and parent. One of the earlier introductions into the aquarium and a dependable showpiece.

With age, the colors of the Dempsey

Cichlasoma meeki

Cichlasoma nigrofasciatum

are particularly prone to become more fixed, brilliant, and less likely to change when the fish is frightened or excited. Our illustration shows an immature fish.

Often a large individual fish is kept as a pet in an aquarium by itself, where it soon learns to beg, in fish language, for morsels of food from its master. Lives for ten years or longer. Our description of breeding of the Cichlids fits this species perfectly. Temperature, 65° to 90°.

Cichlasoma severum
(Heckel)

Meaning of name: Cichlasoma, thrush-body; severum, severe

Length: 5 to 6 inches

Amazon

Reference has already been made to the great changeability in coloring and marking of the various Cichlids. This is particularly true of *Cichlasoma severum*. The background color in any individual may, in a few seconds, change from pale gray to deep green, brown, or nearly black, or any imagined intervening shades. Agitation of one kind or another usually causes the color changes.

While the name *severum* means "severe," it is no more militant than the average large Cichlid.

Undoubtedly this is one of the more difficult Cichlids to breed. It should have a large aquarium, plenty of warmth, about 80°; and be well fed on brine shrimp and other live foods in order to induce mating and spawning. Otherwise, the methods conform to standard. The sex is easily told in

adults, but not in the young. The male has the regular rows of dots on the side, whereas the female has few, if any. When young, they show only dark, distinct vertical bars. Temperature, 72° to 80°.

Cichla ocellaris
Bloch and Schneider

Meaning of name: Cichla, thrush; ocellaris, with round spot

Length: To 2 feet

Widely distributed in South America

This is an important food fish in South America, and young specimens are rarely imported. Nevertheless, we do see them offered for sale occasionally, and we include them here for those hobbyists who have large tanks and who are fond of big, ferocious carnivores. In behavior and food requirements, these fishes are much like the North American Basses. They are loners that preferentially feed on other fishes. Water conditions are not critical, but enough room is a must.

Temperature, 70° to 80°.

Crenicichla lepidota
Heckel

Popular name: Pike Cichlid

Meaning of name: Crenicichla, Cichla with teeth; lepidota, with scales on ear region (gill covers)

Length: To 12 inches

South America

Crenicichlas, of which there are a number of species, are unneighborly fishes and make poor members for a community tank. They are predators of the first order and require live fish

Cichlasoma nigrofasciatum *(A Pair of White Zebra Cichlids)*

Cichlasoma octofasciatum

Cichlasoma severum

for food when adult.

Although lacking brilliant coloring, they are decidedly attractive. The irregular markings on the back, are variable in their intensity.

The genus of *Crenicichla* is occasionally available. They do not tear out plants. Temperature, 68° to 80°.

Geophagus brasiliensis
Heckel

Meaning of name: Geophagus, earth-eater; brasiliensis, from Brazil

Length: 6 inches

Brazil

Some Cichlids might well be the envy of mere man, for they become handsomer with age. *G. brasiliensis* is one of that kind. The highlights on the body and fins are electric blue-green, and they will become much brighter as the fish grows older. This

Cichlasoma severum, *golden variety*

fish has a dark central body spot. Breeds in standard Cichlid manner, but not often.

The fish is rather easily distinguished from the other popular Cichlids by the outline of its body. The head is large, and the body tapers off sharply where it joins the tail fin. This end of the body is called the "caudal peduncle." The eye is dark gold and black. Temperature, 72°-82°.

Cichla ocellaris

Crenicichla lepidota

Geophagus brasiliensis

Geophagus jurupari

Geophagus jurupari
Heckel
Meaning of name: Geophagus, earth-eater; jurupari, after a native name
Length: 7 inches
The Amazon
This *Geophagus* owes its peculiar appearance to a particularly long pointed head and a dorsal fin that is quite high along its entire length. The long, downward arching profile of the snout makes the lower line of the head and body seem somewhat flat. The eyes are very large and placed high and far back on the snout.

Like most Cichlids, their color and markings vary greatly in intensity. The average background is a rather light golden color while the spotted pattern on the body and in the fins is an iridescent green. One of the more peaceful Cichlids. Does not tear out plants.

The eggs of this peculiar mouthbrooder are laid and fertilized on the horizontal surface of a clean, flat, smooth rock. After a day or two, they are picked off by the female—rarely by both parents—incubated in her mouth for about ten days, by which time the young emerge for brief periods to feed. Newly hatched brine shrimp are taken as a first food. At this time the male will also protect the fry against enemies by providing refuge in his cavernous mouth. The young, seldom pursued by their progenitors, enter the mouth of the parent upon a signal of flicking fins or simply when the parent opens its mouth.

Sexes are difficult to determine. In mature fish, the male has slightly larger and somewhat longer dorsal and ventral fins. Temperature, 72°-82°.

Herotilapia multispinosa
(Eigenmann)
Popular name: Rainbow Cichlid
Meaning of name: Herotilapia, resembling Tilapia (anther genus of Cichlids); multispinosa, with many thorns
Length: About 4 inches; females usually smaller
South America
Rainbow Cichlids look very much as if they should belong to the genus Cichlasoma, but certain differences in the teeth justify their classification in a different genus. They do well under the same conditions as Cichlasoma, and breed in the same fashion. Females turn very dark during breeding time. Both parents take an active part in caring for eggs and young. Temperature, 70° to 80°.

Pterophyllum scalare
(Lichtenstein)
Popular names: Angel Fish
Meaning of name: Pterophyllum, winged leaf; scalare, like a flight of stairs, referring to the dorsal fin
Length: 5 to 6 inches
Amazon and Guyana
Three "species" of *Pterophyllum* have been recognized: P. eimekei, P. scalare and P. altum. *P. altum*, from Venezuela, is very rare. It is probable that all three represent only subspecies or geographical races.

To the untrained eye, *Pterophyllum* does not look like a Cichlid, but nevertheless it is one.

Except that it will eat small fishes of suitable size, it is quite a good "happy family" member. While the breeding habits are much the same as we look for in Cichlids, there are two distinct points of difference. Instead of depositing the spawn in or on such objects as flower-pots or stones, they prefer for this purpose a firm aquatic leaf, such as giant *Sagittaria*, or some substitute that will approximate it. They will accept a heavy glass tube for the purpose, especially if it is opaque, or the leaf of a plastic plant. They seem to have no confidence in the clear glass. Sometimes a glass tube is slipped over the aquarium drain pipe. Many commercial breeders use a strip of one-quarter-inch slate, two to three inches wide and eight inches long. It is placed against the aquarium side, sloping a few degrees off the vertical.

Unlike the great majority of Cichlids, Angels do not place their young in prepared holes in the sand. Wherever the baby Angel hatches, there it adheres suspended from the head by a sticky thread, vibrating its tail vigorously. The mass of young produces an appreciable current in this way, thus getting both exercise and a rapid change of water. During this period the parents pick up mouthfuls of young, retain them a few moments and gently spray them on another leaf, repeating the operation at intervals of perhaps an hour, until the babies can swim freely, which is in 3-4 days. One observes that the parents are most solicitous, and use great care to pick up any of the young which did not adhere to a new location. Babies seldom reach the bottom before rescue arrives.

As to how long to keep the parents and young together—if at all—is a matter for each aquarist to decide. Leaving them all together is a most interesting procedure if successful. Some families may remain together until the parents are ready to spawn again.

If the main object is to rear fish and one is willing to forego the pleasure of witnessing their interesting family life, then the best thing to do is to remove the eggs to a hatching tray or aquarium containing water not over 8 inches deep. The container and water should be perfectly clean, for the babies are not to be freed of dirt particles in the laundry-mouths of their natural parents. The water, of course, should be seasoned. If fungus appears, boil the water next time and add 2 drops of 5% Methylene Blue solution per gallon after spawning. (This is bad for plants.)

Returning to the subject of artificial spawn receivers, it will now be apparent where their use is a practical convenience, for they are easily lifted out of the aquarium and laid sloping, egg side down, in the hatching tray. A light current of water about the eggs and young, produced by the mechanical liberation of air, is important. By the time the young have absorbed all of the yolk-sac and become free-swimming, they are able to eat newly hatched brine shrimp.

A number of other Cichlids may be reared in this way. It is worth trying when parents persistently eat eggs or young.

Newly hatched Scalares look noth-

Above: **Herotilapia multispinosa,** *Male*

Below: **Pterophyllum scalare**

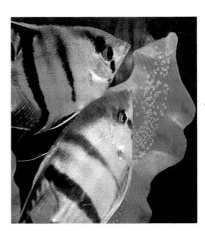

Angel Fish Spawning

ing like their parents, but in a few weeks there is no mistaking their identity. Growth is rapid under the influence of liberal feeding and warmth.

Peculiarities of Angel Fish

Several things about Angel Fish require special consideration. Perhaps the most outstanding one is an unaccountable loss of appetite. Try a change of food. They are particularly fond of live mosquito larvae, *Daphnia,* small or chopped earthworms, white worms and canned shrimp. If these fail to tempt, then try baby Guppies. Pretty bad case if these morsels fail to bring back the appetite. The only thing then left to do is to try a change of aquarium or of water in the present aquarium. Scalares seem to do best in slightly acid water, about pH 6.8. They seldom really starve. There should be plants in the aquarium with Angel Fish. They tend to give the fishes a sense of security. When frightened, Angels may dash against the aquarium glass and injure or even kill themselves.

Ordinarily, when a fish lies over on its side on the bottom of the aquarium, it is preparing to enter fish paradise. The Scalare is liable to do this from shock, fright or chill, but is likely to regain its equilibrium.

This fish is not very susceptible to Ichthyophthirius, but it is liable to a disease that causes the eyes to protrude. This sometimes leads to blindness and usually ends in death.

Under identical conditions, some individuals of the original coloration will have brilliant black bars, while others are gray. Cause unknown. It is no indication of a state of health.

Sex in Angel Fish

This remains difficult to distinguish, but we can make a shrewd guess. Even mating is not a certain sign, for two females sometimes mate and have infertile eggs. One method in use by breeders has reference to the space at the lower edge of the body between the "feelers" and the beginning of the anal fin. In the female, this portion of the body outline is longer and straighter and the angle between the body and anal fin is more pronounced. As with other Cichlids, the breeding tube, which appears in both sexes just before egg-laying, is more pointed in the male and is carried at a more forward angle. Also the female when filled with eggs looks fuller from overhead.

Symphysodon discus
(Heckel)

Meaning of name: Symphysodon, with teeth at middle (symphysis) of jaw; discus, like a disc

Length: 5 to 6 inches

Amazon

At least two species of *Symphysodon* are recognized and imported: *S. discus* and *S. aequifasciata.* All require the same care. They are show fishes. Their showy quality is increased by their large size.

At breeding time, the male rivals the gaudy beauty of the most brilliant marine fishes. Occasionally the female is a brilliant golden yellow.

A considerable study has been made of various possible indications of difference in sex, but the only dependable point is that the blue pattern on the male is more pronounced and more extensive than on the female. Perfectly peaceful, but unexpected, battles may occur between mated pairs.

Black Veiltail Angel Fish

Half-black Angel Fish

Angel Fish, Golden Variety

Black Lace Angel Fish

Marbled Angel Fish

Minimum breeding size, about three inches. The best way of securing a pair is to have say six in a 30-40 gallon aquarium and let them select their own mates. They are fussy feeders and should have a variety of live foods, including, if available, the shrimp-like *Gammarus*. The new young have extremely small mouths. Before we learned that their first food is the slime they pick from the bodies of their parents, many of them died of starvation, because the eggs were hatched separately. The adults at this time seem to secrete a heavier slime on their bodies, an old provision of nature, akin to the fact that pigeons develop a "milk" in the crop as first food for their squabs. This discovery makes it clear

Symphysodon aequifasciata

that the young should be tended by parents, even at the risk of their eating the spawn. Skilled breeders of tropical fishes now provide us with good tank-raised stock of these great beauties.

The species is subject to a few peculiar diseases, particularly abscesses about the head. Their water, especially for breeding, should be slightly acid and at a temperature of about 80°.

Symphysodon discus

Hemichromis bimaculatus
Gill

Popular name: Jewel Fish

Meaning of name: Hemichromis, half-Chromis; bimaculatus, two-spotted

Length: 4 inches

Most of Tropical Africa

One of the typical savage Cichlids. It needs several redeeming traits to justify being kept, and it has them:

temperamental fish, a good parent, fairly hardy, and at times, gorgeously beautiful.

Although the fins and general coloration are the same in male and female, the sex is easily determined. The male has more and larger jewels on the gill plate, and those in the tail fin extend farther and form into a crescent. In her maximum redness at breeding time, the female is a little brighter

Hemichromis bimaculatus

than the male, reversing the usual or-der of things. During courtship, the colors change rapidly, the dark spots become light or disappear altogether, and the jewel facets enlarge.

Out of breeding season both fishes are of a rather dark, nondescript color, lightly lined with blue jeweled scales and displaying a dark spot near the center of the body, one on the gill plate and one at the tail base. It is hard to understand why the specific name of the fish is not t*rimaculatus*.

Mating time is difficult and danger-ous. Whether working by group natu-ral selection with several fishes or using only a pair, it is advisable with this species to have plenty of refuge places for the fish getting the worst of it. In addition to the flowerpot for receiving the spawn, there should be heavy plants like giant *Sagittaria* or some large stones placed in formation for recesses.

The eggs of this species, if in clean condition, can be satisfactorily hatched and reared if the parents are removed, but then the aquarist loses one of his greatest pleasures by not witnessing the instructive and touching family life of the fishes.

The young grow rapidly and when about six weeks old begin attacking each other. For this reason they should be kept in an aquarium of at least ten-gallon capacity.

Temperature range, 60° to 90°. Breeding at 80°.

Hemichromis fasciatus
Peters
Popular name: Banded Jewelfish
Meaning of name: Hemichromis, half-Chromis; fasciatus, banded

Length: 6 to 10 inches

Central W. Africa

We sometimes find a Cichlid that is suited to the aquarium only if the fish is not allowed to grow too big. *Hemichromis fasciatus,* if kept in an aquarium of ten-gallon size, can be held down to five or six inches, but if in a large tank, it reaches a length of ten inches. As it is a fierce digger, it can do a lot of damage when this size. Contrary to *H. bimaculatus,* the colors are not bright. A brassy yellow or olive overlaid with five to six variable vertical bands constitutes the main pattern. Dorsal and tail fins, blue-black with narrow red edge. Ventral fins are clear to yellow and the eye, brown. Black spot on opercle. At breeding time the forward part of the body becomes black and the belly pure white. The nose takes on a mahogany red color, while the anal and tail fins become red. Breeds like *H. bimaculatus.* The fish is a savage fighter.

Pelmatochromis guentheri
(Sauvage)

Meaning of name: Pelmatochromis, Sole-Chromis, referring to a peculiar internal formation of the gill structure; guentheri, after the naturalist, Guenther

Length: 4 inches

Equatorial W. Africa in coastal rivers

The dorsal fin on this fish is most striking and entirely different from that of any other known aquarium fish. It looks as if it were dusted with gold, especially in the female. As the body is a plain, drab purplish hue, devoid of

pattern, the startling fins have the field to themselves. The fish is peaceful and will eat anything.

They are mouth-brooders, and both parents rear the brood. That is, the female will tend the eggs and fry, but the male will join her later in providing refuge in his mouth for the free swimming youngsters. When the young first emerge, they are large. At the slightest sign of danger, they continue to use the mouths of their parents as a refuge, even after they have reached a length of $5/8$ inch. It is quite an amusing sight to see them scamper in, especially when their size makes it impossible for all to enter. It is like a hen who is no longer able to hide all her chicks under her feathers.

Temperature, 70° to 82°.

Nanochromis nudiceps
(Boulenger)

Meaning of name: Nannochromis, small Chromis; nudiceps, with naked head

Length: Females up to 2 $1/2$ inches; males to 3 $1/2$ inches

Congo River

Compared to their South American counterparts, these little Cichlids from the Congo are extremely active fish. They dash with great speed from cave to cave, feeling at home only in a tank suitably set up with lots of rocks and hiding places. They tend to dig, mostly around and under rocks. To avoid uprooting, therefore, plants should be placed a few inches away from rocks. Mature females are a bit smaller than males and, if in good condition, are almost always well-rounded and have

Hemichromis fasciatus

Pelmatochromis guentheri

a beautiful bluish-green patch on their sides.

They spawn in caves or flowerpots, and the females tend eggs and young very carefully. The eggs are large, cream-colored, and attached to the walls of the cave by means of a short stalk. The eggs wave in the current while the female is fanning. Hatching takes place in about three days; thereafter, the fry are often moved by the female from one cave to another. They are free-swimming in another four or five days and are then ready to gorge themselves on newly hatched brine shrimp.

Temperature, 76° to 82°.

Pelvicachromis pulcher
(Brull)

Meaning of name: Pulcher, Pretty

Length: 3 inches

Western Equatorial Africa

This is one of the most popular and beautiful Cichlids from Africa. The females have a more brilliant patch of red on their sides than do the males, have a rounder belly and shorter dorsal. The tail is usually clear and unmarked.

The fish will accept many types of food, but they prefer to feed near the bottom or in midwater. Only reluctantly will they take food off the surface.

Eggs are almost always laid in hidden caves, and a flowerpot laid on its side is readily accepted. The female, rarely both parents, cares for eggs and fry. The male takes a greater interest in guarding the nesting site.

Temperature, 72° to 80°.

Tilapia mossambica

Tilapia mossambica
Peters

Meaning of name: Tilapia, unknown; mossambica, after Mozambique

Length: 8 inches

E. Africa, S. Africa and Mozambique

In this mouthbrooding species, the female carries the eggs. The babies first emerge from her maw in about ten days, retreating as danger approaches much the same as described for *Pelmatochromis guentheri*.

The species is seen in dealers' tanks regularly. They have been introduced into different parts of the tropics as food fish and have multiplied greatly. We give eight inches as the average aquarium size, but the bulletin of the Indonesian Veterinary Association claims that specimens in pond culture reach an incredible six pounds. This fish is a heavy feeder and takes any food. The male at breeding time shows white on lower part of the head, while the tail and pectoral fins become deep red and the body turns a dark charcoal gray. Temperatures, 70° to 80°.

Reports indicate that the fabulous poundage expectation from the fish

Pelvicachromis pulcher

Nannochromis nudiceps

has not always been realized because their very productivity soon overcrowds a pond, resulting in much smaller fish.

Nowhere have we yet found an exception to the axiom that great growth needs not only heavy feeding but also liberal water surface per fish.

Steatocranus casuarius
Poll

Popular name: Bumphead Cichlid, Buffalo Head

Length: Up to 4 inches; female slightly smaller

Congo River

The first thing one notices when observing these fishes in an aquarium is the fact that they do not swim in the normal manner of Cichlids. They dash in short spurts on the bottom or hop from stone to stone in a way similar to the native North American Darters. As the name "Bumphead Cichlids" implies, the male develops a large fatty hump on its forehead, of which the female only shows a trace. Although this does occur to some extent in other mature male Cichlids, it is extremely pronounced in this species. Their natural habitat is the rapids of the Congo River, and they are unquestionably very well adapted to live in such an environment. In captivity, they are happiest in a tank containing lots of gravel and rocks and few, if any, plants. To simulate the natural environment even better, a large volume filter can be used to create a fairly strong current in the tank. At breeding time, which can be any season of the year, they usually move large amounts of gravel as they excavate breeding sites. Eggs are laid in caves and both

Steatocrannus casuarius

parents take an active part in guarding the eggs and fry. It has been reported that this species provides pre-chewed food for the youngsters. This has been observed on other species of Cichlids but only as an individual trait in some females and not as consistent behavior of a species. It is a very touching sight when one is lucky enough to observe it and unique in the world of aquarium fishes.

CICHLIDS OF LAKE MALAWI

The Cichlids of Lake Malawi have been known to ichthyologists for more than half a century, but only since the 1960s have they been imported for the aquarium hobby. Since then, they have become extremely popular, due both to their brilliant coloration and their interesting breeding habits.Their way of life is much different from that of their South American cousins. They are much more active swimmers, and most of them do not establish clearly defined territories, as many south American Cichlids do. Neither do they form pairs, except very briefly for the purpose of propagation.

These fishes live mostly along the rock-strewn shoreline of Lake Malawi, and the majority of them are found nowhere else on the continent. Being extremely agile in their rocky environment, they are very difficult to catch, and, before commercial breeders mass-produced them, were very high priced.

An aquarium set-up for these Cichlids should contain a large rock pile, that is, rocks should be piled up in a random manner to produce many pas-sageways and crevices. In this way, a fight (and there will be many) does not end with the aggressor mercilessly chasing the loser through the aquarium, killing him in the end.

Water conditions are not very important. The fishes have been successfully kept and bred in hard and alkaline water, as well as in soft and slightly acid waters. However, hard and alkaline water is preferred by most species, and acid conditions of 6.0 and below must absolutely be avoided.

For the most part the fishes are omnivorous, feeding on aquatic insects and crustaceans as well as algae and even some higher plants. A few are equipped with mouths specifically adapted for scraping algae off rocks. In the aquarium, they feed on all kinds of live and frozen foods, freeze-dried foods as well as flakes. As a rule, they are happier with frequent small feedings than with one or two heavy meals per day.

The breeding behavior of these Cichlids is a unique and interesting one. Almost all are mouthbrooders with the female carrying the eggs until the fry are hatched and completely formed.

Incubation takes about three weeks, during which time the female takes no food. Some individual females, however, have been observed to grab some food particles during this incubation time and go through chewing motions. Whether this is done to still her own hunger or to provide chewed food for the developing youngsters in her mouth is not clear, but both theories have been advanced. During this period, the female usually stays hidden among the rocks and rarely ventures into open water. At times, a female fails to find a secluded spot in the aquarium and is considerably disturbed by her tank mates. In that case, she should be removed to another tank. This needs to be done very carefully, since she will simply spit out the eggs or swallow them if she is too frightened by the procedure. Some breeders remove the eggs routinely from an incubating female and hatch them artificially. The eggs are placed in a separate container and agitated gently by means of a slow stream of water, using the effluent from the filter.

When the young emerge from the mouth of the female, they are one-half inch long, fully formed replicas of their parents. For the first day or two, they still seek refuge in the mouth of the mother when danger approaches, but after that they are completely on their own. They are amazingly alert and, while searching for food, use the smallest nooks and crannies for protection. It is amusing to watch them— especially at this young age—go through the typical adult fighting behavior. With violent body wagging, fins and gillcovers spread to the utmost, they try to impress one another very much whenever two of them meet.

Newly hatched brine shrimp is the very best food for them, but any food of sufficiently small particle size can be fed.

Spawning takes place on a smooth, flat rock which is cleared of debris by both the male and the female. The pair will circle each other a few times and

then the female will release from one to three eggs. They are large (about $1/8$ in diameter), irregularly shaped and of a dull yellow or pinkish color. The eggs are non-adhesive and often roll about in the current the fish produce while excitedly circling each other. Presently, the female picks up the eggs with her mouth and approaches the male who has taken a position squarely in front of her, presenting a side view of himself. On his widely spread anal fin a few yellowish or orange spots can be observed, which look exactly like the eggs just laid by the female. The female will now peck at those egg spots, as they are called, apparently in the belief that they are more eggs to be picked up. At this very moment, the male will release sperm fluid, which gets sucked into the female's mouth to fertilize the eggs. This process is repeated a number of times until the female is depleted of eggs. The number of eggs varies from about ten to fifty or more, depending on the species and the size of the female. The best temperature is about 80°.

Pseudotropheus auratus
(Boulenger)
Meaning of name: Pseudotropheus, false Tropheus (another genus of Cichlids); auratus, golden
Length: 4 inches
Sexes look very much alike when not mature. Males undergo a dramatical change in color at breeding time.

Pseudotropheus elongatus
Frayer
Meaning of name: Pseudotropheus,

Pseudotropheus auratus

Pseudotropheus zebra *white mottled female*

false Tropheus; elongatus, elongate

Length: To 5 inches

This species is somewhat more quarrelsome than other members of the genus. Males lead a more solitary life. Diet consists predominantly of crustaceans and other aquatic organisms.

Pseudotropheus zebra

(Boulenger)

Meaning of name: Pseudotropheus, false Tropheus; zebra, with stripes

Length: To 8 inches

Solid blue, orange, and white fishes are found in different parts of the lake. They all are P. zebra, and readily interbreed without regard to color. It is not clear how the different strains have evolved and why the different colors remain distinct in the lake. Much research is needed in this field, and hobbyists breeding these fishes can provide much of the information we are now lacking.

Labeotropheus fuelleborni

Ahl

Meaning of name: Labeotropheus, with distinct lips; fuelleborni, a personal name

Length: To 8 inches

L. fuelleborni occur in at least two color varieties: a blue one and an orange mottled one. Orange mottled fish are often females, and there is some doubt as to the existance of mottled males. The fish are well equipped for rasping algae off flat rocks.

Labeotropheus trewavasae

Fryer

Meaning of name: Labeotropheus, with distinct lips; trewavasae, after E. Trewavas, British ichthyologist

Length: 5 inches

As in the foregoing, at least two

Pseudotropheus elongatus

Pseudotropheus zebra

Labeotropheus fuelleborni

Labeotropheus trewavasae

color morphs exist in this species, and, again as in *L. fuelleborni*, mottled males are rarely, if ever, encountered. The fish benefit by the addition of algae in their diet but will accept almost any type of food offered.

THE NANDIDS
FAMILY NANDIDAE

Most spiny-rayed fishes are found in salt water, and very few families of this type are restricted entirely to fresh water. The Cichlids, Sunfishes, true Perches, and Gouramis are among such fresh-water families. The Nandids also share this distinction, and of all such groups they are the most widely scattered in range.

Monocirrhus (one species) is found over most of the Amazon Basin and in the Essequibo River, Guyana. *Polycentrus* (one species) is restricted to Guyana and the island of Trinidad. *Polycentropsis abbreviata* and *Afronandus sheljuzhkoi* represent the family in Africa, where it is confined to a relatively small area about the mouth of the Niger and in Cameroon. In India there are *Badis* (two species), *Nandus* (two species), and *Pristolepis fasciata* in Burma, Thailand, Laos and islands of the Malay Archipelago.

The Nandids differ technically from other related families chiefly in features of the skeleton. All of them (except *Badis*) have large mouths which can be opened out to a tremendous extent and all (except *Badis* again) have the peculiar feature of having the tail fin and the rear ends of the dorsal and anal fins so transparent as to be hardly visible in the live fish. The transparent dorsal and anal fin ends are almost constantly in motion. All except *Badis* are voracious fish-eaters, with large mouths and strong teeth. No member of this family can be maintained on a diet of prepared food. They all require live food.

Badis badis
(Hamilton-Buchanan)
Popular name: Badis
Meaning of name: a native name
Length: 2³/₄ inches
India

Many of our exotic fishes have extensive wardrobes of colored costumes, which they wear according to whim on occasion, and an author attempting descriptions feels that he is helplessly repeating himself in saying very much the same thing about a number of species. However, *Badis badis* is one of the extreme cases. The usual color is brown with black or red bars in a chain-like pattern. Females never deviate from that pattern, but males are capable of considerable color changes. At breeding time, the barred pattern gives way to an overall bluish-black color with iridescent blue spangles in dorsal, anal and tail fin.

Sexes cannot be told positively, but the males are more hollow-bellied and are apt to be darker and larger and have larger fins. Badis badis spawn underneath rocks or in small caves. There is an embrace similar to that of Gouramis, but unlike eggs of Gouramis, *B. badis* eggs are extremely adhesive. The female does not carefully place the eggs as most Cichlids do but scatters them randomly during the spawning em-

Badis badis, *Male*

brace. The eggs then become attached to the walls of the cave and the bottom. The male guards and vigorously defends the spawning site against any fish venturing too close. Eggs hatch in three days, and the young are free swimming in another three days at a temperature of 80°. First food for fry is infusoria.

A ten-gallon tank can be used. Temperature, 78° to 80°.

Badis badis, *Female*

Monocirrhus polyacanthus
Heckel

Popular name: Amazon Leaf Fish

Meaning of name: Monocirrhus, with one whisker; polyacanthus, many-spined

Length: 2 ¹/₂ inches

Amazon and Guyana

Although this extremely odd fish was first described by Heckel as long ago as 1840, for many years the type specimens in the Vienna Museum remained the only ones of which we have any knowledge. In an interesting reprint from the *Biological Bulletin* (November, 1921), Dr. W. R. Allen described a sluggish brook overhung with tropical vegetation from which he captured three specimens. The fishes, of a leaf-brown, irregular

Monocirrhus polycanthus

mottled color, were difficult to see against a bottom matted with fallen leaves. They moved about peculiarly like drifting leaves, and had the collector not thought it strange that leaves should move at all in such sluggish water, he would not have seen them.

The species is most peculiar and is a definite novelty of exotic character. It is really quite striking and is not confined to any particular shade of brown but changes greatly. Whether this is a chameleon-like power of protective coloration, we can only surmise. The eyes are difficult to distinguish, owing to the dark lines radiating from them. Usually the fins are spread, their saw-edges contributing much to the leaf-like effect. The beard on the lower jaw adds a stem to the leaf. Even the natives call the species the Leaf Fish.

They move about sedately and pose themselves at unusual angles, frequently head-down. They do not seem to be particularly bored with life, but they gape or yawn prodigiously. Many fishes do this moderately, but the Leaf Fish puts on a startling act. The mouth seems to unfold from within itself until it becomes a veritable trumpet.

They deposit, fertilize, and fan their eggs somewhat like Cichlids, but their parental care is not nearly so intense. The first spawn of a pair, placed in a dark vertical corner where the aquarium glasses join, was the most successful. Those later placed in pots did not do so well. The youngsters varied greatly in size and after three weeks began to disappear. Removed from the parents and graded for size, the trouble ended. They have barbels for the first months and when quite small are covered with tiny white dots which look like the parasitic disease Ichthyophthirius. This is common to a number of kinds of very young fishes; it is probably protective coloration.

The Leaf Fish is most interesting, but unless one is prepared to feed it exclusively and liberally on small live fishes, all thoughts of keeping it should be abandoned, for it will touch nothing else. As the fish has a voracious appetite, it usually either wears out its welcome or starves to death. Few fanciers are equipped to maintain royalty demanding such expensive food. A thousand grown male Guppies per year just about keeps one of these adult cannibal aristocrats from feeling neglected. It does not attack fishes too large to be swallowed, but one should not underrate its capacity! Temperature, 75° to 82°.

THE GOBIES
FAMILIES ELEOTRIDAE AND GOBIIDAE

The most noteworthy difference between the two families of Gobies is the fact that in the Gobiidae, the two ventral fins are *connected* and form a sort of suction cup. The fishes use it to attach themselves to rocks, plants and other submerged objects. The *Eleotridae* have no such suction cup. Their ventral fins are separated. All Gobies require live foods for their well-being.

Brachygobius xanthozonus
(Bleeker)
Popular name: Bumble Bee Goby

Meaning of name: Brachygobius, short goby; xanthozonus, with yellow zones or bands
Length: 1¼ inches
Malaysia, Borneo, Sumatra, Java

Like so many of the Gobies, this little fish spends most of its time on the bottom of the aquarium hopping about in a droll way. It cannot be called a scavenger, however, since it has a dis-

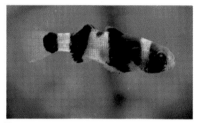

Brachygobius xanthozonus

tinct preference for *Daphnia* and brine shrimp. Reluctantly, it will take some dried foods.

They have rarely been bred. The breeders are conditioned on chopped earthworms and grown brine shrimp. Eggs are laid on the upper side of an empty flowerpot, which is on its side. The female takes an upside-down position in the pot while applying strings of eggs that adhere to the upper side. She drops to the bottom while the male does a "loop-the-loop," fertilizing the eggs as he passes them. Spawn hatches in five to six days at 75°. Male fans spawn and does not eat young. They must be fed on fine infusoria for three days after their yolk sac has been absorbed.

The species prefers live food and they are apt to be fin-nippers.

Dormitator maculatus
(Bloch)

Popular name: Sleeper Goby

Meaning of name: Dormitator, sleeper; maculatus, spotted

Length: In nature, up to 10 inches; Aquarium size, 3 to 4 inches

Coast of tropical America, Atlantic side

Although the color of this species is made up of browns and grays, the fish is not lacking in character. The light spot in back of the gill plate is a sparkle of blue. The anal fin is ornamented with brown and blue spots, and is crisply edged with electric blue. A peculiarity is that in certain lights the center of the eye is a blind-looking stony blue. The fish appears to be able to "close" its eye on the inside, hence the name sleeper. It is often found in brackish water.

A peaceful, sluggish fish that has seldom been bred. Many small eggs are attached to cleaned stones. Tiny young are hard to rear. Especially the adults require large food particles. Temperature, 65° to 85°.

THE ANABANTOIDS

The Anabantoids include the Climbing Perches and Gouramis. All have an auxiliary breathing apparatus, called the labyrinth, in addition to the ordinary gills. Although not capable of independent muscular action, this organ is comparable to the lung of an air-breathing animal and serves the same purpose. It is called a labyrinth on account of its involved structure that brings a great many fine capillaries into contact with the air forced through it. These capillaries absorb oxygen from the air and deliver it directly into

Dormitator maculatus

the blood stream of the fish. The air, however, does not pass through the labyrinth in the same manner as we humans breathe but is taken at intervals by the fish at the surface of the water. Simultaneously, a new bubble is taken in the mouth, and the old one is forced out through the edge of the gill covers, having first passed through the oxygen-absorbing labyrinth. This is in the head.

These fishes use the regular gills for oxygenating the blood to a much greater extent than is generally believed. Experiments have shown that they extract almost as much oxygen from the water as do other species without labyrinths. However, it is a great advantage to a fish to be equipped with both kinds of breathing apparatus for in situations where the oxygen in the water is so deficient as to suffocate ordinary species, the labyrinth fishes maintain life without apparent distress. From this it will be seen why they may be kept in comparatively small containers.

On the mistaken theory that air-breathers take no oxygen from the water, aquarists sometimes add them to tanks which are already over-populated.

The intervals at which air in the labyrinth is changed varies with species and conditions. When excited the fish may come to the surface several times a minute, but at other times, especially in cooler water, it may remain below for several minutes at a time.

Nearly all of the labyrinth fishes are what are known as "bubble-nest build-ers." As the description of this peculiar method of breeding applies to the several species under the heading, it will not be needlessly repeated in each instance, but where individual characteristics vary from the following description, they will be pointed out as occasion requires.

The outstanding feature of the breeding of this group of fishes is the floating nest of bubbles that they construct and in which the eggs are placed, hatched and the young tended. These bubbles are formed by the male as he comes to the surface, draws a little air in his mouth and apparently mixes it with saliva of sorts. When released, many small bubbles float to the surface. Endless repetition of this act piles up what looks like a little mound of very fine soap bubbles. They often select a building spot just under some floating aquatic leaves or a large single leaf. The best temperature for breeding is 78° to 82°. In the breeding tank it is advisable to reduce as much as possible any surface agitation caused by filters or aerators.

When a male starts building a nest, even in a small way, it indicates that he is about ready for breeding. Unless a female is already present, it is the proper time to bring a pair together. It is better to move the male into the aquarium occupied by the female. Most of these fishes are quite harmless to species other than their own, but at breeding time there is danger of one being killed, usually the female. For this reason, it is desirable to have plenty of room and a liberal supply of refuge plants which, by the way, they never injure. The courting is conducted by a grand spreading of fins, first of the male, with ultimate response by the female if his suit is successful. His best holiday attire is used in courtship.

The male is often an impatient courter. After the nest is built, he drives the female towards it. If she is not ready for spawning, her response will be slow, and it is then that he is liable to attack her, tearing her fins. It is at this time that the aquarist needs to be something of a strategist, as well as a diplomat, for the pair should not be separated at the very first sign of trouble. Like the wise judge at a domestic relations court, he should give the contestants a reasonable chance to adjust their difficulties themselves. If matters grow worse, the strong arm of the aquarist should intervene and give the parties an enforced separation. A later trial mating may prove more successful.

But let us assume, as we should, that the courtship has been a normal

Two day old fry of Paradise Fish

one and that the pair is ready for the business of life. She follows him to a position just below the prepared nest. He bends his body into a crescent which encircles her. As they slowly sink through the water, rolling over, she drops several eggs which are immediately fertilized during the embrace of the male. He releases himself, picks up the eggs in his mouth, and pushes them into the nest. This act is repeated for perhaps an hour, at the end of which time there may be anywhere from 100 to 500 eggs in the nest. The male then asserts his rights as a father. He drives the female to the farthest limits of the aquarium and assumes full charge of the nest. At this point she should be removed, for she is likely to be killed, especially if the aquarium is a small one, say under 15 gallons.

To do this with as little agitation as possible, insert a glass divider between the pair. The female is then lifted without trouble.

With the presence of the eggs in the nest, the male redoubles his efforts in producing bubbles, for the old ones gradually burst. In order to retard this evaporation, and for another reason to be explained shortly, the aquarium should be kept well covered with glass. The bubble-nest, originally about three inches wide and half an inch high, becomes perhaps an inch high and spreads out to four inches. The small eggs between the bubble suds can be seen, but sharp eyes are needed.

The eggs hatch in about two days. At first they are like microscopic tadpoles among the foam and are quite helpless. As they fall out of the nest through the water, the vigilant father gathers them up in his mouth and puts them back into their sudsy cradle. This

The female has joined the male underneath the nest, and the embrace begins.

The female, upside down, releases a few eggs which are immediately fertilized by the male.

The pair slowly rolls over until the female is in an upside down position.

After each spawning act, the male, occasionally the female as well, gathers the drifting eggs and deposits them into the nest.

continues about three days, the nest gradually becoming shallower and the young taking a position at the surface of the water just below it. By the time the young have absorbed the yolk sac and gained their balance, the nest is nearly gone. No schoolmaster ever had a busier time looking after his charges, and no children could have a more vigilant caretaker. He looks after the wanderers with an eagle eye, ever alert and willing to give his life in their defense. In perhaps a week he considers his task done and that the young should be able to protect themselves. So thoroughly does he seem to enter

into this idea that he is liable to start eating them himself! Perhaps this is nature's method of eliminating those that can be caught. In the wild state, his protection is no doubt necessary, but in an aquarium in which there are no fish enemies there is no reason to keep the father with the young after they are free-swimming.

There are several points of practical value in raising bubble-nest builders. It is a very, very common experience for beginners to become enthusiastic over prospects of raising a nest of these young, only to have them die off at an age of from two to four weeks.

The principal reason for this is insufficient food of the right kind and aquaria that are too small and too clean. These small fishes require a considerable amount of microscopic food, which can only be developed and maintained in old water. The proper aquarium for this purpose should be at the very least 15 gallons in size, well planted, containing old water from six to eight inches deep, and with a fair amount of natural sediment on the bottom. The presence of a few decaying aquarium plants is desirable. No snails should be used. When the eggs are laid, it is advisable to sprinkle a little dried and crumbled lettuce leaves on the water, and also a very little of any finely powdered fish food. The decomposition of these organic substances keeps up the culture of microscopic life that will later be needed. It is a fact that very small fishes of this character have been raised on a fine flour made of fish food, but it is quite likely that the resulting infusoria which feed on the decomposition of this substance have something to do with the success attained. At any rate, while it is a good idea to have a separate source of infusoria culture, it is also desirable to cultivate a natural supply of it along with the baby fishes, especially when they are of a species that are extremely small. Aside from this suggested aquarium preparation, the young of labyrinth fishes may be raised as per the regular formula for egg-droppers. At the age of five to seven days they can also eat brine shrimp.

A reasonably successful substitute for live food is the yellow of a 20-minute boiled egg. It should be squeezed through a cloth and a bit as big as a pea shaken up in a bottle of about four-ounce size. A few drops of the agitated mixture may be lifted in a medicine-dropper and fed to the fry several times a day. These infusions should always be freshly mixed and should be fed with great care, as they can easily foul the water.

The other cause for losses is the failure to keep the aquarium well covered with glass during the critical period when the labyrinth is forming, for this organ does not begin to develop until the fish is about three weeks old. At this time, they are particularly sensitive to draughts and temperature changes. Slight aeration should be used now to prevent scum from forming at the surface.

In one instance, an aquarist bred five kinds of labyrinth fishes outdoors in a six-foot lily pool, one species each season. Nests were always placed by the fish under a lily pad, with the exception of the Colisa fasciata (Giant Gourami), and Belontia signata, both these species allowing their floating eggs to scatter loosely at the surface, to be freely blown about by the winds. Temperature ranged from 60° to 90°, averaging 73°. Females were never killed. Several overlapping nestings per season were raised, none interfering with or apparently eating the others. Sometimes two pairs of breeders were used. No artificial culture of infusoria was used. *Daphnia* occasionally. These were soon cleaned up by the parents or the young that were large enough to eat them. (The reader should not assume that conclusions from pond breeding are applicable to aquarium culture.)

Members of this fish group are subject to much individual variation in temperament, especially in the action of males in breeding. Some kill one female after another; others devour their babies, while some refuse to mate at all. The most unpredictable is the Betta. Ingenuity by the aquarist is sometimes needed. A change of mates is often the answer.

The labyrinth fishes are by nature carnivorous, living principally on small crustacea and also on insects which fall on the water. They can be trained to take ordinary prepared dried foods, but this should often be supplemented by fresh animal diet, such as *Daphnia,* chopped worms, live and frozen brine shrimp, bits of fish, crab meat, or scraped raw beef liver.

They are all suited to life in a community tank with fishes of approximately their own size. But males of the same species sometimes fight. Male Bettas, of course, will invariably fight. Females may be kept together.

Macropodus opercularis
(Linnaeus)

Popular name: Paradise Fish

Meaning of name: Macropodus, large foot (fin), in reference to dorsal and anal fins; opercularis, with spot on the gill cover

Length: 3 inches

If ancient lineage is the true basis for aristocracy, then the Paradise Fish is undoubtedly the exalted potentate of all tropical aquarium fishes. It was introduced in Paris in 1868 by Carbonnier. This introduction undoubtedly marks the beginning of the study of tropical fresh water aquarium fishes as we have it today, and if any future enthusiasts wish to observe centenaries of the occasion, that is the year on which to base them. Goldfish and a few cold-water species, both fresh and marine, had been kept in European and American aquariums some years previously. It is now difficult to realize that in the mid-1800s, especially in England, the household aquarium was a new and fashionable fad and that many books appeared on the subject. Judging from the now comical misinformation contained in most of them, it is little wonder that the mushroom growth soon passed and left no trace, except for a few musty books. One of the earliest of them (Warrington 1850) contained the first correct statement of the principles of the balanced aquarium and is worthy of commemoration.

For many years following its 1876 introduction to America by the famous Adolphus Busch of St. Louis, the Paradise Fish was regarded as an aquarium novelty of doubtful value, for owners of Lacetail Goldfish rightly feared the presence of this menacing stranger among their highly developed, but defenseless, beauties. The Goldfish fins usually suffered when it was tried.

Because the Paradise Fish is so easily bred and can live in water down to 50°, it is a good beginner's fish. If rare it would be considered a great beauty. When the male's fins are at their best, the long, sweeping fila-

Macropodus opercularis

ments at the tail-ends are blue white at the ends. The females have shorter fin tips.

In contrast with Goldfish, this species early acquired a reputation as a fighter, but in comparison with some other exotic fishes he is really not savage, but is untrustworthy in a small community tank.

A true albino strain of Paradise Fish with pink eyes was introduced from Europe in 1933. The bars on the sides are pinkish, becoming more red as the fish ages. Otherwise it is white or cream colored. It breeds true and is prolific. What fight there is in the original stock seems to have mostly disappeared in the albino, the male not usually attacking the female after she has finished spawning.

M. opercularis, or Paradise Fish, breeds true to standard form as de-scribed for bubble-nest builders. It is particularly suited to pond culture, as it is not injured by moderate chilly spells.

This fish is very tame, and while preferring animal food, it will take anything. Like the Betta, in perhaps a slightly lesser degree, it seems to have no sense of fear. *M. opercularis* is long-lived and can endure very dirty water.

The species has been the subject of an unusual amount of discussion by the systematists, having undergone, since its first description by Linnaeus in 1758, several changes of name and been the subject of many hundred papers by ichthyologists and aquarists.

Paradise Fish are common in the rice fields of China, where they successfully endure a wide range of temperature.

Macropodus concolor

Macropodus concolor
Popular name: Black Paradise Fish
Length: About 4 inches; female smaller
Location: Unknown

Paradise Fishes, the well-known *M. opercularis* as well as this one, are very hardy and durable fishes, able to survive the most adverse conditions. They are gorgeously colored, easily bred and raised, and accept almost any kind of food. Unfortunately, their popularity rating is low, due to the undeserved reputation given them as aggressive and belligerent fishes. However, the risk in keeping them in a community tank is not much greater than that taken with a male Betta, the Siamese Fighting Fish. Of course, their tank mates should be of a comparative

size or be sufficiently agile to be able to escape, if it should become necessary. Only while breeding, and this admittedly might easily take place in the community tank, does the male become so aggressive that he might inflict serious injury on other tank mates. This is the case with many fishes exercising parental care, especially with those who usually are devoted parents.

The outstanding features of Black Paradise Fishes are their deep brown (almost black) body color, the bright blue edging of dorsal, anal, and caudal fins, and their deep orange ventrals. While breeding or guarding the nest and fry, the male's colors are enormously enhanced, whereas the female's colors become a washed out gray. The fish builds a large solid bubble nest, and the fry are easily raised. Infusoria are necessary as a first food, to be followed by newly hatched brine shrimp in five to six days. Temperature, 75° to 85°.

Belontia signata
(Guenther)

Popular name: Comb-tail Gourami
Meaning of name: Belontia, from native name of a related species in Borneo; signata, significant
Length: 3¹/₂ to 4 inches
Sri Lanka (Ceylon)

On reflection, most labyrinth fishes are easily identified; they have marked characteristics. In this one, we have not only a pronounced color pattern, but the long, soft-rays of the ventral fins are split, and the rays of the tail extend beyond the web. The predominating color is reddish brown with some red in the fins, particularly the tail. The male is likely to kill the female unless they have a large tank. Scattered eggs float with no nest. Both parents tend young. Temperature, 70° to 82°.

Colisa chuna
(Hamilton-Buchanan)

Popular name: Honey Gourami
Meaning of name: Colisa chuna: based on two native names
Length: 1 ³/₄ inches
Northeast India

Colisa chuna is a relative newcomer to the aquarium scene. In keeping with its popular name, the male is brick red with a yellow dorsal. A dark line passes from the eye horizontally to the base of the caudal, and a blue-black triangular area fades in obliquely from the eye to the posterior tip of the anal fin. The female shows a more distinct band running from the eye to the peduncle on a washed silver-brown body. The dorsal and anal fins are edged with orange-red.

Breeding this species is accomplished by bringing the temperature of the water down from a normally 83° to 78°. A ten-gallon tank is large enough, and although plants may be present, the male builds his nest independent of plant fronds. Spawning lasts from one hour to two hours, during which time about 400 eggs are released. Within twenty-four hours the eggs begin to hatch, and in seventy-two hours the fry are free swimming. First food consists of infusoria; within three days egg infusion may be offered. Newly hatched brine shrimp is taken five days later. The fry show the dark bands by four weeks. Growth is rapid and the youngsters mature by the time they are four months old, displaying their attractive colors.

Colisa fasciata
(Bloch-Schneider)

Popular name: Striped Gourami
Meaning of name: Colisa, from a native name; fasciata, banded or striped
Length: 4¹/₂ inches
India

While the breeding habits of this *Colisa* are, in general, the same as for other fishes in this group, there are differences. It does not build a very definitely formed nest but blows a few scattered bubbles, preferably under a large leaf. The eggs are lighter than

Belontia signata

Colisa chuna *with Ich*

Colisa fasciata

water and float to the surface where they are more or less scattered.

In the meantime, both before and after the hatching of the eggs, the male takes several gulps of air in his mouth, proceeds to a point below the surface, and expels a fine mist of air bubbles backward through his gills, scattering it with his pectoral fins. For a moment, it seems as though the bubbles are coming from all over his body. He busies himself with this procedure in all parts of the aquarium.

Eggs hatch in two days at 78°. Remove the female after spawning and the male three days after the eggs hatch. A peaceful, beautiful species, easily fed.

Colisa lalia
(Hamilton-Buchanan)
Popular name: Dwarf Gourami
Meaning of name: Colisa lalia, based on two native names
Length: 2 inches
Northern India

Before the discovery of C. chuna, Colisa lalia was the smallest of the genus *Colisa*, but it is still one of the most beautiful. A highly satisfactory and interesting aquarium fish with but a single fault. It is apt to be timid and hide in the foliage. It is too beautiful a flower to be allowed to blush unseen. By associating it with more forward fishes that rush to their master for food, this little beauty soon overcomes its shyness.

In breeding habits, this species varies from the description for bubble-nest builders in one interesting particular. Bits of plant are incorporated into the nest, such as the fine leaves of *Myriophyllum*; also, the female helps build the nest. In addition to his much brighter colors, the male may be distinguished by his orange-red "feelers." Temperature range, 68° to 84°. Breeds at about 80°. They are subject to dropsy. Some males shoot water somewhat like the archer fish.

Helostoma temmincki
Cuvier and Valenciennes
Popular name: Kissing Gourami
Meaning of name: Helostoma, with turned-back mouth, referring to the thick curved lips, which are provided with series of small teeth; temmincki, for C. Temminck
Length: Up to 12 inches
Malaysia, Indonesia

This fish has been publicized both as a "kisser" and as an industrious eater of all kinds of algae. The latter claim is much exaggerated. The purpose of the kissing is not known, but it much more appears to be more of a fighting gesture than a demonstration of affection. The larger ones are prone to persecute the smaller of their own kind. Only one or two in a community tank seems best, provided they are of equal size.

Colisa lalia

Breeding begins at five-inch size. They embrace like other Gouramis, build no nest, and have from 400 to 2,000 floating amber eggs the size of a pin head. Young hatch upside-down in a day. Parents may eat the eggs but will completely ignore young. Babies need infusoria for a week, followed by newly hatched brine shrimp. In two weeks, fine floating food. Thereafter, they are surface feeders. Adults like powdered oatmeal with ground dried shrimp. They also like baby cereal or crumpled dried spinach. They contract few diseases but decline if kept cool or not fed several times daily. There are two color phases: (1) silvery green and (2) a pinkish, iridescent white. It is the latter strain that does most of the breeding. There are no external differences in the sexes. Temperature, 75° to 82°.

Helostoma temmincki

Sphaerichthys osphromenoides

Sphaerichthys osphromenoides
Canistrini

Popular name: Chocolate Gourami

Meaning of name: Sphaerichthys, sphere-like fish; osphromenoides, resembling Osphronemus

Length: 2 inches, rarely larger

Indonesia, Malaysia

Much has been written in the aquarium literature about the Chocolate Gourami, but much remains to be learned about this beautiful, delicate, and still fairly rare fish. The accounts of its breeding habits once varied tremendously, describing it as a livebearer, a bubble-nest builder, and a mouthbrooder. Mouthbrooding accounts outweighed the others, at least, in quantity of material published, and it turned out that these accounts were indeed correct. The fish spawn on the

Opaline Gouramis, A Color Variety of T. trichopterus

bottom, and the female then collects the bright yellow eggs in her mouth. The fry are released after about 17 days.

The water should be fairly acid (the fish are almost never comfortable in alkaline water), soft, and kept at a temperature of 80° or slightly above. A well-planted tank with a loose cover of floating plants to diffuse the light

brine shrimp, and *Daphnia*—in that order. Frozen foods are good substitutes but are rarely eaten as eagerly.

Trichogaster trichopterus

Gold Gourami (another mutant of T. trichopterus)

seems to enhance their well-being and therefore their color. Most types of live foods are accepted, but preference is usually given to mosquito larvae,

Some individuals will take dried foods, but this should never be used as the main diet.

Chocolate Gouramis are very peaceful and can be kept with other small mild-mannered fishes, but care should be taken to select fishes requiring the same treatment.

Trichogaster trichopterus
(Pallas)

Meaning of name: Trichogaster, hair-belly; trichopterus, hair-fin

Popular name: Three-spot Gourami (the third spot being the eye); Blue Gourami

Length: 5 inches

Trichogaster leeri

Malay Peninsula, Thailand

For a time the Three-spot Gourami was known in the hobby only as a silvery fish overlaid with grey markings and with orange dots in the fins. The same species was later found in Sumatra and has become popular as the "Sumatra" or "Blue" Gourami. When the two color phases are crossed, the blue in the babies is apt to be duller.

The species is one of the most easily bred of the bubble-nest builders, although the nest itself is scattered and weak. This makes little difference as both eggs and young float. They are lusty fishes with such big spawns that the young are sometimes used as food for other fishes.

They also make excellent exterminators of that pest few other fishes will touch, hydra. The male has a longer dorsal fin. Temperature, 65°-85°.

Trichogaster leeri
(Bleeker)

Popular name: Pearl Gourami

Meaning of name: Trichogaster, hair-belly; leeri, after Leer

Length: 4 inches

Thailand, Malay Peninsula, Sumatra

If the male fish always maintained its full-breeding color, it could be fairly called the "Robin Redbreast Gourami," but it doesn't. Instead of being a flashy fish, it is one of exquisite refinement. The regularity with which the pearly dots are distributed over nearly the entire fish has given rise to two other popular names: (1) in Europe, Mosaic Gourami and (2) in England, Lace Gourami. Breeding is in the typical style of the bubble-nest builders. The male is not very insistent about driving the female away after spawning is

Trichogaster microlepis

completed. Neither of them eats the eggs or young. The eggs float.

The species share hydra-eating honors with the preceding fish, *T. trichopterus*. It is quite gentle and is well suited to community life among fishes of approximately its own size. Temperature range, 68° to 85°.

Trichogaster microlepis
Guenther

Popular name: Moonlight Gourami

Meaning of name: Trichogaster, hair-belly; microlepis, with small scales

Length: 5 to 6 inches

Thailand

Moonlight Gouramis are softly colored, handsome fishes, perfectly suited for most larger community tanks. While young fishes are often incon-

Trichopsis vittatus

spicuous in the dealer's tank because of their pale silvery color and sometimes unnoticeable dark horizontal line, mature specimens always catch the attention of the hobbyist. Males, especially, have bright red eyes and a deep orange on their feeler-like ventral fins, as well as on the forward portion of their anal fins. Males also have long, fan-like dorsals, as is the case with other species of *Trichogaster.*

These fishes reach maturity at a rather late age. If one starts with young, one- to two-inch fishes, it may take more than half a year before sexes can be determined. They thrive best in slightly acid water at a temperature of about 80°. Breeding can be encouraged by raising the temperature slightly to about 85°. The fishes, however, are not always very cooperative, probably because we are working mostly with wild, imported fishes that are always a little more difficult to bring to breed than those bred domestically for generations. They are bubble-nest builders like most Gouramis, and much plant material is incorporated in their large nests. The young grow very irregularly, which is also quite common with Gouramis. Most complete losses of the fry are probably due to the parasitic disease called velvet which is very hard to detect and, unfortunately, not easily cured.

Trichopsis vittatus
Cuvier and Valenciennes
  Popular name: Croaking Gourami
  Meaning of name: Trichopsis, with hair-like fins; vittatus, striped or banded
  Length: 2 to 3 inches
  Thailand, Malaysia, Indonesia
  These interesting fishes are often neglected by hobbyists and dealers' alike. Admittedly, they often are shy and drab-looking in dealers' tanks,

but given a well-planted tank with fairly soft, acid water, they soon develop a certain grace and elegance of movement. An outstanding feature of *T. vittatus* is their bright green, iridescent eyes. Males have the fascinating ability to produce a sound when sparring with another male or courting a female. With their fins spread to the utmost and the entire body quivering, they emit one or two short vibrating bursts of a somewhat rasping sound. In a quiet room, the sound is clearly audible several feet away from the tank.

The nest is usually built at the surface and passionately tended by the father. Spawning takes place in typical Anabantoid fashion. The young, which are marked with a dark longitudinal line from the time they have hatched, are easily raised and able to take on newly hatched brine shrimp a few days after becoming free-swimming.

They are less demanding in proper pH, hardness, and temperature than *T. pumilus,* a smaller, even more beautiful—but much rarer—species. Temperature, about 80°

Betta splendens
Regan
  Popular name: Siamese Fighting Fish
  Meaning of name: Betta, after a local native name, Ikan bettah; splendens, brilliant
  Length: 2 ½ inches
  Thailand
  With all due respect to the Guppy for having aroused the interest of an

Betta splendens

Cambodia **Betta**

enormous number of persons in the field of aquarium study, there seems little doubt that the modern Betta launched the hobby in a big way in America. Its extraordinary, spectacular beauty made almost instantaneous conquests among those who would never have looked twice at any other fish, but who are now dyed-in-the-wool fanciers and doing everything in their power to interest others in the hobby.

But let us leave superlatives for a moment and have a look at the humble ancestor of this flashy fish. Its body is yellowish brown with a few indistinct horizontal bands. At breeding time the male becomes darker and rows of metallic green scales on his sides become plainer. Dorsal, metallic green tipped with red; anal, red tipped white. Ventrals always fiery red, tipped white. All fins of moderate size, tail fin being rounded.

Suddenly there appeared in our aquarium world a new comet—a cream-colored Betta with fiery, flowing fins. Two varieties, a dark and a

light one, were in the shipment. These were brought into San Francisco in 1927 from Siam. Thinking he had a new species, Mr. Locke, the consignee who received and bred the fishes, called the light one *Betta cambodia*. This has been proved, as have all the now numerous color variants, to be a race of *Betta splendens*. Other importations in varying colors soon followed, some of them coming through Europe. Breeders aimed for the darker colors and soon established the famous "cornflower blue," and finally a solid, rich purplish blue. There are now so many shades of this fish in blues, lavenders, greens and reds that a decorator could almost find specimens to match the color scheme of any room. However, the majority of them have a pair of drooping, fiery red ventral fins.

Over the years there have been numerous accounts, some accurate, some not, of the fighting qualities of this fish, some of it so amusing that we present it, even at risk of too much length.

The late Dr. Hugh M. Smith, ichthyologist and writer, former U.S. Commissioner of Fisheries and one-time Adviser in Fisheries to the then Siamese Government, was qualified to speak on this fish from any standpoint, especially as he had taken a particular interest in the species and personally brought to the United States some of the original long-finned Betta stock. In response to a letter asking to settle the point as to whether the fishes are especially bred for fighting or are caught from the wild for the purpose, the following extracts from his interesting and amusing reply should decide the matter finally, not only for newspaper columnists, but for aquarium writers, too.

A male Betta, attacking his image in the camera lens

"The literature of Betta as a fighting fish is replete with inaccuracies and absurdities. An unusually large number of these occur in a short paragraph in the article entitled 'The Heavenly-Royal City of Siam' by Florence Burgess Meehan (Asia, March, 1921).

Female Betta

" 'The fighting fish are about the size of goldfish. You catch one and put it into a bottle. Your neighbor does likewise. You put your bottle close to your neighbor's. Your fish becomes enraged. So does your neighbor's fish. They both flash all colors of the rainbow. They swell up. You bet on your fish. Your friends back you. After a time one fish or the other, hurling itself against the glass in a vain effort to reach its adversary, becomes so angry that it literally bursts. If it is your neighbor's fish that bursts, you win. If it is yours, you lose.'

"The writer of this paragraph certainly never saw what she was writing about, and the untrustworthiness of the account may be judged from the following facts:

"The Siamese fighting fish cannot properly be described as 'about the size of a goldfish' whatever may be the meaning of the expression. The fish are not matched while in separate 'bottles,' and when not fighting are usually kept in special rectangular jars about 4 inches square and 10 inches high, and a little larger at the top than at the bottom. When fighting, the fish do not 'flash all colors of the rainbow,' do not 'swell up,' do not 'hurl them-

FISHES

The male has constructed a nest in the styrofoam cup provided for the purpose

"With these exceptions, the account quoted is nearly correct, but not quite. For instance, the impression is conveyed that if you wish to stage a fight, you and your neighbor go out and catch wild fish, whereas practically all the combats are between domesticated fish. Fighting fish have been cultivated and domesticated among the Siamese for many years, and all of the noteworthy combats on which sums of money are wagered are with selected, often pedigreed, stock. They have short tail fins.

During the embrace, the pair turns until female is upside down

"There are in Bangkok 10 or 12 persons who breed fighting fish for sale, and about 1,000 persons who raise fighting fish for their own use. A dealer whom I recently visited reports an annual production of 50,000 young, but only a small percentage of these are carried to the fighting age and sold. For the best males the current retail price per fish is 1 to 2 ticals, females half price (1 tical equals 44 cents gold).

From 10 to about 20 eggs are expelled at each embrace. Some eggs can be seen slowly sinking in the water

"The native wild fishes from which the ordinary cultivated fish has been derived rarely exceed 2 inches for the males, the females being smaller. The cultivated fish reach a length of 2 inches for the males.

"The way in which the male fish are matched and their method of fighting are well known. It will suffice to state that the combatants are placed together in a bowl or jar and quickly come to close quarters, expanding their fins and branchial membranes and displaying the gorgeous red, blue and green shades that have made the fighting fish

Eggs are gathered and deposited in the froth nest

famous. They approach one another quietly and may remain in close relation, side by side, for 10 to 15 seconds, or longer, without action. Then, in quick succession, or simultaneously, they launch an attack almost too swift for the observer's eye to follow, and this is repeated at short intervals during the continuance of the combat. The effect of the fierce onslaughts begins to be seen in the mutilation of the fins, which may soon present a ragged appearance and considerable loss of fin substance may occur. The branchial region (gills) may come in for attack, and blood may exceptionally be drawn. On two separate occasions my own fish locked jaws and remained in that position for a number of minutes. That fish is adjudged the victor which is ready to continue to fight while its opponent is no longer eager for the fray."

Dr. Smith's reference to the courage of the cultivated breed of *Bettas* may account for their truly remarkable absence of fear under a certain circumstance which frightens and intimidates nearly all other fishes, especially the fighting sorts. This is the sudden confinement of the fish in a very small space, for instance, a half-pint jar. Placed in such a situation, he calmly surveys his miniature prison, makes a few eel-like turns in it, apparently to see whether it can be done, and is then ready for each or both of his twin interests in life—breeding and fighting. His movements are truly serpentine.

Owing to this intense fighting passion of the males, it is necessary, at the age of about three months, to rear them in individual jars or aquaria. This is the way all fine specimens are produced, for although fish fins recover from injuries, scars remain and the fish is never again perfect. For this reason the price of fine specimens always remain fairly high.

Bettas conform to the described habits for bubble-nest builders. They like acid water, about 6.8, and do best in a well-planted aquarium with liberal light. Water should be clear, but with plenty of natural sediment.

Betta splendens are at their best appearance and vigor between the ages of 10 months and 2 years, and should be bred during that period. Prior to one year it is difficult to select the best specimens, and after 2 years they age rapidly.

There is no way of identifying the sexes until they are about an inch long, when the fins of the males begin to point and lengthen. Soon after this change is noted the males should be kept separately. The females may be placed together. Fin length is the result of inheritance—not food.

This fish is almost as adaptable to foods as it is to its surroundings, but nevertheless it does best on animal substances such as *Daphnia,* brine shrimp, mosquito larvae, chopped worms, bits of fish, crab, shrimp, etc.

A single male may be placed in a community aquarium, and possibly a female also, if the tank is 20 gallons or larger. In general, the sexes should be kept separated; the males singly or else spread around so that two of the species are not in the same tank. Males placed in small adjoining aquariums with a cardboard divider between will always spread themselves when the board is removed. It is a show for visitors that never fails.

The breeding actions of Bettas are unpredictable. Some males are killers, some egg-eaters. None should be trusted with the babies after they become free-swimming. Breeding temperature, about 78°, but stand 68° to 90°.

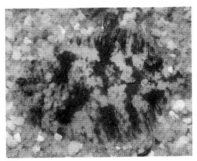

Trinectes maculatus

THE BROAD-SOLES
FAMILY SOLEIDAE

The Broad-Soles belong to the order Pleuronectiformes, all of which lie on one side and have both eyes on the upper side. The Soles differ from other Flatfishes in the shape of the mouth, and other characters. There are several families of Soles. The broad-soles are salt, brackish or freshwater fishes.

Trinectes maculatus
(Bloch)
Popular name: Freshwater Sole
Meaning of name: Trinectes, with three "swimmers" (fins); maculatus,

spotted; also known as Achirus fasciatus, Common Sole
Length: To 8 inches
Coastal waters from Cape Cod southward

Due mainly to their curious method of swimming, an avid interest has developed for the young of this relative of the Flounders. By undulating its fins along the edges of the body, the fish glides in a horizontal position, like a pancake being propelled through

Mastacembelus crythrotaenia

the water. It is also able to bury itself by making wave-like, flapping movements, similar to a blanket being shaken, thereby churning up sand which settles down upon it. This accomplished, it lies in wait for small passing victims, remaining inactive much of the time. They can stick quite firmly to the sides of the tank by body suction.

All fishes of this type—and there are many of them—at first have eyes normally on each side of the head. At an early age, one of the eyes moves over to the other side, so that, eventually, we have a fish blind on one side and with two raised eyes on the other.

They can be fed brine shrimp (either live or frozen), *Tubifex* worms, or bits of chopped clam. A novel and satisfactory fish. Temperature, 60° to 72°.

THE SPINY EELS
FAMILY MASTACEMBELIDAE

The Spiny Eels are not true eels. They are elongated tropical Old World freshwater fishes with numerous spines preceding the dorsal fin.

Mastacembelus erythrotaenia (Bleeker)

Popular name: Fire Eel

Meaning of name: Mastacembelus, with armored beak; erythrotaenia, with red bands

Length: To 2 feet

An odd creature that is often imported today. We include it here for its interesting appearance.

Like the Weatherfish, it spends much of the daytime buried in the sand, head peeping out. Probably, the Weatherfish does this for protection, but with *M. erythrotaenia* it is more likely a camouflage for attack, as it is a strictly carnivorous fish. It swims about the surface of the sand at night. In common with most nocturnal fishes, it can be taught to eat in daytime, but as soon as it has had its meal of chopped earthworms, it quickly returns to its sandy hideout. Not interested in *Daphnia* or in raw meat.

Similar species to the above, but smaller and better suited, belonging to the genus *Macrognathus*, are being imported from tropical Africa and Asia in increasing numbers. Temperature, about 78°.

THE PUFFERS
FAMILY TETRAODONTIDAE

The Puffers are comical fishes. They can blow themselves up with air or water into a veritable balloon. No other fishes possess this remarkable ability. Their fused teeth (two above, two below) form a beak with which

Tetraodon fluviatilis

the larger species can give a dangerous nip. Most of the species are of good size and inhabit salt water throughout tropical and semi-tropical regions, but a few small ones inhabit fresh and brackish water.

Tetraodon fluviatilis
(Hamilton-Buchanan)
  Popular name: Spotted Puffer
  Meaning of name: Tetraodon, four-toothed; fluviatilis, of the river
  Length: 2 to 5 inches
  Most of India, Burma, Malay Peninsula

Puffers of different species have a wide distribution throughout marine waters. This one occurs principally in fresh and brackish locations and in aquarium trade circles is known as the Freshwater Puffer.

The background color is light, with a vivid sheen of green interspersed with large, dark blotches and spots. Belly white, or nearly so.

Although a fish of clumsy, thick appearance, it is extremely active, and never still a moment. It is also quite aggressive towards its own kind but seems to do little harm.

The outstanding feature of these Puffers is their ability when frightened to puff themselves up balloon-like with air or water. Most, but not all, specimens will do it when removed from the water, placed on the hand, and tickled. Air is taken in at the mouth, in about a dozen noisy gulps, until the belly is fully inflated and hard. As the internal pressure increases, little hollow spines are projected from the scale spots. The fish is able to maintain this balloon for only about half a minute. When placed back in the water, it ejects the air with the same gulping valvular contractions and scurries to the bottom.

With ordinary care, it will live well in the aquarium, preferably with its own kind. Eats anything, but prefers meaty food, and lots of it. Never bred. Temperature, 70° to 80°.

Tetraodon palembangensis
Bleeker
  Popular name: Figure-eight puffer
  Meaning of name: Tetraodon, four-toothed; palembangensis, from Palembang in Indonesia
  Length: 8 inches
  Indonesia

This Puffer, together with the well-known *T. fluviatilis*, the Spotted Puffer, is the one most frequently imported. Although it is said to reach a size of eight inches in its natural habitat, specimens measuring over three inches are seldom imported. Their strange common name results from the arrangement of greenish-yellowish lines on their back, which often describe the figure eight. This species is fairly peaceful towards other fishes, but since most Puffers do best in slightly brackish water (i.e., a mixture of fresh and saltwater, which in the aquarium can be duplicated by adding varying amounts of salt, usually up to four teaspoons per gallon) many tank mates are eliminated.

All Puffers are gluttons, requiring copious amounts of live and frozen foods to support their husky frames. Best foods are bloodworms, brine shrimp, some mealworms, pieces of raw or frozen fish, shrimp, or liver and beef heart. Snails are particularly relished and smaller ones need not be crushed, since Puffers have teeth fused into a strong, beak-like structure. Most members of the family exercise some form of parental care. The male parent normally guards the nonadhesive eggs. The young appear to be very difficult to raise, and most breeders report failure in this area. Many hobbyists, however, find it well worth the time, effort, and space to provide a tank for these fascinating creatures alone. Temperature, 75° to 82°.

Colomesus psittacus
(Bloch-Schneider)
Popular name: South American Puffer
Meaning of name: Colomesus. round fish; psittacus, parrot-like
Length: To 4 inches
Northern South America
The most important single factor to be considered when attempting to keep any Puffer is the availability of food. They are bulky fishes with a high metabolic rate and cannot be kept healthy and vigorous on a diet of dried foods, although some Puffers will take them. Large amounts of live and frozen foods are required, and they especially relish bits of frozen or fresh shrimp (the kind used for cocktails), lean meat, fish, earthworms, mealworms, snails, etc.

South American Puffers are the most active members of the family and the only ones found in South America. With powerful strokes of their pectoral fins, as well as their dorsal and ventral fins, which are set far back on their bodies, they can sustain a speed far greater than that of their Far Eastern counterparts. Large, roomy tanks are, therefore, necessary to maintain this species.

When very young and about an inch long, they have four broad black bands across their white backs. These bands change into irregular black and green patterns as the fishes mature. These Puffers sometimes bury themselves up to their heads in sand, if that is used in the tank. Coarse gravel usually prevents them from doing this. Water conditions do not seem to be very important as long as extreme acidity is avoided. They will live equally well in either fresh or saltwater, as well as all stages in between.

Sex differences have not been observed, and there is no record of them having spawned in captivity. Temperature, 73° to 78°.

THE TRIPLETAILS
FAMILY LOBOTIDAE
These are mostly marine fishes of tropical regions. *Datnioides* is an exception, being found in freshwaters of Thailand, Malaysia and Burma.

Datnioides microlepis
Bleeker
Popular name: Tiger Fish
Meaning of name: Microlepis, with small scales
Length: To 15 inches
Tiger Fishes can only be kept with other fishes of approximately the same

Tetraodon palembangensis

Colomesus psittacus

size. They have cavernous mouths and are capable of swallowing a surprisingly large fish. However, *Datnioides* do not need a diet only of fish. Earthworms, frozen or live, ghost shrimp, and even chunks of freeze dried brine shrimp will be accepted. They require large amounts of food, and grow at a very fast rate. They are a little happier in slightly brackish water (about 5 oz. of salt for ten gallons of water). Temperature, 72° to 82°.

THE NEEDLE FISHES
FAMILY BELONIDAE

Most members of this family are marine fishes. All are strictly carnivorous, feeding on other fishes. Very few enter freshwater. Few have ever been bred in captivity.

Xenentodon cancila
(Hamilton)

Popular name: Needle Fish

Meaning of name: Xenentodon, with odd teeth

Length: 12 inches

These are easily frightened fishes, and extreme care is necessary while handling them. They are capable of tremendous speeds and often injure themselves by crashing against the aquarium glass. They should be kept in large, well covered tanks. Live fishes are their only food.

Temperature, 70° to 80°.

Datnioides microlepis

Xenentodon cancila

INDEX
Page numbers in boldface refer to illustrations.